RIEN.

Vos en zet. Voor elk ten zet.
tut Cokar met ....

KETEL

Tout ou Rien.
FOLIÉ publique.
...é comme un feu de Paille.
... hausse des Actions.
baisse.

Der... ...re,
l'Envie avec sa noire dent
Grugeoit la tête d'un serpent.
La flame d'un boteau de paille
Représentoit naïvement
Le court éclat de la canaille.
. Armé de Torche et d'un poignard,
Le DESESPOIR d'une autre part
Attendoit pour saisir un homme,
Qu'il eût fondu toute sa somme.
Sur une truie un faquin nu
Crioit: Hélas! j'ai tout perdu.
Me revoila donc dans la crasse.
Un SATIRE à laide grimace
Pestoit contre les actions,
Qui comme d'affreux SCORPIONS.
Ont une queue envenimée.
Troupe digne d'être enfermée,
Cria DIOGENE en couroux,
Un ANE est moins bête que vous.
Vous recherchez une couronne
De Plumes de Paons, de chardons;
c'Est la SOTISE qui la donne!
c'Est pour elle qu'en vos maisons
Vous introduisez la famine.
Vos ustenciles de Cuisine
Sont des meubles à retrancher.
Vous meritez qu'on vous assomme
& Loin de vous je vais chercher

The Moneymaker

Also by Janet Gleeson

THE ARCANUM

The Moneymaker

Janet Gleeson

BANTAM PRESS

LONDON · NEW YORK · TORONTO · SYDNEY · AUCKLAND

TRANSWORLD PUBLISHERS LTD
61–63 Uxbridge Road, London W5 5SA

TRANSWORLD PUBLISHERS
c/o Random House Australia Pty Ltd
20 Alfred Street, Milsons Point, NSW 2061, Australia

TRANSWORLD PUBLISHERS
c/o Random House New Zealand
18 Poland Road, Glenfield, Auckland, New Zealand

TRANSWORLD PUBLISHERS
c/o Random House Pty Ltd
Endulini, 5a Jubilee Road, Parktown 2193, South Africa

Published 1999 by Bantam Press
a division of Transworld Publishers Ltd

Copyright © Janet Gleeson 1999

The right of Janet Gleeson to be identified as the author of this work has been asserted in
accordance with sections 77 and 78 of the Copyright Designs and Patents Act 1988.

A catalogue record for this book is available from the British Library.
ISBN 0593 044983

Typeset in Bembo by
Phoenix Typesetting, Ilkley, West Yorkshire.

Printed in Great Britain by
Mackays of Chatham Plc, Chatham, Kent

3 5 7 9 10 8 6 4 2

To my parents Jill and Michael

An engraving by W. Greatbach from a rare print by Leon Schenk (1720) showing John Law at the height of his fame as Controller General of Finance.

The chapter-opening illustration shows a plaster replica of a silver and pewter coin (1720) satirizing John Law. The legend reads 'Mélac revived, without fire and wood, raiding the purses of Europe, empty and utterly turned inside out. Therefore, John Law, you need expect nothing here.' The inscription likens Law to the infamous Comte de Mélac, a French general and field-marshal during the German war of 1689 noted for his slaughter of the inhabitants and the burning and devastation of the country under his occupation (from *Medallic Illustrations of the History of Great Britain and Ireland*, 1909).

The endpapers show a French broadsheet lampooning John Law after the collapse of his Mississippi scheme. 'A true portrait of the renowned Mr Quinquenpoix' – John Law is seen in a cauldron fuelled by the burning of banknotes and shares. He is surrounded by Vanity, Envy and Folly, and a foolish investor in search of wealth pours more gold into the pot but receives only paper in return. (*Courtesy of the National Portrait Gallery, London*)

Contents

Within the last twenty years commerce has been better understood in France than it had ever before been, from the reign of Pharamond to that of Louis XIV. Before this period it was a secret art, a kind of chemistry in the hands of three or four persons, who actually made gold, but without communicating the secret by which they had been enriched . . . It was destined that a Scotchman called John Law should come into France and overturn the whole economy of our government to instruct us.

Voltaire, Essay on Commerce and Luxury

MONEY HAS EVER POSED PROBLEMS. NOT EVEN LOVE, SAID Gladstone, has made so many fools of men. Throughout time the most obvious but universal dilemma – that there is never enough of it – has confounded everyone, from mendicants to monarchs, and their ministers.

Rarely, however, had the problem seemed more pressing than it did in the late seventeenth century. Money, as most people had always understood it, was silver or gold – precious metals whose value lay in their intrinsic scarcity. But the fact that coin supplies were limited by the metal that could be dug out of the ground was proving a serious hindrance. Throughout Europe, warfare of vast scale and expense coupled with the extravagant lifestyles of kings had emptied treasuries, while the growing population, expansion of trade and colonization of foreign lands demanded more cash to progress. As rulers plotted invasions, perused peace treaties, yearned to sponsor new industry, build new palaces and develop their domains overseas, money, and how to create more of it, became a marked obsession. In an age poised between superstition and enlightenment, it became as fashionable to ponder the subject that would soon be christened political economy as the disciplines of philosophy, mathematics and nature. While on the one hand alchemists strove futilely to turn base metal into gold, on the other entrepreneurial projectors proposed a plethora of ingenious schemes to sidestep the shortage. At the lowliest level, small-change coins made from base metal alleviated the lack of coins in the streets. On a grand scale, banks and joint-stock companies used the magical device of credit to fund royal debts and colonial expansion by issuing paper banknotes and shares of token rather than intrinsic worth. By a multiplicity of new monetary expedients the frustrating limitations of gold and silver evaporated, but at the same time a new, even more baffling problem emerged: the question of how to maintain public confidence in the value of intrinsically valueless paper.

Among monetary philosophers and innovators to confront the problem, John Law stands alone as the most improbable, controversial but visionary of financial heroes. He was big in every sense, over six foot tall with ambitions that were larger and more daring than anyone else's. On one level his story is the stuff of romantic legend. He turned his attention to finance after killing a man in a duel over an unfortunate liaison and escaping prison to save his neck. A congenial chancer, prepared to punt on the turn of a card yet burning with mathematical brilliance, he exuded a glamorous, dangerous magnetism.

Women were spellbound by his impeccable dress, charming manner and sexual charisma, men by the ease with which he was able to demystify complex subjects, his nonchalant wit, and willingness to linger for hours over games of cards and dice. But his ideas and actions invest his life with far more significance than that of a beguiling and ambitious playboy: the things Law made happen still have resonance today.

In an ironic reversal of the concept of the philosopher's stone, he founded the first national bank of issue in France that made money from paper on a previously unprecedented scale to revive the ailing economy. He formed the most powerful conglomerate the world had yet seen – the Mississippi Company – and encouraged an audience of private investors of unprecedented numbers to dabble in its shares. Once initial hesitation had been banished, investors from England, Germany, Holland, Italy and Switzerland stampeded to Paris to play the markets, and share prices rose from 150 livres to 10,000 in a matter of months. In comparison, the best bull market of the twentieth century, between 1981 and 1987, when the UK stock market rose by 366 per cent, seems paltry. Law sparked the world's first major stock-market boom, in which so many made such vast fortunes that the word 'millionaire' was coined to describe them. Almost overnight he had become rich beyond expectation, a heroic figure, fêted throughout Europe, and promoted in recognition of his achievement to the position of France's financial controller – the most powerful public position in the world's most powerful nation.

Pioneers, so they say, usually end up with arrows in their backs. In Law's case, enemies, inexperience, greed and destiny conspired against his unconventional genius. The idea that money could be made from speculation rather than drudgery was printed indelibly on the popular consciousness. But having made their fortunes, many began to look for alternative invest-ments, or to feel that paper was no long-term substitute for more traditional, tangible assets. When speculators began to cash in shares and withdraw paper funds to buy estates, jewels or gold, or to speculate in other escalating foreign share markets, Law, hampered by jealous rivals, was unable to hold back the tide and the stock plummeted as rapidly as it had risen. People who rushed to the bank to convert paper back into coin found insufficient reserves and were left holding an asset that had become virtually worthless.

Over half a million people, equivalent to two-thirds of the entire population of the city of London at the time, claimed to have lost out as a result of John Law. Having sparked the first international stock-market boom, he had also sparked the first international bust. As loudly as, months earlier, he had been lauded a financial saviour he was branded a knave and ignobly demoted. Sadder, wiser, immeasurably poorer, he spent the rest of his life unsuccessfully trying to convince the world of his integrity, and that the idea behind his schemes was sound. His fall cast long shadows. It was eighty years before France dared again to try to introduce paper money to its economy. For years afterwards history judged Law harshly. In the story of money, the chapter on his life embodies the perils of paper, his economic foresight largely negated by the failure of his schemes.

Today, if John Law or his critics could witness commerce conducted on any high street with credit cards, banknotes and cheques – not a gold or silver coin in sight – they would see, incontrovertibly, his vision achieved, but recognize also the same inherent weakness. The survival of any credit-based financial system still hinges on public confidence in a way that one based on gold does not. Spectacular financial breakdowns have peppered history ever since the advent of paper credit.

Three centuries on, an age of comparably varied and ambitious financial innovation unfolds – witness the introduction of the euro, the opportunity to trade shares on the Internet and a panoply of monetary instruments, from foreign-currency mortgages to inventive use of derivatives in equity, bond and currency markets. Scanned from this perspective, Law's story still holds uncanny relevance.

During the period covered in this book English and French currency was based on a similar structure: 240 pennies or deniers = 20 shillings or sous = 1 pound or livre tournois. Coins in common current use in France included the gold louis d'or and the silver écu, which were measured and varied widely against the value of the livre. Another common coin was the pistole, a Spanish silver coin worth approximately 10 livres. Exchange rates also varied enormously: a livre was worth between a shilling and 1s. 6d. According to the Bank of England a pound in 1720 is equivalent to about £73 today. Therefore a sum quoted in livres can be converted to its approximate equivalent in pounds sterling today by halving it then multiplying by seven.

Chapter One

A Man Apart

He came to Paris, where he cut such a fine figure, that he held the bank at Faro. He usually played at the house of a famous actress, where they played for high stakes; although he was in as great demand with Princes and Lords of the first order, as in the most celebrated academies, where his noble manners and even temper, distinguished him from other players.

Barthélemy Marmont du Hautchamp,
Histoire du système de finances (1739)

IN THE PARISIAN SALON OF MARIE-ANNE DE CHATEAUNEUF, 'La Duclos', it is an evening in November 1708. La Duclos, celebrated actress of Paris's Comédie Française, is entertaining Parisian society, but this evening, despite the lustrous presence of sundry *ducs*, *marquis* and *comtes*, talk is uncharacteristically desultory. France is in the throes of the world's first global war, the War of Spanish Succession, which has raged already for seven years and will endure for another six. This country, the most powerful and populous in Europe, has been ruined by the perpetual conflict. But this cocooned Parisian circle is scarcely conscious of it: the talk is not of the devastating defeats

France has suffered at the battles of Oudenaarde, Turin, Ramillies and Blenheim, it focuses instead on the move of the elderly Louis XIV, the Sun King, and his court from Versailles to Marly, and the love affairs of the glamorous but dangerous Duc d'Orléans.

Those who find these topics less than engaging find themselves drawn instead to watch the cluster of players engrossed in a game of faro. Most are habitués of the tables – at this level of society everyone knows everyone else – but among them one man stands apart. He is fashionably clad as one would expect in a wide-skirted velvet coat, unbuttoned to reveal a damask waistcoat and cravat of Brussels lace, while a periwig of black curls cascades over his shoulders. But at over six feet tall – a remarkable stature in these diminutive days – he is a man of 'grand and imposing looks' that according to one acquaintance 'without flattery puts him among the best made of men'. Amid the twitchy players, he is also remarked for his 'gentle and insinuating manners', a serenity of temperament that, observers say, amply reflects his outward appearance.

During a lull in play La Duclos proudly presents the stranger as John Law, a Scottish gentleman, visiting Paris. Her guests soon realize, however, that although Law is as charming and witty as he is physically attractive, he displays a singular reticence when questioned on his circumstances. They also discover, as the evening progresses, that he is a masterly gambler.

According to the rules of the game, the players must defeat a single opponent, the tallière, or banker, to win. This evening Law has been permitted to pit his wits against the rest and adopt the solitary role of opponent. He is the bank. As the stakes grow higher, the players' mood shifts from studied composure to overt unease and a crescendo of voices pledge increasingly reckless sums. But no matter how great the amount at risk, Law never relinquishes control over his outward expression.

Each player chooses one, two or three from a deck of cards

on the table before them using gold louis d'or as their stake. Slowly the croupier takes his pack, discards the uppermost card, plays the next two – the loser and the winner – and places them in front of him. Winning depends on players having selected the same number as the second card dealt by the croupier (suits are irrelevant), so long as he does not deal two cards of the same face value, in which case the banker also wins. The dealing continues, players betting on every draw until three cards remain. The room is transfixed for the final turn, when the players must guess the cards in order of appearance. Inevitably, Law triumphs over most. He scoops the gold coins he has accumulated into the leather purses he has brought with him, leaving the losers, ruefully, to review their depleted wealth. Once again he has apparently defied the laws of chance and emerged spectacularly victorious.

Few among those present perceive that he has been assisted by anything more than unusual good fortune. Years later his closest acquaintances, such as the Duc de Saint-Simon, failed fully to understand his gaming victories, and described him as 'the kind of man, who without ever cheating, continually won at cards by the consummate art (that seemed incredible to me) of his methods of play'. In fact, success on this scale has almost nothing to do with luck or consummate art but in ensuring that the odds are stacked heavily in his favour. Even when not in the lucrative role of banker, by marshalling a remarkable mathematical intellect and employing his understanding of probability theories, of which few are aware, Law is able to measure with astonishing accuracy the likelihood that a given card will appear. To him there was little doubt about the evening's outcome.

Not far from the opulent interior of La Duclos' salon, in a plain but comfortably appointed apartment of the Benedictine Priory in Faubourg St Antoine, was one of the few men in Paris to whom John Law's success was of pressing concern. Marc

René de Voyer de Paulmy, Marquis d'Argenson, Paris's super-intendent of police, was as physically unattractive as Law was outwardly engaging, with sallow skin and deep-socketed eyes. He was noted chiefly for his 'subtle mind' and 'natural intelligence', and his business – others' secrets – was a métier at which he excelled. As the eagle-eyed Duc de Saint-Simon remarked, 'There was no inhabitant [of Paris] whose daily conduct and habits he did not know.'

D'Argenson relished sophisticated company and felt easy in the élite world to which John Law's gaming skills had given him access. During the decade he had held his position, Law's sporadic appearances and extraordinary successes had grown increasingly perturbing. D'Argenson was convinced that John Law was fulfilling some secret role for the British, or that he constituted some other even more insidious threat. Unease deepened when, despite every attempt to find out more about him, intelligence proved worryingly sparse. Some said he was a fugitive from British justice, that he had escaped from prison where he had been sentenced to death by hanging for killing a man. His fortune was variously rumoured to have come from the gaming tables of Vienna, Rome, Venice, Genoa, Brussels and the Hague, or from an inherited Scottish estate. But all this was hearsay and speculation. A year earlier, when d'Argenson discovered Law intent on masterminding a dangerous scheme that might undermine France's economy, the introduction of paper money to France, he had expelled him from Paris. Now the King's foreign minister, the Marquis de Torcy, had informed him that not only was Law back without a passport but that 'his intentions are not good, [and that] he is serving our enemies as a spy'. Torcy was worried and wanted to know more. D'Argenson, equally disturbed, had attempted for some weeks to track Law down. The quarry had proved elusive.

Chapter Two

Gilded Youth

In an island near the Orcades a child was born, whose father was Aeolus god of the winds, and whose mother was a Caledonian nymph. He is said to have learnt all by himself to count on his fingers, and, at four years of age, to have been able to distinguish between the different metals so exactly that when his mother tried to give him a ring made of brass, instead of gold, he realised that it was a trick and threw the ring on the ground.

As soon as he was fully grown his father taught him the secret of catching the wind in balloons, which he then sold to travellers. However, since his wares were not greatly appreciated in his own country, he left, and began to lead a wandering life in the company of the blind god of chance.

Baron Secondat de Montesquieu, *Persian Letters* (1721)

THERE IS LITTLE IN JOHN LAW'S BACKGROUND TO SUGGEST the professional gambler, beau, murderer, adventurer or international celebrity he would one day become. The family came originally from Lithrie in Fifeshire and for generations had followed careers as men of the Church. John Law's great-grandfather Andrew and his grandfather John Law of Waterfut, after whom he was christened, were both ministers of Neilston, a small, unremarkable village in Renfrewshire. The local archbishop of Glasgow, James Law, was probably also a relative.

Long-standing clerical family tradition was not, however, inviolate. During the Civil War and Commonwealth, Presbyterian extremism was ruthlessly enforced in the Scottish Church. John Law of Waterfut was too tolerant to fit in with the prevailing mood and in 1649 was ousted from his post 'for inefficiency'. Bereft of home and income, and with no profession to pass on to his two young sons, he was left with little alternative but to seek employment in Edinburgh.

Writing of the city, which he visited towards the end of the century, the English chaplain Thomas Morer observed that it was 'very steepy and troublesome, and withall so nasty (for want of bog houses which they very rarely have) that Edinburgh is by some likened to an ivory comb, whose teeth on both sides are very foul'. Daniel Defoe described it as a place of 'infinite disadvantages', that 'lies under such scandalous inconveniences as are, by its enemies, made a subject of scorn and reproach; as if the people were not as willing to live sweet and clean as other nations, but delighted in stench and nastiness'. In other words, it was like most other large cities of the time, a foul, stinking metropolis – stark contrast to the uncontaminated though bleak country ministry of Neilston.

The transition to such an environment for Minister Law and his family must have been painful and distressing. The city was recovering from the ravages of the worst plague in its history that had left it 'never in a more miserable and melancholy situation than at present'. Pestilence, coupled with draconian Commonwealth rule, had depleted the population, provoking mounting poverty and dwindling trade. For the next decade the family lived a penurious hand-to-mouth existence while their father tried to secure a pension from the Church and find a suitable occupation for his two young sons, John and William. There was an obvious solution to the second dilemma: members of the Law family not involved in the Church had been goldsmiths since the early sixteenth century, and with the help of family contacts, soon after their arrival in Edinburgh, the two young Laws were apprenticed to prominent goldsmiths. In the late seventeenth century the profession enjoyed an elevated status that set goldsmiths apart from most other craftsmen. As well as fashioning jewels, trophies and household valuables, many had developed an even more valuable and influential sideline business as money-dealers.

Money, perhaps more than any other human artefact, has a multiplicity of meaning. To a modern layman's eye it might signify security, power, luxury, freedom, temptation. But its more prosaic prime function, economists tell us, is as a medium of exchange. Without it we would be forced to barter for anything we could not provide for ourselves with any surplus we wished to sell. Money lets us separate the buying of one thing from the selling of another. It means we need not swap eggs for oranges, carpets for bricks, a book for a bowl of rice. Almost anything can and has served as money: a herd of cows, a wife or two, a bundle of tobacco leaves, a pouch of shells. Form matters little; what counts is that both buyer and seller trust that if they exchange it for whatever goods or services they are selling, it will hold its value and, at some later stage, they will be able to buy something else with it.

Of all money's chameleon masks, gold and silver are its most recognizable, widespread and enduring. Ancient Mesopotamians used precious metals according to standards set by the king and the temple and invented the earliest forms of writing to keep accounts; Egyptians measured their pharaoh's wealth or a servant's worth in Nubian gold, silver and copper ingots and slivers. In ancient Greece gold and silver were similarly esteemed. Herodotus claimed that the first coins – pieces of metal of a standard weight and fineness – were invented in the sixth century BC, in ancient Lydia, the kingdom of Croesus, whose name still embodies riches beyond compare. In fact, archaeologists have since discovered coins from a century earlier used by Ephesians, and that coins were similarly employed by Greeks in the realm of Ionia.

Banking, too, extends its reach to the ancient past. The first bankers lived three millennia ago in the ancient city of Babylon, a site in modern Iraq; in ancient Athens in the fifth century BC, there were bankers who changed foreign visitors' money and accepted deposits, and in ancient Rome money-lending bankers wielded huge political clout. The first modern banking institutions were born in the great medieval Italian trading cities of Genoa, Turin, Pisa and Milan. The word 'bank' comes from the Italian *banco*, meaning the bench used by money-dealers. But in a world in which coin was made from precious metals, the system's overriding disadvantage was that sources of precious metals were finite, whereas greed and aspiration were not.

A breakthrough came with what the eminent economist J. K. Galbraith has called 'the miracle of banking': the discovery of credit. If money was lodged in a bank vault for safekeeping, the person who owned it could take away a piece of paper testifying to his ownership of the sum, which he could use as a form of currency, while the guardian of the cache could lend part of it to others (keeping some reserve to pay to those who wanted to withdraw their deposits for whatever reason) and profit by charging interest for the service he offered. In this way money could be multiplied and the problems of limited supplies of gold and silver overcome. The only pitfall was an outside event that intervened to make everyone want to withdraw their deposits at once. Then the guardian of the treasure would find himself unable to repay the depositors because the reserves would be exhausted – much of their money would still be on loan and therefore inaccessible – and he would be bankrupt. Thus, it was realized, political stability and healthy reserves were the key to successful money-dealing.

Britain was far from enlightened when it came to credit. Money-lending for profit was deemed usury, a crime against God; its perpetrators were hanged, drawn and quartered. During medieval times the trade was thus monopolized by foreigners, first by Jews and later by entrepreneurial gold merchants from Italy, known as the Lombards. In London, the early Italian financiers were permitted to lend and trade in money, provided they confined themselves and their businesses to a London street that still bears their name. Lombard Street remains to this day at the heart of international financial dealing. Many of the Lombards who set up their businesses in medieval London were also goldsmiths, using surplus bullion to make objects from which they could also profit and, after the relaxation of the usury laws in the mid-sixteenth century, English goldsmiths began to join the lucrative business. The so-called 'father of English banking', Sir Thomas Gresham, broke new ground with his sophisticated money-lending business, which operated at the Sign of the Grasshopper in Lombard Street, offering loans to private individuals and the Crown at set rates of interest, paying interest on deposits, arranging bills of exchange and dealing in coin and bullion. Largely by such services he became one of the most powerful courtiers of Henry VIII, Edward VI, Mary I and Elizabeth I. Much of the vast fortune he accumulated was kept in gold chains wrapped around his body; he detached a link or two to serve as cash when he needed it.

By the late seventeenth century, wars, wages, burgeoning commerce, a growing population and expanding overseas trade combined to create a vast demand for credit. In England, gold-smiths continued to dominate the field of money. They lent tens of thousands of pounds to the Crown, and kept records of these transactions by notching wooden sticks (usually made from hazelwood) known as tallies, a form of accounting used from ancient times until the nineteenth century. A tally might measure anything between 3 inches and 5 feet in length, and the carved notches varied in width to represent the sum advanced: an incision the width of a hand might correspond to a loan of £1,000; a thumb, £100; a barley stalk, £1. The stick was then split, half to be kept by the lender and half by the borrower as a record of the loan.

But the life of a seventeenth-century banker, in these politically volatile days, was perilous, and runs on reserves were a particular hazard. In 1667 when a Dutch squadron entered the Thames to open fire on Sheerness, frightened depositors feared invasion was imminent and besieged Edward Backwell, one of London's famous goldsmith bankers. The diarist Samuel Pepys was among those who frantically withdrew his gold and gave it to his wife to take out of the city. She buried it in her father's garden on a Sunday morning, a safe time, she said, because everyone else would be in church. Pepys was 'almost mad about it' when he learned what had happened, and came at dead of night to retrieve the money, only to find that his wife and father-in-law had forgotten where it was buried. Eventually, 'by poking with a spit', they located the money-bag, but during the lantern-lit excavations it ruptured and nearly a hundred pieces of gold were lost. Pepys only retrieved them the next day after several hours' sieving soil.

One supposedly secure stronghold to which both goldsmiths and private investors entrusted money was the Royal Mint, then located in the Tower of London. This had proved even less secure than Pepys's garden when, in 1640, Charles I had appropriated £130,000 worth of privately owned bullion to pay his debts. Three decades later, in 1671, when Charles II was similarly strapped for cash and unable to meet the interest payments on his loans, he abruptly confiscated over £1.3 million that had been loaned to the royal exchequer at 8 per cent interest. Misappropriation on this scale had drastic consequences: numerous goldsmiths, plus hundreds of their clients whose money they had invested, were ruined overnight.

By the time that John Law of Waterfut apprenticed his sons to goldsmiths in Edinburgh, money-dealing had grown sophisticated and the most successful goldsmith bankers commanded notable power and influence, parading the chilly, malodorous streets of Edinburgh clad conspicuously in scarlet cloaks and cocked hats. To the recently impoverished father, life as goldsmiths promised his sons financial security and elevated social status. William, the younger, was apprenticed to George Cleghorne and seems quickly to have made the most of his opportunities; in 1661, as he was nearing the end of his training, the bond between master and favoured pupil was formally acknowledged when he married Cleghorne's nineteen-year-old daughter Violet. A few months later William qualified as a goldsmith and set up his own business.

William Law's new shop was surrounded by similar premises and stood close by the Goldsmiths' Hall, to the south of St Giles, the hub of Edinburgh's commercial district. Space was at a premium. 'In no city in the world,' Defoe wrote, 'do so many people live in so little room as at Edinburgh.' Goldsmiths' shops to the north of the square were little more than tall narrow buildings, known as luckenbooths, made of wood with projecting superstructures that hung out over the street. Law's was grander, but still cramped. Ground-floor space might have measured only seven feet square, yet this and similar buildings telescoped up several storeys. Family life went on in upper rooms, while below pride of place was given to the tools of the trade: the forge, bellows and crucibles where the precious molten metal would be raised and wrought into spoons, tankards, rings, church plate or intricate drinking cups formed from silver-mounted nautilus shells.

The Laws' nuptial bliss was short-lived. Within a year of their marriage Violet died giving birth to a baby son, who died not long after; a mortal legacy, perhaps, of Edinburgh's insanitary conditions. A year later, the widowed William's affections were recaptured by Jean Campbell, the formidably intelligent and robust twenty-three-year-old daughter of a prosperous merchant from Ayrshire; she became his second wife. With her dowry William expanded his business and acquired a second shop. He and Jean had twelve children – seven sons and five daughters – only four of whom survived childhood. John Law, the child destined to become the financial wizard of his age, was their fifth child and eldest surviving son. He was born, lusty, large and bonny, in April 1671, in all probability in one of the cramped rooms perched high above the goldsmith's shop in Edinburgh.

For his father, the arrival of a healthy heir must have seemed a crowning moment in a stellar career. A year before John was born his pre-eminence among goldsmiths had been acknowledged when he was appointed assay master for Edinburgh, responsible for supervising the testing and hall-marking of silver and gold objects made within the city precincts. In 1674, when the Scottish Parliament tasked a commission to report on the Royal Mint he was called in to advise – further evidence of the esteem in which he was held in the city; the following year he was promoted to Dean of the Goldsmiths of Edinburgh.

William Law was as ambitious for his children as for himself. Adamant that John should have every opportunity that his father's misfortunes had denied him, he ensured that he was raised and educated as a gentleman. John's early education took place at Edinburgh's High School where presumably he received the usual grounding in religion, mathematics and Latin, which allowed pupils to enter university. He may also have had some instruction in Greek and French, although these were more frequent additions to the curriculum of Scottish schools in the following century. According to his early biographers – who may have been following the fashion for investing the famous with special qualities as young children – he was noted almost immediately for his intelligence and outstanding aptitude for numbers.

He grew up in a rapidly changing city. When John Law was eight, he would have witnessed the pomp and ceremony that attended the appointment of the King's brother, James, Duke of York, as viceroy of Scotland. With James's arrival, the city savoured a limited period of renewal. Holyrood Palace became the focus of grand entertainments: '. . . vast numbers of nobility and gentry . . . flocked around the Duke and filled the town with gaiety and splendour', recorded the historian Robert Chambers. As young John learned to read and solve elementary mathematical problems, James pushed the city towards modernity: the Merchant Company was founded, the physic garden extended, coffee-houses opened, an attempt made at street-lighting and, in the following years, a new Exchange in Parliament Square was built.

Amid these developments William Law's money-lending business flourished. Alert, quick-witted and perceptive, John must have been fascinated by the lucrative financial business his father was building, as he watched deals struck over stoops of ale supped within the shadowy confines of John's coffee-shop or the ancient baker's Baijen Hole. His curiosity must also have been sparked by the skills of the craftsmen his father employed, while his love of the arts and patronage of craftsmen perhaps sprang from watching sheet metal formed into works of exquisite beauty.

By 1683, when John was twelve, his father's wealth was enough to establish him as a man of substance. He acquired Lauriston Castle, a three-storey fortified building with two corbelled turrets that had been built by Archibald Napier in the late sixteenth century, and 180 acres of land fringing the southern shore of the Firth of Forth. But before the family could move from the confines of Parliament Close and take up residence on their estate, tragedy struck.

Years of hard work had taken their toll on William's health. Now in his middle years and at the peak of his success, he was stricken with increasing regularity by agonizing pains in his abdomen and diagnosed as suffering from stones in his bladder, a common seventeenth-century complaint. Soon after he had bought Lauriston he left Edinburgh for Paris, a city so famed for pioneering advances in this field and 'men well practised in the cutting for it' that several leading hospitals displayed chests filled with the stones they removed – one such trophy was apparently as large as a child's head. The French surgeon advised a lithotomy, one of the oldest surgical procedures known to man – vividly described by Dr Martin Lister – a zoologist and later physician to Queen Anne – who watched an expert surgeon perform the operation: 'He boldly thrusts in a broad lancet or stiletto into the middle of the muscle of the thigh near the anus, till he joins the catheter or staff, or the stone betwixt his fingers; then he widens his incision of the bladder in proportion to the stone with a silver oval hoop . . . then with the duck's bill [a surgical implement] he draws it out.' Nine similar operations, Lister observed, were 'very dexterously' performed within three-quarters of an hour.

The speed with which experts could complete the procedure did little to reduce the risk. Samuel Pepys, who was 'cut of the stone' in London, celebrated his recovery from the operation with an anniversary party. In William Law's case, the procedure proved fatal. He died without seeing his family or homeland again, and was buried in the Scots College in Paris, in the heart of the city that his eldest son would hold one day in his thrall.

★　　★　　★

It was left to Jean Law to unravel the complexities of her husband's will. The document revealed the extent of his financial business, which totalled over £25,000 of outstanding loans. There were pages of debtors' names, among them many from Scotland's most eminent families. This intricate web of indebtedness was evidently not easy to resolve: many were slow to repay the sums outstanding and letters from Jean to her debtors were still being exchanged years after her husband's death.

According to the terms of William Law's will, the newly acquired estate of Lauriston and its rental income was bequeathed to his twelve-year-old son John. He also left ample provision for his children to be educated as their mother deemed appropriate to their status. Perhaps because John was already displaying a worrying waywardness as well as mathematical brilliance, Jean removed him from his school in Edinburgh and sent him 'far away from the temptations of the city', to Eaglesham in Renfrewshire, a distant boarding-school run by a relative. In this remote but pleasant environment John Law completed his formal education. Along with his remarkable ability in mathematics he also emerged as a skilled exponent of 'manly pursuits'. These must have included fencing, which was soon to play a pivotal role in his career, and tennis, which was popular all over Europe and particularly in Scotland. By now he had matured into a strikingly attractive man – contemporaries euphemistically characterized him as of 'marked individuality'. A description of him by a later acquaintance recalls his 'oval face, high forehead, well placed eyes, a gentle expression, aquiline nose, and an agreeable mouth'. He took such keen interest in his clothes and appearance that friends dubbed him 'Beau Law' or 'Jessamy [meaning fop or dandy] John'.

With no father to guide him, John Law, who later confessed that he 'always hated work', did not attend university but succumbed to adolescent indolence, happily passing the days in the pleasurable pursuits of gaming and womanizing. There had always been a dare-devil strand to his personality, and the risk-taking of gambling perhaps appealed as much, if not more, than any money he might win. The poker-faced gamesmanship necessary to do well in games of chance must also have become second nature to him. Perhaps it was in these early days that he learned the chameleon knack of playing his cards close, shrouding his feelings, and having the confidence to follow a hunch. With women, his handsome face, sartorial finery and nonchalant charm apparently combined to yield innumerable easy conquests. One of his friends from these Edinburgh days, George Lockhart of Carnwarth, said, with a tinge of jealousy as well as reluctant admiration, that he was already 'nicely expert in all manner of debaucheries'.

Before long, however, the life of self-indulgence palled, and John Law began to hanker for new challenges and the world beyond Edinburgh's city walls. London – ten uncomfortable days distant by coach – drew him. His mother probably raised no objection when he told her of his wish to travel, perhaps hopeful that a change of environment might entice her son to involve himself in something other than hedonistic pursuits. Perhaps it was with a small sigh of relief as well as a shiver of foreboding that she bade him farewell as he set out on his long, hazardous journey south.

Some in clandestine companies combine,
Erect new stocks to trade beyond the line;
With air and empty names beguile the town,
And raise new credits first, then cry 'em down:
Divide the empty nothing into shares,
To set the town together by the ears.
The sham projectors and the brokers join,
And both the cully merchant undermine;
First he must be drawn in and then betrayed,
And they demolish the machine they made:
So conjuring chymists, with their charm and spell,
Some wondrous liquid wondrously exhale;
But when the gaping mob their money pay,
The cheat's dissolved, the vapour flies away.
  Daniel Defoe, *Reformation of Manners* (1702)

LONDON WAS A REVELATION. LARGER THAN ANY OTHER
Western European capital (only Paris could come close), it was
home to some 750,000 inhabitants, many of whom, like Law,
had gravitated from elsewhere. Streets thronged with markets,

shops and hawkers noisily touting oysters, oranges, whalebone stays, patch-boxes, glass eyes, ivory teeth and mandrake potions. Amid the bustling street life, workmen toiled to complete vast building programmes begun after the Great Fire. A grand new Royal Exchange had already replaced the old one founded by Gresham, a new Dutch-style customs house now flanked the Thames, while forty-five livery company halls, fifty-one city churches and innumerable private houses were emerging to replace those that had been destroyed. It was an energetic, exciting milieu, but one in which the gulf between affluence and poverty was starkly evident. To the north and east, factories and workshops drew workers who lived in stinking, insanitary shanty-town hovels. Westwards, framed by green fields, St James's, the Strand and Piccadilly were inhabited by aristocrats and entrepreneurs who were transforming once rural sites into elegant piazzas, arcades of shops and avenues of grandiose mansions.

One imagines that the sharp-witted, rapacious Law must have greeted the city as James Boswell, a fellow Scotsman, did when he caught his first glimpse almost a century later: 'When we came to Highgate Hill and had a view of London, I was all life and joy . . . my soul bounded forth to a certain prospect of happy futurity. I sung all manner of songs, and began to make one about an amorous meeting with a pretty girl . . .'

He set himself up in lodgings in London's newly fashionable suburb of St Giles. Surrounded by countryside it was virtually a village, on higher ground than the city and encompassing Holborn, Covent Garden, Seven Dials and Bloomsbury. The area was renowned for its verdant surroundings; the grand Bloomsbury Square, the bustling flower-filled Covent Garden market with its church – well known as a meeting-place for unfaithful wives – and its 'sweating house', the Hummums Bagnio, where for five shillings one could find oneself 'as warm as a cricket at an oven's mouth'.

From the outset Law was determined to make his social and intellectual mark. Immaculately dressed, he presented himself as a new beau about town. He visited theatres such as the Drury Lane to enjoy the latest drama and admire the most celebrated actresses, strolled in the elegant walks of St James's and Vauxhall Gardens, shopped in the fashionable New Exchange – a favourite with beaux who, according to Ned Ward, a chronicler of London's less well-publicized customs, were happy to 'pay a double price for linen, gloves or sword-knots, to the prettiest of the women, that they might go from thence and boast among their brother fops what singular favours and great encouragement they had received'. He ate in taverns such as the Half Moon or Lockets – notorious for charging such high prices that 'many fools' estates have been squandered away' – breakfasting perhaps on ale, toast and cheese, or dining on roasted pigeons, goose, boiled calf's head and dumplings, or mutton steak. Alternatively, he might visit famous coffee-houses such as Will's in Covent Garden, the Royal near Charing Cross or the British in Cockspur Street – a favourite with visiting Scots, where he could catch up on foreign news, exchange ideas . . . and, if so inclined, procure the services of a prostitute.

London life was not without its pitfalls. Neither his fondness for female company nor his penchant for gambling had deserted John Law on his journey south. Gambling provided his entrée to society, women a refuge from its demands and disappointments. Both were to lead him astray. At some point after his arrival in London he was joined in his lodgings by his mistress, a Mrs Lawrence. Little is known of the woman who was to play a crucial part in his future career. What were her circumstances? Who kept whom? Perhaps they met in Duke Humphrey's Walk, St James's Park, 'a rare place for a woman who is rich enough to furnish herself with a gallant that will stick close, if she will allow him good clothes, three meals a day and a little money for usquebaugh [whisky]'. In which case she probably provided for Law who, though reasonably affluent, did not have the means to support an expensive mistress.

He must also have encountered many of London's most illustrious inhabitants. Although documentary evidence of this period of his life is sparse, among his probable acquaintances was Thomas Neale, the seedy Master of the Mint and Groom Porter to the King, and a keen property speculator. As part of his royal responsibilities Neale provided the cards, dice and other gambling equipment for the royal palaces, settled squabbles at the card table, licensed and supervised gaming-houses. He was not well suited to the role. Neale was a compulsive gambler who is said to have run through two fortunes at cards. Like Neale, Law quickly discovered the seamier side of London. The prevailing passion for gambling had created an entire social group, of gamesters whose fortunes depended on the roll of the dice or the cut of a pack. It was a life 'subject to more revolutions than a weathercock' in which, according to Ward, most 'die intestate, and go as poor out of the world as they came into it'. At Christmas Neale was allowed to keep an open gaming table, a chaotic and disorderly scrum where 'Curses were as profusely scattered as lies among travellers . . . money was tossed about as if a useless commodity . . . every man changed countenance according to the fortune of the cast, and some of them . . . in half an hour showed all the passions incident to human nature.' Already drawn to gambling in Edinburgh, Law was mesmerized by this frenetic, dangerous existence. Mingling with aristocrats and opportunists he joined in high-rolling games of hazard, brag, primero and basset – and predictably found himself dogged by ill-fortune. Bad luck and bad company took rapid toll. By early 1692, before his twenty-first birthday, Law's inheritance was exhausted and debts had mounted. Incarceration in a debtor's prison loomed, unless he could raise money. He had no option but to ask his mother to sell the Lauriston estate.

Jean Law now knew that her son was continuing his life of profligacy, but she did not despair. With formidable self-possession and business acumen she used her own well-managed legacy from her husband to buy the tenancy of the estates from her son and could congratulate herself that his reputation was salvaged, debtor's prison avoided, and her husband's money preserved.

The episode marked a turning point in Law's approach to gambling. Always intensely proud and private, he must have hated having to ask his mother for help. He began to see how easily he, like Neale, could lose all he possessed at the tables. And, unlike Neale, he had no lucrative royal position with which to rebuild his fortune. At the same time abstention from gambling was impossible. The pastime was almost *de rigueur* in polite society and provided a sociable beau such as Law with an easy way to infiltrate the glamorous circles to which he was drawn. To reduce the risk, without losing the frisson, he began to search for ways of loading the chances of success in his favour.

He became circumspect, almost academic in his approach to gambling. He studied various newly published pamphlets detailing theories of probability. Study in this field had long preoccupied scientists: Gerolamo Cardano had studied the science of dice-throwing at Padua University in the sixteenth century and had worked out that the reason it was easier to throw a nine than a ten with two dice was a matter of probability (1 in 9 for nine: 1 in 12 for ten). Galileo had also, reluctantly, tackled similar problems for his employer, and a century later new ground had been broken in France when mathematician Pascal was able to explain to his friend the Chevalier de Mère, that to have a marginally better than even chance of throwing a double six with two dice he would need to allow twenty-five throws. One of the first books on the subject was published anonymously in 1662 at a French monastery patronized by Pascal. *La logique ou l'art de penser* contained four chapters on probability and was widely translated and disseminated throughout Europe. The Swiss mathematician Jakob Bernoulli, whose *Art of Conjecturing*, a pioneering study of combinations and analysis of profit expectations from various games of chance, would be published posthumously in 1713, had also visited London at around this time, and Law may have known about Bernoulli's research.

Law's formidable mathematical talents must have made it easy for him to absorb the 'science' of chance, and he began to try out his new skill at the gaming salon. Over games of dice and cards he taught himself to calculate, often at incredible speed, the odds on a certain sequence of numbers being rolled at dice or a certain card appearing in the pack. 'No man understood calculation and numbers better than he; he was the first man in England that was at the pains to find out why seven to four or ten was two to one at hazard, seven to eight six to five, and so on in all the other chances of the dice, which he bringing to demonstration, was received amongst the most eminent gamesters, and grew a noted man that way,' recalled Gray, an acquaintance and Law's earliest biographer. The approach rapidly paid off and Law's luck turned. He ceased to be the stereotypical compulsive gambler, addicted to the frisson of gain but invariably losing. He had mastered the art of risk in much the same way a bookmaker is able to calculate odds. Betting became a serious business.

Nevertheless, even a master of odds cannot guarantee to win as much as Law seemed to do without cheating or drawing on some other advantage. Law's friends and contemporaries invariably describe him as a gambler, and either suspected him of card sharping or were simply amazed by his luck. How did he manage it? With hindsight, most biographers now feel that

Law's wins were not a result of luck but of wiliness. His large gains were made when he was able to adopt the role of banker – where the odds were stacked heavily in his favour – rather than punter. Most of the time when not playing banker he was presumably canny enough not to bet excessively. He is also known to have invented his own gambling games – where again he could ensure the odds were stacked in his favour.

Showpiece routines for the rich reaped hefty rewards, but they were not demanding enough to satisfy him for long. Law's study of probability must have reawakened his natural mathematical talent, and the urge to use it drew him to one of the new obsessions of the age: the science of economics.

At the time London was poised on the brink of economic and financial revolution. A flurry of publications had recently appeared penned by writers such as Sir William Petty, Nicholas Barbon and Hugh Chamberlen, who had debated monetary theory, commodities and currencies. There were two strands to the emerging material: some writers concentrated on ways of assisting mercantile trade, usually for their own profit; others blended the role of the state and issues of morality with the theme of money. All were anxious to solve, or at least explain, the nation's overwhelming shortage of cash and suggest ways of making it more prosperous.

William III was frantic for money to pursue his war in Europe but the royal record for failing to repay loans made London's goldsmiths and money-lenders reluctant to help. Memories lingered of Charles II's unreliability. And there was such an acute lack of coins that money was hard to come by. The treasury had tried threats and bribes but could raise only a paltry £70,000. It was not nearly enough to prop up the desperate King.

In 1694 Neale partly saved the day by instituting a government lottery that would provide a sixteen-year loan for the Crown. His scheme, something like today's premium bonds, sold tickets for £10 each, paid annual interest of 10 per cent, and also entitled the holder to a chance of winning some of the £40,000 annual prize money. The idea, borrowed from Venice, captured Londoners' imaginations – there were much-publicized stories of big wins – but failed to reach its target of raising £1 million. The diarist John Evelyn's coachman was one of the lucky ones: he won £40.

Law, perhaps surprisingly, deplored the use of lotteries to raise money. A few years later, when Victor Amadeus of Savoy asked for his advice on the subject Law's disapproval was unmistakable: 'Public lotteries are less bad than private ones, but they are injurious to a state. They do harm to the people, take the paltry sums they earn by their labour, make them dissatisfied with their lot, and give them a desire to grow rich by gambling and luck. Servants lacking money are tempted to steal from their masters to obtain means to play in the lottery.' What inspired such strongly voiced censure of 'gambling and luck'? Could it have been the humiliation of having to ask his mother to help him out with his gaming debts, or revulsion at recalling his seedy life as a London gamester?

Law's fascination with money taught him other crucial lessons. The Crown's chequered track record on repayment was only part of the reason why William found it hard to raise money. Equally to blame was the fact that the coinage was in disarray. At the Tower of London, Neale, in his role as mint master, was supervising a massive upheaval. Minting had remained virtually unchanged since the Middle Ages and much of the currency in circulation was over a century old. Coins varied hugely in weight and size because shavings of gold or silver had been pared from their middle or edges – a crime known as clipping – and used to make counterfeit coins or sold as bullion. All in all, by the late seventeenth century John Evelyn reckoned that England's coins contained less than half the silver or gold of their face value. The penalty for counterfeiting or clipping was death, but many were desperate enough to try it.

The unreliable coinage created difficulties for everyone: Ward was typically enraged when his money-dealer 'attempted to pay me in scrupulous diminutive pieces that I thought nothing but a knave would offer to pay, or a fool be willing to receive'. At times the situation was so acute that traders returned to bartering or charging inflated prices to compensate for the dubious value of the money available, and civil unrest frequently erupted. One remedy was to introduce new coins with a metal content closer to their face value, and with clipper-proof milled edges. At first the treasury circulated new coins without withdrawing the old ones and the situation grew even worse: money-dealers rushed to melt down the old coins and smuggle the resulting bullion on to the European market, where it fetched a higher price than in England – which proved a theory put forward a century earlier by Gresham and immortalized as Gresham's Law, that bad money drives out good. The financial pandemonium taught Law a valuable lesson: he began to see that for a country to prosper and maintain its political status quo, sound money was essential.

While the theoreticians and 'projectors' – entrepreneurial proposers of new financial schemes – wrestled with how to manufacture and maintain an adequate money supply, King William needed money to pay, feed and equip his soldiers against the French, and to build and fit new ships. But, infuriatingly, every request for a loan was thwarted. The only way out was to authorize one of the flurry of inventive money-raising projects. Many were hare-brained or deceitful, but a few held real promise. Watching from the sidelines, Law took note.

The ingenious scheme that William eventually sanctioned was proposed by William Paterson, a Scot. It was simple, as have been many of the most effective innovations throughout history. Basing his ideas on the highly successful national banks of Amsterdam and Venice, Paterson proposed that money could be raised for the King by the formation of a bank funded by a large number of private investors. Each would subscribe to a total value of £1,200,000, and this sum would then be loaned to the King for eleven years at 8 per cent interest. To allay fears of a repetition of Charles II's waywardness, the government would guarantee repayment of the loan. Depositors were to be given handwritten banknotes, signed by one of the bank's cashiers, which contained a promise to pay the bearer on demand the sum of the note – in other words, the note could be exchanged for gold or silver coin at any time by anyone presenting it for payment. Thus banknotes would circulate in a limited way as paper money.

The subscription list of the institution, known ever since as the Bank of England, was opened for investors on 21 June 1694. Within twelve days the total was subscribed. The King had enough money to pursue his war – for the time being at least – and the limited issue of banknotes as a new medium of exchange helped alleviate the shortage of coin.

Even if he had had the resources to do so John Law could not have invested in what turned out to be a financial landmark that underpinned the rapid advances of his age. He was in prison, convicted of murder.

Twill be in vain to make a long defence,
In vain twill be to plead thy innocence.
His breath concludes the sentence of the day,
He kills at once, for tis the Shortest Way.
Daniel Defoe, *More Reformation* (1703)

AS THEIR CARRIAGE DREW INTO BLOOMSBURY SQUARE, the two men must have seen John Law waiting. Perhaps, hearing the clatter of carriage wheels, he turned expectantly and watched as one of them descended from the carriage and strode purposefully towards him. It was just past midday on 9 April 1694.

Bloomsbury Square was a celebrated architectural landmark on the fringes of a rapidly advancing city. Three sides were framed with gracious brick-fronted façades, the recently completed residences of the well-to-do, who had escaped the stench of the city and gravitated to this district in search of 'good air'. Spanning the northern limit stretched the imposing, multi-pedimented Southampton House. Beyond, formal gardens avenued with lime trees led on to open fields that separated the square from nearby St Giles.

In spring and summer months this meadowland divide was filled with flowering grasses and scattered with cowslips, foxgloves and heartsease. Amorous couples wandered among the peach trees that, according to the great nineteenth-century historian Macaulay, improbably flourished here; snipe nested safely among grassy tussocks of damp undergrowth. Yet a more menacing convention overshadowed this urban Arcadia: the stretch of open terrain was renowned in seventeenth-century London as a place where duels were regularly fought.

It was on this ground that John Law paced apprehensively as the man from the carriage approached. It appeared – as several witnesses later attested – that a meeting had been prearranged between them. As he came face to face with Law, perhaps with a flourish of drunken confidence, the man drew his sword. Instantly and, he would later say, unthinkingly, John Law responded. Drawing his sword – 'a weapon of iron and steel that had cost five shillings' – with unexpected speed he made a single, defensive lunge. With a brief, anguished cry his opponent fell, mortally wounded, to the ground.

History does not record what happened next. We can surmise, however, that as in any metropolis a crowd gathered, and that among the cluster of ghoulish spectators and concerned passers-by was a sheriff's officer. John Law seems to have made no attempt to escape. Answering the officer's questions, he declared himself to be twenty-three years of age, presently a resident of the nearby parish of St Giles-in-the-Fields, where he had settled several years ago having moved from Edinburgh. The constable's attention turned next to the victim and his companion, who introduced himself as Captain Wightman. The dead man, noted the constable, was of similar age to his assailant and grandly dressed. Examining the corpse more closely, or asking Wightman to identify it, he must have flinched with surprise: the body was that of Edward Wilson, one of London's most enigmatic, flamboyant and talked-about beaux. His death, the stalwart constable might have reflected, could only serve to fuel the blaze of gossip already surrounding him.

While Law settled into London, he had not only pondered mathematical and financial conundrums. In his idle hours he had continued to gamble and philander. Practice had increased his winnings in both spheres, but along with the fashionable friends, enticing *amours* and triumphant gains had come enemies too. At some stage Law crossed the path of Edward Wilson, the fifth son of an impoverished gentleman from Keythorpe in Leicester, whose estate was heavily mortgaged. In his youth Wilson is believed to have served as a humble ensign in Flanders, but recently in London he had led such a flamboyant life that he had caught the eye of London society. John Evelyn described him living in 'the garb and equipage of the richest nobleman for house, furniture, coaches, saddle horses'. Another eighteenth-century writer recalled that he 'took a great house, furnished it richly, kept his coach and six, had abundance of horses in body clothes, kept abundance of servants, no man entertained nobler, nor paid better'. But where had the money come from? Even in the gossipy circles that both he and Law frequented no one could discover its source, though many hours were wasted talking about it.

Wilson paid off his father's debts and took care of his sisters by introducing them to polite society in the hope that they would make good marriages. One Miss Wilson moved into the same lodgings where John Law and his mistress Mrs Lawrence were living. At some point Wilson and Law clashed. Angry letters were exchanged over the impropriety of Law's living arrangements. Tempers ignited further when Miss Wilson, doubtless with her brother's encouragement, flounced out of the lodgings and took rooms elsewhere. Law was roundly scolded by his landlady who, egged on by Wilson, fussed that Law's libertine lifestyle might damage the reputation of her hitherto respectable establishment. She did not want scandal. Law retaliated by writing more angry letters to Wilson and, when these did not improve matters, paid a visit to his mansion. Over a glass of sack he warned him, unequivocally, to stop spreading rumours.

But animosity continued to brew. Events came to a climax on the morning of 9 April 1694, the day of the duel, when Law entered the Fountain tavern in the Strand and found himself face to face with Wilson and his friend Captain Wightman. Significantly, Wightman never divulged precisely what was said in the crucial exchange leading to the fatal duel. He commented only that 'after they had staid a little while there, Mr Lawe* went away, after which Mr Wilson and Captain Wightman took coach, and were drove towards Bloomsbury', which implies that Wilson was the aggressor. If not, as a friend of Wilson, Wightman would have said so.

John Law was arrested and taken to Newgate prison to await his trial. Prison life in the late seventeenth century was redolent of menace. 'The mixtures of scents that arose from tobacco, dirty sheets, stinking breaths, and uncleanly carcasses, poisoned our nostrils far worse than a Southwark ditch, a tanner's yard or a tallow chandler's melting room. The ill-looking vermin with long rusty beards . . . came hovering round us, like so many cannibals, with such devouring countenances as if a man had been but a morsel . . .' one eye witness recalled of a terrifying night spent in a typical London gaol. Newgate, its cells crowded with prisoners awaiting execution or sentence for capital offences, was the most fearsome

---

*Law's name is variously spelled in seventeenth- and eighteenth-century texts – Lawe and Lawes often appear in England and in France Lass is a common alternative.

of all London's gaols. Later Daniel Defoe was incarcerated there on charges of seditious libel, and an inkling of the horrors to which inmates were subjected may be gleaned from his novel *Moll Flanders*, ''Tis impossible to describe the terror of my mind, when I was first brought in . . . the hellish noise, the roaring, swearing and clamour, the stench and nastiness, and all the dreadful crowd of afflicting things that I saw there, joined to make the place seem an emblem of hell itself,' Moll recalled.

Law was almost certainly spared Newgate's worst extremes because he had at his disposal two potent weapons that Moll did not: money and friends in high places. Though far less famous than his victim, he moved by now in elevated circles, and when word of his arrest spread, wealthy friends rallied to his support, offering guidance and, more importantly, money to make his stay in prison more bearable. For a considerable fee he could enjoy the relative luxury of rooms in the King's block, away from the misery and corruption of life 'commonside'. But though gratefully availing himself of the benefits of wealth and influence Law failed to grasp their more fundamental advantages. In seamy seventeenth-century London, they offered not only a comfortable cell, but a buffer against the corrupt wheels of justice. Against his friends' advice, Law never attempted to deny his part in Wilson's death. His story never changed: Wilson had drawn his sword first, Law had acted in self-defence. He was not guilty of murder, he claimed repeatedly, but of manslaughter.

Yet in the eyes of seventeenth-century justice the case was not so clear cut. The question of who initiated the fight was irrelevant. What counted was whether the fight had been premeditated, and whether Law had 'with malice afore-thought' planned to kill Wilson. There was plenty of evidence to support this hypothesis, Wilson's relatives claimed. Wightman testified that earlier in the day the two men had quarrelled bitterly. Then Wilson's manservant revealed their long-standing rivalry over Mrs Lawrence and letters were found among the dead man's belongings that proved a lengthy and acrimonious disagreement had existed. Thus, after several days in Newgate, Law was informed that he would be charged not with manslaughter but with the capital offence of murder.

The case came to court at the routine sitting of the King and Queen's Commissions at the Old Bailey a few days later. A typical mixture of cases was to be heard; most were routine charges of stealing – jewellery, gold, silver, silk dresses, petticoats, tippets, scarves and stockings (textiles feature high in lists of seventeenth-century burglars' loot). A further five prisoners faced capital charges of counterfeiting and clipping coins. There were two alleged rapists and, strangely, a man accused of road-rage, usually assumed to be a late-twentieth-century phenomenon: one Matthew Pryor was indicted for driving the near wheel of his coach against the left leg of a lady who later died of the injury. (He was acquitted: there was no proof he had driven with deliberate lack of care.)

Law must have shuddered when he learned that his case was to be heard by the ageing Sir Salathiel Lovell, who prided himself on his high conviction rate, and who is remembered for his appalling memory, questionable integrity and the sadistic pleasure he derived from tormenting those who came before him. Lenient sentences were conferred on defendants who offered bribes, and he was happy, if necessary, to take a share of a criminal's booty. Those unable to pay experienced a brutality only exceeded by his notorious contemporary Judge Jeffreys. Daniel Defoe stood before Lovell and lampooned him in the *Reformation of Manners*:

> *L— the Pandor of thy Judgment Seat*
> *Has neither Manners, Honesty nor Wit,*
> *Instead of which, he's plenteously supplied*

With nonsense, noise, impertinence and Pride . . .
But always serves the hand who pays him well;
He trades in justice and the souls of men
And prostitutes them equally to gain.

Law, by now just twenty-three, was an opportunist with an idealistic streak who had not, as far as we know, come before the judiciary before. With all the naïveté, stubbornness and recklessness of youth, he refused to doubt the system, having never previously experienced it. Now, faced with Lovell's mercenary brand of justice, he was disillusioned.

Lovell instructed the jury that everything rested on whether the two men had prearranged their duel: 'if they found that Mr Lawe and Mr Wilson did make an agreement to fight, though Wilson drew first, and Mr Lawe killed him, he was [by construction of the law] guilty of murder'. Legal procedure of the time meant that, as defendant in a Crown case, Law was not entitled to a legal representative, or to testify or to call witnesses. His solitary means of defence was an unsworn statement that was read out in court. In it he claimed that the meeting in Bloomsbury 'was an accidental thing, Mr Wilson drawing his sword upon him first, upon which he was forced to stand in his own defence'. Therefore, he argued, 'the misfortune did arise only from a sudden heat of passion, and not from any propense malice'. Numerous character witnesses 'of good quality' testified at length to Law's unquarrelsome nature and general good character.

But nothing could detract from the judge's damning influence: 'This was a continual quarrel, carried on betwixt them for some time before, therefore must be accounted a malicious Quarrel, and a design of murder in the person that killed the other,' he said, in summing up the case. Law's friends claimed later that both judge and jury had been bought off by Wilson's powerful and vengeful relatives, which seems highly probable, bearing in mind Lovell's reputation. In any event Law's case was lost. After 'having considered the verdict very seriously' the jury declared that he was indeed guilty of murder as charged.

A total of twenty-eight defendants were convicted during the three-day hearing. Of these, twenty-one, mostly burglars and thieves, were to be punished by branding or 'burnt in the hand' as it was termed. One was to be transported. The remaining five were sentenced to death by hanging. Three were forgers and clippers of coins. The fourth was the rapist. The fifth was the twenty-three-year-old duellist John Law.

Chapter Five

Escape

Mr Laws knows best how he made his escape. Many odd storys were then told, particularly that he took the sleeping of the sentinel for some hours at his door to be a trick and that he bought an underkeeper . . .

James Johnston, *Earl of Warriston* (1719)

AFTER THE TRAUMAS OF THE DUEL, THE TRIAL AND HIS murder conviction, Law could do little but wait for events to unfold. His mood was surprisingly sanguine. A seventeenth-century man of privilege expected justice to be pliant and merciful, particularly if his crime was widely regarded as honourable.

In the privileged world of both Law and Wilson, duelling was one of the unwritten rules of membership – a nobleman's way of settling a dispute and thus, in some deep-rooted sense, a ritualistic badge of rank. It was expected that a gentleman would issue a challenge if his honour was in any way impugned. If he did not, or if his opponent resisted such a challenge, it would be tantamount to an admission that he was not a gentleman – which the dashing John Law would never have countenanced. Since the restoration of the monarchy duelling had flourished. Among the journals of the day there are numerous examples of fatal conflicts arising from the most trivial of slights. Shades of Law's escapade echo in John Evelyn's diary note of a duel involving a young spendthrift, Conyers Seymour, who 'had a slight affront in St James's Park, given him by one who was envious of his gallantries, for he was a vain foppish young man'.

The covert respectability of duelling was reflected in the way surviving protagonists were treated. Charles II had issued a proclamation against duellists but invariably pardoned those convicted, and a blind eye was turned throughout William's reign. Duellists made frequent appearances in the courts, but were never put to death for their crime. 'I neither heard before nor after that killing a man in a fair duel was found murder,' remarked Law's friend James Johnston, the Earl of Warriston. In his Newgate cell, Law must have concluded calmly, therefore, that there was no cause for alarm. A reprieve was certain. Over the following weeks and months his optimism began to seem misplaced.

Wilson's cousins – the Townsend, Ash and Windham families – were eager to avenge the death of their kinsman. All were prominent courtiers and as such 'strangely prepossessed King William'. They anticipated, correctly, that Law's supporters would try to secure a royal pardon so they besieged the King with counter-demands. In this particularly brutal duel, they insisted, Law had shown himself a man of dishonour. Premeditated malice had been proven, therefore no mercy should be shown. Within days of the trial, a haze of subterfuge and intrigue pervaded the cabinets and corridors of Whitehall Palace. Caught in its midst King William became uneasy and increasingly irate whenever the matter was raised.

Law's most stalwart supporter was the Earl of Warriston. A fellow Scot, intelligent, honest, and a brilliant lawyer,

Warriston had been brought up in Holland, and studied law in Utrecht. His bond with King William was long-standing – Warriston had helped to set up an intelligence network before the Glorious Revolution of 1688, which had brought William to the throne. At the time of Law's imprisonment, Warriston was Scottish Secretary, having replaced the disgraced Earl of Stair in the aftermath of the massacre of Glencoe.

How or where Law and Warriston met is not known, but the bond between them must have been close because Warriston braved the King's wrath more than once to help. First he accosted William at his morning levee with the claim that Wilson's supporters had bought off the jury, and that Law was being made unjustly to 'suffer for his ingenuity'. His legal expertise told him that 'without Mr Law's confession the fact could not have been proved, for those that saw it being strangers to him when brought to prison to see him, could only swear that it was one like him'. In other words, if Law had denied his presence he would probably have escaped sentence of death.

The King's antipathy to his Scottish subjects was immediately apparent in his scathing retort: 'What . . . Scotchmen suffer for their ingenuity. Was ever such a thing known?' The more Warriston attempted to reason with him, the more the royal anger smouldered: 'When I reasoned the matter . . . I was more rudely treated by him and the nation too than we ever had been upon any occasion.' The King was convinced that money lay at the root of the quarrel. 'He could not but believe . . . that Mr Laws had quarrelled with Wilson who, he said, was a known coward, in order to make him give him money.' This placed a sordid complexion on the matter and he saw no reason for the death sentence to be lifted.

Warriston realized he would need help to overcome the King's antagonism and enlisted the help of the dashing Duke of Shrewsbury, who at the time 'had more power . . . with the King than any man alive', and, fortunately for Law, also owed Warriston a favour. Shrewsbury cannily advised Warriston to play for time and let the King's temper subside – 'he would keep it out of the cabinet for a week', he promised. In the meantime, Warriston should try to find evidence 'that it was not a money business'.

Somehow Warriston made contact with one of Law's money-dealers who confirmed that 'a little before' the duel Law had received '£400 from Scotland by Bill, which the Banker's book could show'. Law, therefore, had plenty of money and no reason to resort to extortion. Shrewsbury was convinced by this testimony and passed the information to the King with the confident assurance 'that there was nothing of money in the case'. But to the King the dilemma still seemed insoluble. Now that his original objection was disproven Warriston and Shrewsbury were pestering him to release Law; yet he had promised the Wilsons he would never pardon Law without their consent, and he could not risk upsetting them. Eventually he took the middle ground: Law was reprieved from the death sentence but not released, pending the Wilsons' reaction.

They retaliated dramatically, issuing an 'Appeal of Murder', an ancient legal procedure that allowed the heir to a murder victim to oppose a royal pardon. If they succeeded the King could have no further jurisdiction over the outcome. They would be able to demand Law's death and not even a royal pardon would save him.

The case was now a civil one and came under the jurisdiction of the Court of the King's Bench at Westminster Hall. Without tasting freedom, Law was transferred from Newgate to the King's Bench prison in Southwark – from one grim hell-hole to another – to await this second trial. Opinion had swung markedly in Wilson's favour. Even Warriston privately admitted the worst: 'Mr Law's case is very doubtful, all indifferent men are against him; and I never had so many reproaches for any business since I knew England, as for concerning myself for him: my Lord Chief Justice is earnest to have his life, the Archbishop owns to me that he himself pressed the King not to pardon him, as being a thing of an odious nature, and which would give great offence,' he wrote gloomily.

On 22 June, almost two months after the first trial, Law came before the King's Bench. To his relief, he found Chief Justice Sir John Holt officiating. Unlike Lovell, Holt is remembered for his fair-mindedness, humanity – he ended the practice of bringing defendants to the dock in irons – and for the exceptionally profligate and debauched friends he made while at Oxford. Years later one of them came before him on a charge of felony. Holt inquired after the rest of the circle to be told, 'Ah, my lord, they are all hanged but myself and your lordship.'

Since this was a civil action, Law was now entitled to his own defence and enlisted some of the most eminent lawyers of the day: Sir William Thompson and Sir Creswell Levinz with Thomas Carthew as junior. As soon as the case opened it became apparent that, even with this support, his prospects were even worse than everyone had feared. Wilson's legal team had prepared a damning case, claiming that Law had committed murder '. . . violently, feloniously, wilfully, and of his malice aforethought', and furthermore that he had cowardly attempted to evade arrest. Robert Wilson said he had been forced to give chase 'from vill to vill into the four nearest vills and further . . .'. Bearing in mind that this is the only mention of Law's attempt to evade justice, Wilson's version of events rings hollow and was probably just another malicious attempt to manipulate the court and make the case against Law even blacker.

Law's defence team opted to use technical quibbles to demolish the Wilson case. There were serious discrepancies in the writ against their client, they complained: the time and place of the incident had not been precisely given; the charge against Law was indirect and thus there was 'no necessity, nor is he [Law] bound by the law of the land to answer' the Wilson appeal. Clearly the argument carried weight because Holt and his learned colleagues needed time to consider the complexities raised and deferred judgment for a week. But by late June, Trinity term was drawing to a close and the hearing was postponed until the following autumn.

Law now faced the prospect of several months in the King's Bench prison, a loathsome penal establishment. But, unlike the fortress Newgate, where the turnkey locked the prison gates and did not reappear till morning, King's Bench was notoriously insecure. Ever since his removal there friends had urged him to try to escape. Even Warriston, pillar of the establishment though he was, whispered that Law was 'a blockhead if he make not his escape which he may easily do considering the nature of that prison.' So far Law had resisted, hoping that he would be legally released. Now, faced with what seemed an interminable wait and a doubtful outcome, he listened. Friends offered to smuggle in tools, and by mid-October he was surreptitiously filing down the bars of his prison cell, dreaming of freedom.

It was a short-lived illusion. On 20 October the diarist Narcissus Luttrell noted that Law's filed bars had been discovered by one of his guards. To prevent any further attempts he was manacled in irons. Even the stalwart Warriston now despaired. 'I am afraid Mr Law shall be hanged at last, for I am in a manner resolved to meddle no more in the matter; had he had his senses about him, he had been out of danger long before now,' he wrote despondently. A tragic conclusion seemed even more certain when Judge Holt decided that Law's legal objections had failed. He would face the Wilson appeal as charged in the new year of 1695.

So much for the record. At this point traditional legend and probable fact diverge. According to the usual story, which Law did nothing to discourage, somehow he laid his hands on powerful opiates and more tools. Shortly before his trial, he broke free of his irons, drugged his guards, filed down the bars of his cell, scaled the prison wall – and suffered no more than a sprained ankle in the process. A waiting carriage then whisked him to the coast, where he sailed to safety on the Continent.

The truth was almost certainly rather more complex and much more astonishing. By autumn of 1694, Law had given up hope of legally escaping the death sentence, but his friends had not forgotten him and his case was still debated in court circles. The King remained irresolute but eventually, with royal blessing, the Duke of Shrewsbury announced to Warriston that the only satisfactory conclusion would be for Law to be saved, 'provided it can be done in such a manner, as that his majesty did not appear in it, nor must I [Shrewsbury]'.

Warriston reacted quickly. Assuring them 'that nothing was more easy than to give a verbal order to the keeper to let him make his escape, as had been done in many a thousand cases', he began to plot Law's escape himself. Secrecy was paramount: if either the King, the Duke or Warriston was known to have sanctioned the escape of an already notorious convicted felon a huge public scandal might result. This time the plan succeeded. Warriston, having witnessed the bungled first attempt, knew that Law would need help to escape successfully. He found two underkeepers 'to offer . . . services to Mr Laws'. One night, soon after New Year, the underkeepers drugged the guards on the door, took turns to file down Law's manacles and released him from his cell. A few days later Warriston met the Duke, who 'whispered to me in a crowd, that my friend was at liberty . . . and prayed me to keep his secret'. Warriston was as good as his word and never spoke of the matter 'till King William's death, or at least that the duke was out of all business'.

To Law the freedom of which he had dreamed and despaired

came as a shock. He did not expect to be pushed to liberty and, fearful that the open door and sleeping guards were merely another example of Wilson chicanery, was bemused when it happened. Years later he would own that 'though he knew nothing nor does yet know of the truth . . . that he himself was surprised with the zeal and forwardness of the underkeepers who relieved one another in sawing off his irons'. The truth was that Law was happy for the world to believe what it liked of his escape because even he did not fully know how it had happened.

The escape, announced a few days later in court, aroused the Wilson family's outrage. They immediately ensured that Law was declared a fugitive from justice, and a reward for his apprehension was offered in the *London Gazette* of Monday 7 January 1695. But here, too, their attempts to recapture Law were thwarted. The publication was produced under the auspices of the Secretary of State – none other than the Duke of Shrewsbury. Doubtless with his connivance, the advertisement was worded as follows: 'Captain John Lawe, a Scotchman, lately a prisoner in the King's Bench for murder, aged 26, a very tall, black, lean man, well shaped, above six foot high, large pock holes in his face, big high nosed, speaks broad and loud, made his escape from the said prison. Whoever secures him, so as he may be delivered at the said prison, shall have fifty pounds paid immediately by the Marshall of the King's Bench.'

The unidentified person who placed the notice ensured that the description of the handsome fugitive was wildly inaccurate. John Law was not a captain, nor was his face pock-marked, nor was his voice 'broad and loud'. If anything, the unattractive picture it painted helped his successful escape.

Public interest, already avid at the time of the trial, was whipped up further by the drama and romance of Law's flight. Everyone expected that he would make for his native Scotland and attention focused on roads to the north. There was at least one false alarm. Narcissus Luttrell noted a writ of Habeas Corpus issued 'for bringing up hither Mr Lawes, who killed Mr Wilson, he being apprehended in Leicestershire as he was riding post for Scotland.' Then, a few days later on 26 January, he disappointedly recorded the latest instalment: 'The report of Lawes being taken in Leicestershire proves a mistake; 'twas another person.'

Even years later the details of the duel and escape were still picked over. Most agreed that there was more to the matter than evidence in court had suggested, and that the origins of Wilson's money lay at the root of the matter. Many bizarre theories were put forward to make sense of the scant facts. John Evelyn wrote, 'It did not appear that he was kept by women, play, coining, padding, or dealing in chemistry; but he would sometimes say that if he should live ever so long, he had wherewith to maintain himself in the same manner.' *The Unknown Lady's Pacquet of Letters* published in 1707 offered one solution. According to their author, Wilson had accidentally met a masked woman in Kensington Gardens and, without knowing who she was, embarked on an illicit affair with her. The woman forced Wilson to agree that he would never attempt to discover her identity and in return paid him a generous retainer. But the temptation for Wilson was too great. When he discovered that the woman was Elizabeth Villiers, the King's boss-eyed, unattractive mistress, she was furious that he had broken his word and enlisted the help of her friend Law, whom she knew to be already embroiled in a quarrel with Wilson, to avenge them both. Villiers assured Law that, with her royal connections, he would escape the usual punishment.

This extraordinarily far-fetched account was countered a decade or so later by another outlandish and recently rediscovered theory. A pamphlet thought to have been published around 1723, entitled *Love Letters Between a Certain Late Nobleman and the Famous Mr Wilson: Discovering the True History of the Rise and Surprising Grandeur of that Celebrated Beau*, suggested that Wilson's money came secretly from a homosexual lover and that Law had been involved in the intrigue and had fallen out with Wilson over it. But by the time this version of events was published, Law was an internationally famous figure, who had rocked the financial structure of the Western world. Europe was full of satirical and slanderous attacks on his character and background – and this, in all probability, was one of them.

The truth remains enigmatic.

What is not in doubt is that the duel and the events surrounding it formed a template for the rest of John Law's life. His blinkered high principles and refusal to compromise, his willingness to wager everything – life itself – in a matter of honour landed him in similar dire predicaments, when he had to rely on prominent friends to propel him to safety. It is possible, too, that while it was the duelling convention as much as reckless courage that induced him to respond to Wilson's challenge in the first place, the violence of the encounter, his brush with death and the horrific experience of prison unsettled him more than he revealed. Years afterwards, it may have been these disturbing memories that spurred the loss of control that surfaced in similarly stressful situations.

Certainly, too, the inscrutable John Law had resolved that the duel's full story should be left untold. As he stood on the deck of the packet ship crossing to the Continent and savoured his freedom, he forgot his past and prepared for a new life.

Flushed with success and skill at all manner of play, he goes from Genoa to Venice, where his good fortune continues so, that he was worth twenty thousand pounds sterling.

With this foundation he began to look about him, and consider how to improve this stock in a solid way of trade . . . having made himself entirely master of these things he frames a paper scheme of his own, and resolves with it to make himself happy and great in his own native country.

W. Gray, *The Memoirs, Life and Character of the Great Mr Law and his Brother at Paris* (1721)

WHAT EXACTLY LAW DID AFTER LEAVING LONDON REMAINS mysterious. As if deliberately to separate himself from his past, the trail of documentary evidence he has left of his life during the next two decades is sparsely and confusingly scattered throughout Europe. He appears in France, where predictably the gambling salons of Paris proved a magnet. He is noted in prison in Caen – his papers were apparently not in order. There was also a lengthy stay in Holland and visits to various cities in Italy. Everywhere he went, his life followed a familiar pattern, with gaming and perilous romance recurring themes. But there are also signs that the lure of the gaming salon and boudoir were not alone in absorbing him: John Law quickly rekindled his fascination with economics.

His growing obsession is underlined by the places he visited: Amsterdam, Venice, Genoa and Turin offered tantalizing cultural and social attractions. All were cities well stocked with rich tourists and residents, where a gamester of Law's superior ability knew that there would be ample scope to supplement his income. More tellingly, all were key financial centres. Amsterdam, his home for several years, offered idyllic country-side resembling 'a large garden, the roads all well paved, shaded on each side with rows of trees and bordered with large canals full of boats'; it had fine civic buildings, immaculate houses, and women 'more nicely clean' than their English counterparts. But Law was attracted to it chiefly because the city was the commercial capital of Europe, and its success was due to a bank.

Amid the monetary confusion of the time, the Bank of Amsterdam had achieved the seemingly impossible: it had brought economic stability to the country, boosted trade and, for a time, made the Netherlands the commercial superpower of the world. Founded in 1609, the bank's governing principles were simple. Adulterated coins were the same scourge in main-land Europe as they were in England, and a vast variety – some eight hundred different denominations of gold and silver coins – circulated. Currency could be exchanged in every town and at every fair throughout Europe, but in Amsterdam the bank took deposits in local and foreign coinage, weighed and assessed them for their purity and in return issued credit notes or bank money – a form of paper money – representing the *intrinsic* value of the metal content of the coins rather than their nominal face value. The bank money, Law astutely observed, provided hefty benefits: 'Besides the convenience of easier and quicker payments . . . the bank save[s] the expense of cashiers, the expense of bags and carriage, losses by bad money, and the money is safer than in the merchants' houses, for 'tis less liable to fire or robbery.' The bank guaranteed credit notes and in its turn was endorsed by the state. Since the value of the notes was assured, the public preferred them to conventional coins and they usually changed hands for more than face value.

Amsterdam's bank was not the first to turn to paper as a substitute form of money. Paper notes were invented, like so many ingenious artefacts, by the ancient Chinese, who are known to have used them in the seventh century. In Europe, nearly a thousand years later, tentative trials had been made in 1656 in Sweden, where a Livonian, Johan Palmstruch, was given a royal privilege to found a private bank, provided that half of his profits were paid to the Crown. Sweden was rich in copper but poor in silver and gold, and its currency included massive copper sheets, of equivalent worth to silver coin, but so heavy – as much as fifteen kilograms – that people carried them lashed to their backs or needed a horse and cart to transport them. In 1661 Palmstruch and his Stockholm Banco overcame this inconvenience by printing paper notes that represented the value of the metal currency, the first true circulating European banknotes as we understand them today. The project blossomed initially but the temptation to over-issue notes proved irresistible. Six years later, unable to redeem the notes it had produced, the bank foundered and Palmstruch landed in prison, only narrowly escaping execution.

Three decades later in America, there was a further foray into paper money. In 1690 the Massachusetts Bay Colony was forced to use banknotes to pay its soldiers after the failure of a military incursion into Quebec, which had been expected to yield enough plunder to pay them. In place of gold and silver salaries the men were given paper notes that would be redeemed, they were promised, as soon as taxes were paid by the local community. Predictably the shortage of hard cash continued to beset the colony, and two years later, citing 'the present poverty and calamities of this country, and through scarcity of money, the want of an adequate measure of commerce', the paper was made legal tender. Other colonies, beset by similar cash shortages, soon followed suit.

Of all the unpromising and disparate seeds from which the paper revolution grew, Amsterdam stood out as a shining exemplar of prudence. Loans to private individuals were offered only against deposits of silver and gold and were carefully restricted; there was no mass circulation of notes without metal reserves. The result was that everyone had faith in Amsterdam's bank. One visitor, Sir William Temple, remarked, 'Foreigners lodge here what part of their money they could transport and know no way of securing at home.' Overseas investors, including English, Spanish and other governments, gladly used it, and their vast deposits were then advanced as loans at modest rates of interest. In this way fleets were financed, and trade thrived. In 1609 the bank had 730 accounts; by the end of the century it had 2,700, with over 16 million florins held on deposit. Trust in a bank had secured an entire nation's fortune.

In 1697, two years after Law's life of exile began, peace temporarily descended on Europe. The treaty of Ryswick brought to a close the bitter Nine Years War between France and Austria, Holland, England, Spain, Sweden and Savoy. France became more accessible to foreign tourists and around this time Law made what was probably his first visit to Paris.

The city must have captivated him. During the past forty years of Louis XIV's reign, Paris had become 'one of the most beautiful and magnificent [cities] in Europe', according to Dr Martin Lister, who visited the same year as Law, 'in which a traveller might find novelties enough for six months for daily entertainment'. It was a city of stone-paved streets and ornately carved façades replete with hidden treasure. 'As the houses are magnificent without, so the finishing within and furniture answer in riches and neatness; as hangings of rich tapestry, raised with gold and silver threads, crimson damask and velvet beds or of gold and silver tissue. Cabinets and bureaus of ivory inlaid with tortoiseshell, and gold and silver plates in a 100 different manners; branches and candlesticks of crystal,' the overawed doctor reported.

For the visiting beau, city life offered much. By day he might choose to follow the familiar tourist route, visiting the Louvre, or the King's Library, promenading in the Tuileries, the Luxembourg or Physic Garden, or hiring a coach to drive to 'a great rendezvous of people of fashion', the Cour de La Reine, a triple-avenued park bordering the Seine. As night fell, there was the opera at the Palais Royal or the Comédie Française or, during the season, the bustling fair of St Germain, where stalls remained open long into the night.

Once settled, Law gravitated to the court of the erstwhile King James II. Reliant upon the generosity of Louis XIV for his subsistence, James was currently living in impoverished exile in St Germain-en-Laye, a château outside Paris. The Jacobite court seethed with covert plots to reinstate him, and it is impossible to be certain how genuine Law's sympathies were with his cause. He may have visited the court merely because he hankered for the company of fellow Scots; or, as he later suggested, to rejoin some of the friends who had helped him to escape from London; or, more questionably, to infiltrate the court in the hope of gathering intelligence of Jacobite schemes. Performing such a service might gain him favour with King William and help secure a pardon – which preoccupied Law throughout his years of exile.

Gaming, 'a perpetual diversion here, if not one of the debauches of the town', claimed his interest, and even more so than in London offered the easiest way to meet high society.

As one visitor put it, 'It is a great misfortune for a stranger not to be able to play, but yet a greater to love it. Without gaming one can't enter into that sort of company that usurps the name of *Beau Monde*, and no other qualification but that and money are requisite to recommend to the first company in France.' Predictably, much of Law's time was spent in stylish salons mingling with the élite, gaining their confidence with his insinuating charm and impeccable manners, before fleecing them at faro and basset, two of the most fashionable and high-rolling games of the day, at which he excelled. The odds in both games are stacked heavily in favour of the banker – a role Law adopted whenever he could, possibly paying his hostess for the privilege. One acquaintance remembered that Law 'never carried less than two bags filled with gold coins worth around 100,000 livres' and that the stakes were so high that his hands 'were unable to contain the coins he wished to stake' and he had his own tokens minted, each worth eighteen louis d'or.

Travel, and the unfortunate affair with Mrs Lawrence, had done nothing to blunt Law's enthusiasm for romance. Perhaps it was after a particularly successful evening at the tables that he was introduced to Madame Katherine Seigneur, née Knowles, an expatriate outsider in the court of St Germain who had married a Frenchman. Katherine was of noble birth, a descendant of Anne Boleyn, Henry VIII's second wife, and the sister of the Earl of Banbury. Law had probably met her brother, and if not had certainly heard of him while in the King's Bench prison in London: he, too, had been involved in a fatal duel. There are no surviving original portraits of her, although she sat at least once for her friend, the famous Italian pastellist Rosalba Carriera, but a Dutch engraving, possibly made after one of them, shows an immaculately dressed woman with dainty features, a generous bosom and minuscule waist. Judging by descriptions of her she was not, however, an obvious target for Law's attentions. The Duc de Saint-Simon recalled candidly that she was 'rather handsome', but that her beauty was flawed by a birthmark like a winestain 'covering one eye and the upper part of her cheek'. Katherine had another crucial distinction: among the over-powdered, over-rouged, coquettish ladies of fashionable Paris, Saint-Simon noticed, 'She was proud, overbearing and very impertinent in her talk and manners, seldom returning any of the polite attentions offered to her.' Although in England overtly intelligent women were not generally esteemed – most men would have tended to agree with Samuel Johnson's later quip that 'a man is in general better pleased when he has a good dinner on his table than when his wife talks Greek' – in France it was different. Amid Parisian society women enjoyed a greater level of in-dependence. 'It is observable', wrote one visitor, 'that the French allow their women all imaginable freedoms, and are seldom troubled by jealousy; nay, a Frenchman will almost suffer you to court his wife before his face, and is even angry if you do not admire her person.' Perhaps Law, having learned to respect his mother's formidable business acumen, had an unusual regard for clever, outspoken females and this daunting, difficult, striking woman reminded him of the awe-inspiring Jean – or, accustomed as he was to easy conquests, he simply found her hauteur challenging. In any event, he pursued Katherine with determination, and she, evidently dissatisfied by her marriage, must have responded. Yet even had she not been married, such a relationship would have caused consternation: Katherine was of noble birth while Law was a gamester, whose family circumstances were shrouded in mystery. Society frowned on such alliances and most people sympathized with Lord Sandwich, who later remarked that a father would rather see a daughter 'with a pedlar's bag at her back' than marry beneath her. To Law and Katherine, however, far from home and their families, there was little to stand in the way of their mutual attraction. Certainly, Katherine's husband (about whom nothing is known apart from his name) seems to have offered no impediment – although the most obvious explanation for his apparent inertia is that he was absent when she and Law met. The liaison blossomed.

Meanwhile, Law's mastery of dice and cards had unfortunate but unsurprising repercussions. No one wants to stake money against someone who hardly ever loses and, as it had in London, Law's knack of winning brought him enemies along with gains. Whispers of his 'sharpness' at cards, his dubious past and his possible involvement in espionage began to circulate and brought him to the attention of the authorities. Clearly the time had come for Law to move on; only Katherine held him back.

In the sophisticated world of which both Law and Katherine were habitués, discreet infidelities, however ill-advised, could be quickly forgotten – but there was a chasm between a clandestine affair and an elopement. Both must have known that the latter would cost Katherine her reputation and that there would be no turning back. It is, therefore, a mark of the usually guarded Law's feelings that he asked Katherine to leave Paris with him. The decision cannot have been easy, but, perhaps feeling that travel offered the only way for such an unconventional partnership to evade the usual social restrictions, she agreed, in Gray's words, 'to pack up her awls, leave her husband, and run away with him to Italy'. From now on Katherine Seigneur was known as Mrs John Law even though marriage, for the time being at least, was impossible. As no doubt they had feared, the story of their flight made headlines in the Paris press and Horace Walpole later wrote of 'an account in some French literary gazette, I forget which, of his [Law] having carried off the wife of another man.'

Their destination was Italy, the birthplace of European banking. They went first to Genoa, where, according to Gray, Law was able to find 'cullies enough to pick up a great deal of Money from', and later to Rome, Florence, Turin and Venice.

In each city he visited he played the tables and worked at his research into finance. The great public banking institutions of Italy had been born in the Middle Ages from the need to fund crusades, commerce and war. By the late sixteenth century Venice's state banks – the Banco di Rialto and the Banco del Giro, operated much like the bank in Amsterdam, which had followed the Venetian lead, accepting deposits in adulterated coin and issuing notes in 'bank money' with the guarantee of the state. Law also learned much about foreign-exchange dealing in Venice. According to Gray, 'He constantly went to the Rialto at change-time [when the exchange was open], no merchant upon commission was punctualler, he observed the course of exchange all the world over, the manner of discounting bills at the bank, the vast usefulness of paper credit, how gladly people parted with their money for paper, and how the profits accrued to the proprietors from this paper.'

Along with its bank, Venice had much to attract John Law and his beautiful companion. They arrived in time for the famous carnival, which began on Twelfth Night, when some thirty thousand foreigners invaded the city to enjoy a bacchanalian extravaganza of acrobatics, music, animal fights, fireworks, dancing in the streets and, according to one spectator, 'Women, men and persons of all conditions disguise themselves in antique dresses, with extravagant music and a thousand gambols, traversing the streets from house to house, all places being then accessible and free to enter.'

Venice was famed for sex and gambling. The city dubbed 'the brothel of Europe' had gambling houses or *Ridotti*, 'where none but noblemen keep the bank, and fools lose their money'. One rueful English visitor described a typical *soirée*: 'They dismiss the gamesters when they please, and always come off winners. There are usually ten or twelve chambers on a floor with gaming-tables in them, and vast crowds of people; a profound silence is observed, and none are admitted without masks. Here you meet ladies of pleasure, and married women who under the protection of a mask enjoy all the diversions of the carnival.' With Katherine at his side, Law presumably ignored sexual distractions and capitalized on the plentiful opportunities for making money instead.

By the end of his tour of Italy, his financial expertise had opened numerous doors: the Duc de Vendôme and the Duke of Savoy were among his royal friends. After ten years of economic research, he had accumulated formidable financial knowledge as well as £20,000, from gambling, money-lending and foreign-exchange trading. Yet for all this he was dissatisfied. Perhaps ambition made moneymaking for personal gain seem no longer sufficiently satisfying. Perhaps the glamour of travel had dimmed and Katherine, tired with the discomforts of their itinerant life, was pressuring him to settle. Certainly by now his observation of banking systems in Amsterdam and Italy, coupled with what he had seen of London's financial innovations, had fired within him a grand vision: he wanted to use his understanding and ingenuity for the benefit of the populace, to play a key part in Europe's financial evolution.

Law's interest in economy was leading him, like many others of his age, to reflect on the role of the state, or of large-scale enterprise, in national prosperity. He saw money as a scientist might an array of laboratory equipment and chemicals, as substance for experiment and a subject for theory. In this sense, he was reflecting the new, enlightened age. Just as the mysteries of mathematics and nature had been explained by the researches of scientists like Newton, Huygens and Boyle, Law's confident aim was now to use his knowledge to take on the challenge of experimenting with a nation's fortune.

Scotland, the land of his birth, he decided, was where his ideas would be unveiled. In about 1704, according to Gray, he made the long journey home, leaving Venice 'with his Madam and family' to journey 'through Germany down to Holland and there embark for Scotland'. Throughout the voyage, worries about his past constantly intruded. In England he was still a fugitive with a death sentence hanging over him, but Scotland, although ruled by the same monarch, had a separate government and he could not be arrested there for a crime committed in London. However, should union between Scotland and England take place – and there were many in favour of such a change – his safety would no longer be assured.

Law was tired of being on the run. After nearly ten years of travelling he saw that unless he wanted to spend the rest of his life as a fugitive, a royal pardon was essential. The Wilson family's animosity might be defused if he compensated them generously for their loss – and he now had the money to do so. Royal assent, the other criterion for a pardon, depended on the new monarch, Queen Anne, who had succeeded to the throne after William's death. A flicker of hope grew that if he could convince her of the benefit his ideas could bring to her country, she might spare him the gallows and give him the longed-for reprieve.

On arrival in Edinburgh, Law was reunited with his mother, whom he had not seen since he left the city as a young man. What did the redoubtable Jean make of the equally determined Katherine? Did her son hide from her the true nature of the liaison? Whatever their feelings, it seems that within this settled domestic background, Law was able to work with new purpose.

He decided to tender his knowledge to the Queen in the traditional way, by writing a proposal. His first work, only recently identified by scholars, was entitled 'Essay on a Land Bank'. In it he proposed a bank issuing paper money based on the value of land. This was a more stable basis for credit than silver, he contended, since history had shown that precious metals could fluctuate in value according to their scarcity whereas land's value was less volatile. The idea was not entirely original: since the mid-seventeenth century numerous writers had put forward similar schemes – even Defoe felt 'land is the best bottom for banks'. The same idea still flourishes today in the form of building societies.

However, Queen Anne was not impressed. Law's arguments might be ingenious and succinctly expressed but he could not erase his past. As a convicted felon and a notorious gambler, he was a far from obvious candidate to trust with the nation's purse. After cursory consideration, the idea was therefore quickly rejected. The list of petitions and memorials to the Queen in August 1704 recorded that Law, presently residing in Scotland, 'by the intercession of friends' had managed to secure the Wilson family's agreement to annul the appeal. It continues circumspectly, '. . . yet your petitioner is debarred from serving your majesty (as he is most desirous) in the just war wherein your majesty is now engaged', requesting royal pardon, 'not only for the death of the said John [*sic*: it should be Edward] Wilson, but also for his breach of the said prison that he may be able to serve the Queen for the rest of his life'. The application is marked with the single word 'rejected'. In the eyes of the Queen and her government, Law's financial genius would never be acknowledged.

Faced with this setback, Law's determination did not waver. Certain that the scheme's soundness was not in question, he decided to adapt it for Scotland. Here he was confident that his influential friends, including the Duke of Argyll, who was the Queen's Commissioner in Scotland, would ensure a fair hearing.

Scotland desperately needed someone to cure her economic ills. At the turn of the eighteenth century the country languished in an economic nadir, with currency in short supply, trade in the doldrums, unemployment and poverty widespread. The situation was exacerbated by a financial fiasco called the Darien scheme. The brainchild of William Paterson, founder of the Bank of England, the idea had been to found a colony in Panama, which would provide a base from which cargoes would be carried across the isthmus from the Pacific to the Atlantic and back, avoiding the long, treacherous route around Cape Horn. Touting the idea as a fail-safe investment that would yield fabulous rewards and make Scotland the richest country on earth, he raised £400,000 – nearly half the capital of Scotland – from optimistic private investors all eager to participate. In 1698, after ejecting scores of desperate stow-aways, five ships set sail from Leith with 2,000 passengers aboard, including Paterson, his wife and son. Three months later they dropped anchor at the settlement of New Caledonia.

The expedition was a disaster. Malaria, dysentery and other disease was rife; the Spanish besieged the settlement; the English refused support because they were worried about competition with the East India Company and, as a conse-quence, trade was blighted. Two years later, when the project was finally abandoned, the lives of 1,700 colonists, among them Paterson's wife and son, were lost, numerous investors were ruined and the Scottish economy was in such crisis that even the survival of the Bank of Scotland, set up a year after the Bank of England, was threatened.

John Law was convinced he could rectify the situation. Within a year he had completed a 120-page pamphlet entitled *Money and Trade Considered with a Proposal for Supplying the Nation with Money*. It was published anonymously in 1705 by Andrew Anderson of Edinburgh, a company owned at the time by Law's aunt. A poster advertising the main points of Law's argument was prominently displayed in local meeting places. His name did not appear on the proposal, perhaps to avoid marring its chances of success with his tarnished reputation; but in circles of influence, Law's authorship was soon common knowledge.

Economic historians still marvel at the extraordinary clarity of expression, that is, they say, remarkable for its time. Law begins by explaining the meaning of value which he says is related to rarity rather than use. 'Water is of great use, yet of little value, because the quantity of water is much greater than the demand for it. Diamonds are of little use, yet of great value, because the demand for diamonds is much greater than the quantity of them.' He then looks at the meaning of money and argues that 'Money is not the value *for* which goods are exchanged, but the value *by* which they are exchanged: the use of money is to buy goods, and silver while money is of no other use.' This vision of money as a functional medium – with no intrinsic value but backed by something of stable value, the gambler's chips that can be cashed in at the end of the evening – leads him to his central suggestion, for a bank with the power to issue notes using land as security.

To his friends the argument was convincing and the Duke of Argyll brought it to the attention of the Scottish Parliament. At the next sitting on 28 June 1705, the main business under consideration was the question of union between Scotland and England: in view of Scotland's economic ills worsened by the Darien scheme, the union was now widely seen as advantageous. Law's scheme was also to be discussed, along with another proposal by the eminent Dr Chamberlen, who was already well known in Scotland and England for his financial schemes.

Despite Law's hopes, the past weighed heavily against him, and his proposal sparked an explosive response. William Greg, an agent working for the English government who watched proceedings, was highly dismissive of Law, 'a gentleman who of all men living once was thought to have the worst turned head that way', and wrote off the pamphlet as the 'homespun' proposal of a 'rake'. Two days later, when Parliament again convened to discuss the two schemes, Law became ensnared in the complexities of Scottish politics.

One of the parliamentary factions, the Squadrone Volante, opted to support him, but he was fiercely opposed by the national party, headed by Andrew Fletcher of Saltoun. George Baillie of Jerviswood, a member of the Squadrone, proposed Law's scheme, 'in his opinion, a more rational and practicable scheme than that of Dr Chamberlen'. Few agreed. Fletcher, an irascible man, scornfully retorted that he thought it 'a contrivance to enslave the nation' and demanded that the two men be brought before Parliament to reason and debate the matter openly.

Rushing to Law's defence, the Earl of Roxburghe, also of the Squadrone, declared he did not see why Law, who had spent 'some considerable time purely to serve his country', should be forced to appear against his will; he should be treated 'with good manners if not encouragement'. According to one witness, Fletcher was so furious at what he took to be an accusation of ill manners, that had he been near Roxburghe 'they would have gone together by the ears'.

Argyll, who was presiding over the meeting, ordered that Fletcher and Roxburghe be confined in their chambers to avoid the row continuing after the debate. Roxburghe, 'mannerly and respectful', allowed himself to be arrested. Fletcher, who famously boasted 'that he never made his court to any king or commissioner', proved more elusive. Surreptitiously leaving the house he made his way to a nearby tavern and sent a challenge to Roxburghe to meet him at Leith, a popular spot for duels.

With Baillie as his second, Roxburghe talked himself out of confinement, responded to Fletcher's challenge and rushed to Leith at six in the evening. Before the two men could draw swords Baillie intervened. The fight would not be fair, he said. His lordship had 'a great weakness in his right leg so that he could hardly stand, 'twas not to be expected that this quarrel could be decided by the sword'. Fletcher had foreseen such an objection, produced a pair of pistols and offered them to Roxburghe to take his choice. Baillie again objected that his lordship's weakness would 'equally disable him from firing on foot'. Meanwhile, in the distance a party of mounted constabulary was spotted – both men were still supposed to be under arrest. The seconds immediately fired their pistols in the air and everyone returned to Edinburgh.

The ludicrous quarrel did nothing to help Law. His scheme, though interesting enough for William Greg secretly to dispatch a copy south to his superiors (London was already watching the progress of John Law), was damningly rejected for being 'too chimerical to be put in practice'. And while the wranglings dragged on, union drew ever closer. Law, reluctant to leave his homeland and still optimistic of securing a royal pardon, again lodged an appeal for clemency. His petition re-iterated his intention to work for 'the ease and honour of the government and the good and prosperity of his country'. Again he was turned down.

Exile was now the only way to avoid imprisonment. As Katherine made preparations to depart, Law passed his final days on Scottish soil at the gaming tables. Among his recorded successes was an estate worth £1,200 won from Sir Andrew Ramsay, 'one of the finest Gentlemen of his time', who after his encounter with Law had only £100 left.

The earliest known likeness of John Law, a miniature in the Earl of Derby's collection, dates from around this time. The image shows a dreamy young man in a short wig with Madonna-like oval face, heavy-lidded eyes, long hawkish broken nose and generous mouth. His expression of poker-faced calm calls to mind his contemporary du Hautchamp's description of him playing cards, 'a serene temper without transport [that] made him master of himself when fortune ran against or for him, so he generally came a gainer, seldom a considerable loser'. Perhaps Law gave the miniature to his mother on his departure. He was never to see her again; she died two years later. For the time being, however, such sorrow was far from his thoughts. Finding some way of putting his schemes into action was now his overriding aim; his resolve had never been greater.

Chapter Seven

The Root of All Evil

In his travels he learnt that in Betica everything shone with gold, which made him hurry to get there. He was made very unwelcome by Saturn, who was then on the throne, but once the god had departed from the earth he had an idea, and went out to every street-corner where he continually shouted in a hoarse voice: 'Citizens of Betica, you think yourselves rich because you have silver and gold. Your delusion is pitiable. Take my advice: leave the land of worthless metal and enter the realms of imaginations, and I promise you such riches that you will be astonished.'

Montesquieu, *Persian Letters* (1721)

LATE IN 1705, LAW AND HIS FAMILY RETURNED TO A continent riven by conflict. The War of the Spanish Succession pitched the armies of France and Spain against an alliance of England, Holland and the Holy Roman Empire. A year earlier, at the Battle of Blenheim, the English general Sir John Churchill, later Duke of Marlborough, had vanquished the French, killing, wounding and imprisoning almost three-quarters of their army, some forty thousand men. That year the

British captured Gibraltar, and allowed their ships to sail into the Mediterranean 'like swans on the river'. Over the following months the allies triumphed also at Ramillies, Barcelona and Turin. As if to underline France's waning fortunes, a total solar eclipse on 11 May 1706 signalled that seemingly even God had deserted the Sun King.

Amid the unfolding political drama the Laws based themselves in The Hague to await the birth of their first child. John Law hankered to make his next move, and the difficulty of travelling in war-torn Europe must have worried him since he needed free passage to be able to sell his schemes. However, over the next nine years he crossed enemy lines with apparent ease, ignoring the usual formalities if necessary, reaching the enemy heartland of Paris several times, as well as visiting Vienna, Turin, Milan, Brussels and Utrecht.

Soon after the birth of their baby, a boy they named John, the Laws visited Vienna. Here, according to du Hautchamp, 'he proposed his system to the Emperor, and although he was unsuccessful he did not leave without playing heavily and making large winnings'. Law did not shed many tears over his failure. By now he had focused his sights on Europe's largest, most populous but severely impoverished nation: France.

Superficially France seemed hardly to have changed for the past half-century. Louis XIV had reigned for sixty-three years, during which he had raised his country to commercial heights that made it the envy of Europe, then ruined it with his penchant for military aggression, religious intolerance and un-rivalled extravagance. Lack of money lay at the root of all France's evils. In the countryside the impoverished masses lived in abject misery, unshod, dressed in rags, forced to scavenge to survive. During severe famines, which happened in 1694 and again in 1709, following the worst winter in living memory, the poor made flour from bracken and grass stalks or roots such as asphodel. Children lived on 'boiled grass and roots' and, according to one account, 'crop the fields like sheep', while the Princess Palatine, sister-in-law of Louis XIV, wrote: 'The famine is so terrible that children have devoured each other.' A fortunate few could barter: a cabbage for a bag of corn, two pigs for a cow, and so on. In Versailles it was not so easy. In a feverish bid to pay for his army and feed his people, the King had to resort to sending his gargantuan golden dinner services and silver furniture to the mint to be melted down for currency. Now he ate off enamel or faience pottery, and his entourage was expected to follow suit.

Various vain attempts had been made to replenish the coffers. Additional venal offices were created and each position, mostly entirely spurious, sold off to the highest bidder. Interest-bearing paper credit notes called *billets de monnaie* had been offered in return for coins and were later converted into government bonds. New taxes were introduced, old ones raised – there were so many taxes that it was feared even marriages and births would be taxed. The coinage was constantly tampered with. Between 1690 and 1715 the currency was revalued forty times.

But the situation did not improve. By 1715 France would be over 2 billion livres in debt, largely to a group of forty private financiers, who also controlled the collection of taxes. The government could not afford the interest repayments on its notes, let alone repay them in coin. They had become so discredited that when Louis wanted to raise a loan of 8 million livres in coin from one of the financiers of Paris he had to pay 32 million in notes. In the provinces few could afford the taxes; people even resorted to marrying or baptizing their children without a priest to avoid the extra levy they felt might soon be demanded.

Law knew he had the answer. The problems of the country, he promised, all stemmed from a lack of available money. 'Trade and money,' he had written in Scotland, 'depend mutually on one another; when trade decays money lessens;

and when money lessens, trade decays.' The only way out of the downward spiral was through credit and by increasing the circulating money. Since there was a shortage of gold and silver in the country the answer was to establish a national bank and issue money made from paper.

It was a beguilingly simple solution. The hard part was getting through to the King. In November 1706 Law managed a journey to Paris, where he submitted a four-part memorandum to Chamillard, Louis XIV's incompetent and overworked controller general, who headed the ministries of finance and war. Law tried to keep his argument brief and to the point. 'I know', he wrote, 'that these proposals are long and boring, because it is necessary to explain many aspects of money . . . what I will present will be shorter and easier to follow, I will attempt to include nothing that is spurious.' The harassed Chamillard tried to appear diligent, scribbling annotations in the margin. In truth he did not understand and only laughed at Law's vision. The King was never told of the proposal and without his approval Law reached an impasse. 'Apparently the opinion is that what I propose does not merit discussion at the council. I am not surprised: a new type of money more suitable than silver seems impracticable,' he wrote disconsolately. But the visit was not entirely wasted. During his stay in Paris he met the King's nephew Philippe, Duc d'Orléans. Their friendship was to change the course of history.

The two men had much in common. They were of similar age – Law was just three years Orléans' senior, aged thirty-six in 1707 – both were handsome, athletically built and brilliant tennis players. Both enjoyed extraordinary success with the opposite sex, although Orléans far outstripped Law in his sexual appetites. His numerous mistresses, whether stars of the opera, actresses from the Comédie Française, serving girls, daughters of diplomats or, more rarely, aristocrats, were selected for good humour, voracious appetites for banqueting, drinking and lovemaking, and lack of interest in politics. Looks mattered little – even the Duc's mother remarked wryly, 'They do not have to be beautiful. I have often reproached him for choosing such ugly ones.' At night, in his Paris residence, the Palais Royal, he dismissed his servants and held *soupers*, notorious all-night revelries at which an eclectic assortment of courtesans, actresses and his inner circle of dissolute male friends – the *roués* – gorged, drank to excess and, according to Saint-Simon, 'said vile things at the tops of their voices'. It was, said Saint-Simon, a ritual that 'when they had made a vast deal of noise and were dead drunk they went to bed and began it all over again the next day'. Meanwhile they stimulated enough gossip to entertain the rest of Paris.

But Orléans was far more than just another debauched aristocrat. A multi-talented man of abundant if mercurial intellect, he was a free-thinker who was fascinated by developments in music, literature, philosophy and science, including the science of money. Chemistry enthralled him, and he passed long hours experimenting in his private laboratory with the eminent Dutch chemist Wilhelm Homberg. He was intrigued by necromancy; his penchant for conjuring spells and summoning spirits late into the night elicited much criticism in court circles. He was also a connoisseur of art. He learned to paint with the famous decorative painter Antoine Coypel – who decorated the ceiling in the Palais Royal – and festooned the walls of his home with masterpieces by Raphael, Titian, Rembrandt, Veronese, Caravaggio and leading French artists. He patronized writers and poets, composed operas and played the flute. Yet for all his abundant gifts and interests Orléans was frustrated. Louis XIV distrusted him and had consistently denied him a fulfilling role. His dissipation was largely inspired by boredom. Underneath the louche exterior, like Law, he was an idealist who longed for change.

Law willingly spent long hours explaining his ideas and

in Orléans found someone with the intellect and vision to understand. Perhaps also Orléans' regard for Law was strengthened by secret admiration for his life of opportunistic adventure, a world away from the protocol and formality of the French court. Both men were fast thinkers and witty talkers, and with mutual intellectual respect, personal affection grew.

Encouraged by his royal friend, Law optimistically revised his proposal and resubmitted it to the King. But for all Orléans' help and Law's high hopes, Louis eyed it icily. This time, according to Orléans' mother, the Princess Palatine, the stumbling block was not the scheme's complexities but the author's religion. Law was a non-Catholic and therefore, to Louis, inherently untrustworthy. Police superintendent d'Argenson was instructed to hasten Law's departure.

Law did not give up hope. He based himself in Holland from where he continued the roving quest for a ruler willing to listen. The nomadic life must have been arduous for Katherine, with a baby to care for, but the relationship does not seem to have suffered. On the contrary, it seems likely that the fortitude and loyalty she later displayed resulted from the closeness that developed during this extended period of rootlessness. In unfamiliar environments, and during long journeys across Europe, she and Law spent much time together, and must have relied on one another for companionship. At each new city, Katherine's dignified bearing perhaps worked in Law's favour, for political advancement depended upon social success as much as worthy ideas. Her glamour, allied to his charm, might well have helped forge the alliances on which his career depended.

In the spring of 1710 he was in Italy, accompanied as usual by Katherine, who was pregnant. Their second child, Mary Katherine, whom Law called Kate, was born in Genoa. In Turin, Law presented a scheme for a bank similar to the Bank of England to Victor Amadeus, Duke of Savoy, whose domain was in dire need of cash after the siege of the city. The Duke, a great admirer of Law, liked his scheme and Law's spirits rose. As he waited to be given the go-ahead, he involved himself in speculative dealings and currency trades so successfully that a year later he was able to open a bank account in Amsterdam with a deposit of £100,000.

But as the months passed, it became obvious that Victor Amadeus's support did not mark the turning point for which Law had hoped. The Duke's ministers were stubbornly conservative and eventually, after lengthy arguments, Victor Amadeus was forced to reject Law's idea with the lame explanation that his dominions 'were too small for the execution of so great a design'. He added that 'France was the proper theatre for its performance, if I know the disposition of the people of that kingdom I am sure they will relish your schemes.' Law agreed, but knew that with the present administration intact there too the door was closed.

Even in exile John Law's success gripped the English authorities. By now he had decided that his ambitions would be helped if he presented himself to the world as a man of substance. In the spring of 1712 he left Italy to return to The Hague, 'the handsomest, the most fashionable and the most modern looking town in the Netherlands', according to one writer of the time. He invested his winnings in a grand residence and filled it with paintings and works of art. Lavish living on such a scale brought instant acclaim. With Katherine happily playing the role of society hostess, numerous visitors came to call. Everyone wanted to know exactly how his fortune had been made. In April 1713, the diplomat John Drummond wrote to the Earl of Oxford from Utrecht mentioning 'a famous man in this country . . . This Mr Law has picked up in Italy a great estate, some say by army undertakings at Genoa, and some say partly by gaming . . . I should be sorry to see him settle at The Hague, where he has bought a fine house, seeing he is rich, and can be very useful . . . the service he may be able to do his country really deserves his pardon.' Law enjoyed his reputation as a man of mystery and did nothing to discourage the gossip. He was as convivial and charismatic as ever: 'He is really admired by all who know him here . . . and I should always wish the Queen's subjects of such good estates and sense established at home,' wrote Drummond.

He was still adding to his substantial fortune. According to Gray, the Dutch were renowned as 'a very close wary people, but will give in to anything where there is any prospect of Gain'. Law, said Gray, seized the opportunity to introduce them to the delights of a national lottery, based on the one his old friend Neale had set up in London but 'improved' to his own advantage. In Rotterdam Law's ploy was discovered: he had 'calculated these lotteries entirely to his own benefit, and to the prejudice of the People, having got about 200,000 guilders by them'. He was asked to leave the country. However, recent research suggests that Law was in fact operating a form of insurance scheme offering investors a way of reducing their losses should all their tickets lose: for a fee of 100 guilders, investors could lodge ten tickets with Law, and claim three times the sum if all ten lost. Later the scheme was modified so that the price dropped but all winnings over a certain level were payable to Law, who was employing his understanding of risk to his own profit, in much the same way as he did in games of chance. Such ventures were highly lucrative because two years later his fortune was said to have grown to £500,000.

In France, meanwhile, his luck had begun to turn. The signing of the peace of Utrecht in April 1713 had brought the long war to a close. Louis XIV, now seventy-five and still in remarkably robust health, brooded over the ruins of his kingdom. His sense of loss was compounded by a tragic sequence of events that had transformed the French succession. In the space of three years, three heirs – his son the Dauphin, his grandson the Duc de Bourgogne and his great-grandson the

Duc de Bretagne – had died. The heir to the throne was now Louis' second great-grandson, a four-year-old child, and Law's ally, the Duc d'Orléans, stood in line as regent.

Louis' sorrow promised opportunity for Law. More than ever France needed an answer to her financial problems. Sensing that the King's contempt for him might now have mellowed, Law returned to Paris. On Christmas Eve he wrote to Nicolas Desmarets, Louis' new finance minister, begging for an audience 'to discuss matters, which I trust will be agreeable, being for the service of the King and the well-being of his subjects.' Orléans' support was beginning to work in Law's favour and his request was received slightly more favourably. Desmarets scribbled a note to his clerk, 'when he comes I will speak to him,' at the top of Law's letter. But either the office was inefficient and no word was sent to Law, or some of the old distrust lingered and Desmarets dragged his feet. Nearly a fortnight later, having heard nothing, Law wrote again, this time more impatiently: 'On 24 December I took the liberty of writing to your lordship to beg you to allow me a private audience to discuss the service of His Majesty. As my business affairs oblige me to leave shortly I would like to know if this honour will be granted.' Again the honour was not granted, but Law was still convinced that a breakthrough was close. He returned to The Hague to prepare to move his family to France.

By May 1714 he was back in Paris, still denied the formal audience to make his presentation. He wrote confidently, 'You had the goodness to say you would let me know when you had time to give me an audience. I await your orders.' Katherine, meanwhile, was in The Hague supervising the packing of furnishings and personal effects, a formidable task, with their extensive collection of art and furniture. They suffered a setback when they were held up by French customs officials at Rouen. Law wrote to Desmarets, confidently requesting the assistance he felt was due to a man who would soon be playing a key role in French affairs: 'Several chests and crates with the valuables and furnishings that I used during my stay there are being dispatched from Holland. As among these there are some crockery and other fragile objects that will be easily damaged if they are opened *en route* and as I have no one to look after them, I am taking the liberty of begging your lordship to grant permission for them to pass through Rouen without being opened, and that they can be examined when they arrive at my house.' Desmarets was not unsympathetic but neither would he allow Law to ignore the usual formalities. He gave instructions that Law should be told 'that I can't arrange a visit at his home . . . this is only usual for ambassadors . . . but if he likes I will send an order to have the chests and crates sent to the customs in Paris, where they can be opened in front of him'.

A month or two later the Law family were comfortably settled in their new residence, a mansion staffed with 'a sizeable retinue of servants', in the Place Vendôme (then known as the Place Louis le Grand), one of Paris's newest and most fashionable squares where many of the capital's most powerful financiers lived. The move had been noticed by d'Argenson, who remained extremely wary of Law and alerted foreign minister Torcy: 'A Scot named Law, gambler by profession and suspected of evil intentions towards the King appears at Paris in high style and has even bought an impressive home in the Place Louis le Grand, although no one knows of any resource except fortune in gambling, which is his whole profession. I cannot believe that the motives which have aroused just suspicions against him have ended with the peace'. Torcy, however, must have caught wind of the shift in the establishment's regard for him and scribbled on the letter, 'He is not suspect. One can leave him in peace.'

The move had just been completed during the summer of 1714 when Queen Anne died. Still hankering for a role in

England, Law immediately lobbied an old Scottish friend, John Dalrymple, 2nd Earl of Stair, the recently appointed British ambassador to France, to bring his case to the attention of the new king, George I. The son of the disgraced earl held responsible for the massacre at Glencoe, Stair shared the youthful Law's passion for gambling and high living; he may have met Law over the tables in Edinburgh or London. When Stair arrived in Paris in January 1715, Law was the first person he visited.

The encounter left him deeply impressed. Now forty-three, Law had retained his good looks and athletic physique but his youthful appetite for self-indulgence had been replaced by lofty ambition. Stair was dazzled by Law's grasp of finance and his ability to explain complex subjects lucidly. He had little hesitation in taking up Law's case and wrote to the statesman and Secretary of State in England, James Stanhope, to recommend Law as 'a man of very good sense, and who has a head fit for calculations of all kinds to an extent beyond anybody'. He was, said Stair, 'certainly the cleverest man that is', who might be 'useful in devising some plan for paying off the national debts'. Stair also recommended Law to Lord Halifax at the Treasury. Halifax, who had met Law in The Hague and seen the proposal he had written in Scotland, needed little convincing of Law's talent: 'I have a great esteem for his abilities, and am extreme fond of having his assistance in the Revenue,' he said. But his good opinion was not enough. Later he wrote, 'There appears some difficulty in his case, and in the way of having him brought over. If your lordship can suggest anything to me that can ease this matter, I should be very glad to receive it.' Stanhope's reply to Stair confirmed the objections: 'I did not fail to lay it before the king,' he wrote. 'I am now to tell your lordship that I find a disposition to comply with what your lordship proposes, though at the same time it has met, and does meet, with opposition, and I believe it will be no hard matter for him [Law] to guess from whence it proceeds.' According to Law, Stanhope was furious that the petition was turned down, and 'speaking to the King on my subject said that England's debts during two wars were £50 million, but that she had lost more in the form of one of her subjects the day that engaged myself in the affairs of France.' Twenty years on, the ghost of Wilson still hindered Law's rise.

He did not waste time lamenting. Having resolved instead to prove to England what she had lost by his success in France, in May he made the long-awaited proposal to Desmarets for a state bank issuing paper money against deposits. But Desmarets, still distrustful, strung him along in a state of constant suspense, demanding endless explanations, pointing out pitfalls. In early summer, perhaps worn out with frustration, Law fell ill and was not sufficiently strong to revise his scheme again until July. By then word of it had filtered to Paris financiers, who, fearing that their profits would suffer, noisily voiced their opposition. A state bank of issue would never work, said Samuel Bernard, one of the wealthiest, 'in a country where everything depends on the King's pleasure'. Faced with yet more hostility Law remained cool and surprisingly optimistic. But Desmarets, still playing for time, raised more queries. How soon could Law begin? What guarantees would he offer? How would it be administered? Patiently Law answered every question. He was ready to open the bank on 10 August or even earlier if he could. He was so sure it would succeed he would put up 500,000 livres of his own money as guarantee. In this grand new institution Desmarets should certainly hold an official role. Eventually, in early August, Law's persistence paid off. Desmarets approved. There remained only the King to convince.

Louis was enjoying a quiet summer at his summer residence at Marly. On 10 August, the day on which Law hoped to open the state bank, the King's health suddenly deteriorated. According to contemporary reports, discoloured blotches on his leg enlarged and the doctors, fearing gangrene, tried magical elixirs, multiple incisions and swathing it in brandy-soaked bandages. But he was beyond help. On Sunday, 1 September 1715, at a quarter to nine in the morning, having reigned for seventy-two years, Louis XIV, France's most glorious king, died.

Orléans, like most of France, spent little time grieving. The day after Louis' death he made a compelling address to the Parlement in which he coerced the representatives to reject the right of a council of noblemen and the Duc de Maine to assist him in his regency, a scheme of joint rule laid out by Louis to restrain Orléans' power. He emerged triumphant. From now until the five-year-old Dauphin came of age he would rule France as regent. For John Law, the opportunity of which he had long dreamed had never seemed so close.

Chapter Eight

The Bank

Your Royal Highness will have no difficulty in reaping success from what I have the honour of proposing, the best actor is not the one with the largest role, but the one who acts the best. I know my strengths and I love pleasure too much to occupy myself in affairs that I do not understand in depth. My ideas are simple, the principles on which I have worked them out are true, and the conclusions I draw from them are correct . . .

Letter from John Law to the Regent, December 1715

AT THE BANQUE GÉNÉRALE THE MASSIVE DOUBLE DOORS TO the rue St Avoye stood open. Inside, a handful of clients conversed idly in the vestibule before drifting towards the *grande salle* to conduct their commissions. It was late summer 1716 and, as usual, business was quiet.

Later that morning a carriage arrived that was far from ordinary or expected. Perhaps a few customers glimpsed it slowing to turn into the narrow, arched entrance to the street. They must have recognized the livery of the coachman and the servants inside as that of the Duc d'Orléans. The servants got out carrying metal-bound coffers, which they took into the bank and placed on the counter. Then an equerry stepped forward to unlock them. Inside each chest was a mass of gold louis d'or and silver écus, which the Regent wished to entrust to the bank. The total value was a million livres.

The bank's other customers must have been transfixed. For the Regent to invest such a sum in a bank that was at present the subject of mockery in many quarters was astonishing and significant. They did not know that the Regent and the bank's director John Law had contrived that the deposit be made as conspicuously as possible: public awe was precisely the effect for which they strove. It would boost confidence in the ailing bank and its paper banknotes.

The ploy worked. Within days the press had reported that the Regent had such faith in John Law's new bank that he had deposited a million livres in its vaults. The previously hostile *Gazette de la Régence*, which had predicted '[Law's] bank will not succeed' and 'no one talks of Mr Law's bank except to joke about it', now remarked on 'an order the other day from the mint to send a million to M. Law's bank, that the Regent supports and is really his bank under the name of this Englishman. Everyone believes that it will hold up because royal funds are going in to it.' Royal patronage, as John Law was only too aware, was the most potent of marketing tools.

Yet after Louis XIV's death, Law had been disappointed by the protracted process of establishing his bank. On his accession as Regent, Orléans had dismissed Desmarets and, in line with his new system of government by aristocratic councils, made the Duc de Noailles head of the finance council. Noailles was energetic, shrewd, ambitious, but indecisive, and innately distrustful of anyone who might threaten his position. Louis de Rouvray Saint-Simon, a French writer, courtier, member of the Regency Council and friend of the Regent, whose forty-one volumes of memoirs provide a fascinating insight into the key personalities and events of the time, observed that 'In spite of his intellect, the multitude and mobility of his ideas and views, which successively chased each other off either wholly or in part, made him incapable of concluding any work of his own; neither was he ever satisfied with work done for him.' He was a hard and insidious taskmaster and when the Regent introduced Law as someone whose ideas were worth considering, Noailles was instantly suspicious. He nodded and muttered superficial encouragements but inwardly viewed Law as 'an intruder put by the hand of the Regent into their administration' and hence, according to Saint-Simon, 'long bandied [him] from pillar to post'.

Noailles found France's financial crisis far worse than anyone had imagined. The country's debts, estimated at over 2 billion livres, incurred interest repayments of 90 million; the tax system that should have covered the repayments of interest on the debt was so staggeringly inefficient and riven with corruption that the income was swallowed up three or four years in advance. Having studied the books, Noailles summed up the monetary morass: 'We found the estate of our Crown given up, the revenues of the state practically annihilated by an infinity of charges and settlements, ordinary taxation eaten up in advance, arrears of all kinds accumulated through the years, a multitude of notes, ordinances, and allocations anticipated of so many different kinds which mount up to such considerable sums that one can hardly calculate them.'

Some advisers suggested that France should simply declare herself bankrupt and start again. Law convinced Orléans that to do so would pitch the country into even worse distress. He had a better way. In October, bubbling with enthusiasm, he proffered his newest proposal to the Regent: a plan for a state bank administered in the King's name that would handle all revenues and issue paper money backed by coins. 'The convenience will be such that everyone will be charmed to have these bank bills rather than money, because of the facility of making payments in paper, and the certainty of receiving the value whenever they wish.'

While Orléans perused the scheme, Law lobbied the Regent's closest advisers for support. A brave few murmured wary encouragement, among them the Duc d'Antin, who said he was 'struck by his ideas, they appeared to merit a most detailed attention'. At the end of the month the scheme was formally put to the council and a panel of thirteen of Paris's most illustrious bankers and financiers. But still Law's star failed to rise. Members of the business community remained scornful and distrustful, their criticisms concealing their underlying concern that if a state bank was allowed to open its doors it would be at great cost to them. Nine of the thirteen voted against it. Noailles, defensive and resentful of Law's effortless influence with the Regent, also thwarted him. As Law waited, naïvely expecting to be told to proceed, his betrayal took place behind the closed doors of the council chamber.

Confronted by the massed hostility of the business community as well as his own advisers, Orléans concluded, regretfully, that he could not afford to back such a controversial scheme and risk upsetting so many at this delicate early stage of his regency. For the time being the scheme must be sacrificed. He made his closing pronouncement ceremoniously. 'He had come there persuaded that the bank ought to be established; but, after the opinions he had just heard, he agreed wholly with that of M. le duc de Noailles; and it would be announced to everyone that same day that the bank would not be carried out.'

Law's prickly response to the Regent's abandonment hid profound disillusionment. 'The use of banks is so recognized in all commercial countries that it seems to me extraordinary that they are called into question,' he raged. The Regent, all too well aware of the truth of this, and probably lamenting his *volte-face* even as he made it, dreaded that Law might return to his wandering, gambling life or, worse still, take his expertise elsewhere. While Law brooded in his Paris mansion, the Regent ordered Noailles to pacify him. Law said later that Noailles made a few vague promises on the Regent's behalf, and that 'I could still be useful to the state, and he hoped that this rejection would not make me want to leave France, that he wished to make my stay a pleasant one in every way he could, and that it was even the opinion of the council that he should engage me to stay, being able to be useful with the knowledge that I have.' Still bristling, Law retorted, 'I have need of nothing having enough to live with ease, that my intention in proposing to serve His Royal Highness was to make myself useful to the state and not augment my own good. The truth of this was obvious by the nature of my proposition.' But as the Regent had hoped, he simmered down, secretly flattered by all the attention. 'I would not have even thought of making a second proposition if he had not pressed me to do so,' he later wrote, with manifest self-righteousness.

In fact, the fire burning in Law was unlikely ever to have been extinguished by the rejection of a single council: he had been dreaming for far too long to give up. Yet again, he told himself, it was merely a matter of modifying his ideas, and waiting. If the Regent was uneasy with the idea of a state bank, Law reasoned now that the answer must lie in a private scheme. The revised plan that emerged was for a privately run bank, similar to the Bank of England, issuing banknotes and financed by shareholders. Throughout a winter so cold that, according to the Princess Palatine, the Regent's mother, even the sea at Calais froze, Law briefed Orléans with renewed enthusiasm in conferences held at the Palais Royal and at Marly. In December he equated the introduction of credit with the discovery of the Indies, remarking that 'if Spain had ceded the Indies [he meant the Spanish Americas] to the English, they would not have profited as much from them as they have from the use of credit . . . My banking project . . . will not bring the least prejudice to the King nor to the people; it is the quickest, safest and most harmless method of restoring the good faith and confidence of commerce; it is the true foundation of power in a state and the way by which one must begin to establish order.' When Law talked like this, money became the stuff of dreams, a magical cure-all, the embodiment of universal happiness rather than of sordid temptation. Orléans was captivated.

While the Regent and Law were closeted together, it was left to Noailles to initiate more painful methods of improving the country's finances. A year earlier, he had instigated the Visa, a drastic form of financial surgery, by which large swathes of royal debt were amputated. Long-term debt, which had largely financed Louis' wars, mostly took the form of annuity bonds sold by Paris's city government, the Hôtel de Ville, to financiers and other private investors. The bonds paid a set interest rate that was covered traditionally by an agreed source of government revenue. One of Noailles' money-saving measures was to reduce the interest on bonds from 7 per cent to 4 per cent. He also converted the various forms of short-term debt into *billets d'états*, state notes worth only two-thirds of their former value. He cut salaries and pensions, and revalued the coinage at 50 per cent of its previous worth.

In systems of currency based on the value of gold and silver, especially in France, adjusting the value of the coinage was a frequent royal scam. The French monetary system was based on the livre tournois, a unit of account (like the pound sterling in England) used to express prices, contracts and wages, for which there was no single coin, and against which the value of gold and silver coins could be adjusted. French coins included the gold louis d'or and the silver écu, equivalent in England to the gold guinea and the silver shilling. In this case, Noailles raised the value of the louis d'or, stating that its value would increase from fourteen to twenty livres (and the écu from three livres ten sous to five livres), thus effectively devaluing the livre.

This was an inflationary measure that would cause prices to rise, even though it reduced the value of the state's debt by diminishing the amount of coins needed to repay it. Revaluations worked by demanding that the public bring all their coins to the mint either for endorsement with a new stamp, representing the increased value, or by reminting lighter coins with a higher valuation against the livre. In both cases the state appropriated part of the bullion in the process of stamping or reminting it, but concealed it against the adjustments in value. The public, well aware that the Crown was profiting from such transactions, was understandably reluctant to hand over coins and see them altered in this manner, hence the tendency to hoard, adulterate or smuggle them abroad and sell them as bullion.

Noailles' measures made the balance sheet look better, but plunged the nation into further financial distress. By encouraging people to send coins abroad, they worsened the shortage; by reducing interest payments and the value of government securities, they forced people to sell to maintain a level of income and the market price plummeted 80 per cent. Businesses already foundering from a shortage of money fell deeper into debt and shopkeepers closed their doors – how could they agree to buy or sell something when they were unsure from one day to the next what the livre would be worth? Hundreds were bankrupted, which led in turn to mass unemployment. Many had no option but to turn to crime. The *Gazette de la Régence* recorded the climate of wretchedness: 'It is not possible to express the misery of the provinces. The countryside is full of robbers; we dare not go out of the towns for fear of robberies which happen every night . . . nowhere else is there a country like it, and if the King does not pay we run the risk of a revolt. There are several officers who went charitably to dinner with some capuchins and even the capuchins made a collection for them. It is utter desolation.'

Not only was the entire country foundering in an economic abyss, the very fabric of society was threatened.

Then Noailles instigated his most drastic remedy yet. In March 1716, a so-called Chamber of Justice was charged to investigate and bring to book the financiers, tax collectors and other officials who, it was felt, had profited unlawfully and on a vast scale from France's economic distress. To assist the courts in their quest, people were tempted to inform with the bait of a fifth of any recovered money or property. Treachery ensued on an unparalleled scale. Disgruntled servants betrayed their employers; wives and mistresses whispered of their lovers' financial misdemeanours; children cited their parents' transgressions; and, fearful of being reported, anyone who had coins hoarded them, unwittingly worsening the monetary shortage. People who panicked and tried to flee the country found that innkeepers and postmasters had been ordered to refuse horses to anyone they suspected of evading justice. Some turned back, admitted their crime and relinquished properties or large sums of money to avoid the rack or the pillory. Others committed suicide rather than subject themselves to the horrors of investigation.

The Chamber of Justice was installed, somewhat inappropriately, in the convent of the Grands Augustins and a sinister torture chamber was set up next door. Many successfully bribed their way out of trouble, some courtiers and the Regent's mistress, La Parabère, profiting vastly as a consequence. One tax collector, fined twelve million livres, was approached by a courtier and offered a reduction if he was paid a *douceur* of 100,000 livres. 'You are too late, my friend,' the financier is said to have responded. 'I have already made a deal with your wife for fifty thousand.'

For the unfortunates who could not escape, the procedure often appeared to have been as terrifying as feared. The financier Samuel Bernard, one of Law's most vociferous opponents, offered some 6 million livres but was still sentenced to death. The profiteers La Normande and Monsieur Gruet were heavily fined, and sentenced to 'make amends' by parading in front of Notre Dame and Les Halles, La Normande wearing a shirt and a placard reading '*voleur du peuple*' (fraudster of the public), before being condemned to spend the rest of their lives on the galleys. La Normande was eventually spared the final punishment, and most reports were merely propaganda exercises to pin the blame on the unpopular financiers, many of whom acted only as middlemen for the court élite. Nevertheless, fear of the chamber of justice was all too real.

Among the frightening panoply of French punishments – being broken on the wheel, hanged, racked, whipped and pilloried – life on the galleys was among the most horrific. The condemned were chained, naked to the waist, in rows of half a dozen at each oar, while their supervisors strode on platforms above and whipped them to make them row harder for ten or twelve hours at a stretch. Hundreds died in excruciating agony at the oar, to be flung overboard like so much rotten meat. Like many forms of punishment, the galleys were regarded as an entertaining tourist attraction: the slaves were made to dance, sing and row for the delectation of the crowd. The diarist John Evelyn was among the travellers who saw them in the seventeenth century. He recorded, 'Their rising forwards and falling back at their oars, is a miserable spectacle, and the noise of their chains with the roaring of the beaten waters has something strange and fearful in it, to one unaccustomed. They are ruled and chastised with a bull's pizzle dried upon their backs and soles of their feet upon the least disorder, and without the least humanity.'

Against such a backdrop of horror Law's scheme seemed suddenly to offer painless salvation. By spring the stage was set: his new proposal laid out plans for a private bank, funded by himself and other willing investors, which would issue notes backed by deposits of gold and silver coins and redeemable at all times in coins equivalent to the value of the coin at the time of the notes' issue, 'which could not be subject to any variation'. Thus, Law pledged, his notes would be more secure than metal money, a hedge against currency vacillations, and therefore a help to commerce. Moreover, paper notes would increase the amount of circulating money and trade would be boosted. In short, he vowed, his bank would offer hope and the promise of a better future.

The Regent listened avidly. Harried with other concerns of state, exhausted by all-night excess, exasperated with interminable financial dilemmas and Noailles' ineffectual, unpopular remedies, he wanted a speedy, effective answer. Law now had his unstinting support. Before the meeting at which the new proposal was due to be presented to the council, the Regent spoke to each member individually to make his wishes clear. Conscious of the menacing Chamber of Justice, almost all fell into line. A solitary exception was the Duc de Saint-Simon, who dared to speak out against Law's scheme. He knew little of finance but was sharp and honest enough to point out two main pitfalls: 'First to govern the bank with enough foresight and wisdom not to make more bills than they ought . . . ; second, that what was excellent in a republic . . . became dangerous in an absolute monarchy like that of France, where the necessities of war ill-undertaken and ill-sustained, the rapacity of ministers, favourites, mistresses, the luxury, extravagant expenditure, and prodigality of a king might soon exhaust a bank, ruin the holders of bills, and overthrow the kingdom.' The objection, in other words, was the same as that voiced by Bernard in Louis XIV's day: since the King was above the law, in difficult times there was no guarantee that the bank would not be abused.

Orléans fobbed him off with woolly reassurances, although neither he nor Law had any real answers to this flaw. The bank was to be unregulated and answerable only to Law and his shareholders. Anything could happen.

In May 1716, Law, having adopted French nationality as required, was finally granted a charter for his Banque Générale for a term of twenty years. But even with its seal of official approval it failed to generate much interest. Its stock consisted of 1,200 shares each valued at 5,000 livres (£250). Its capital should have been 6 million livres or £300,000 sterling, but it was far less: only a quarter of the shares were taken up and these transactions were not straightforward. Investors could pay three-quarters of the cost of shares in *billets d'états*, the unpopular government securities that were currently worth 60 per cent less than their face value. In real terms the bank's working capital was thus little more than 800,000 livres.

Public suspicion shone through the lacklustre response. Law was still branded a dubious foreigner, a gambler and, some said, a charlatan. Few trusted him, let alone his paper money. The establishment, who had been the chief investors in the painful disaster of the annuity bonds and *billets*, remembered the experience ruefully. To the wider French populace banks of issue were mysterious institutions and the press compounded their entrenched misgivings, deriding the Banque Générale as 'a vision . . . one can only laugh at it, no one believes it will last'. Undercapitalized, ridiculed and distrusted, Law's bank battled for its existence.

To save it Law resorted to both subtle and headline-grabbing tactics. His goal was first to ensure that the Regent's trust in him was unwavering, second to make his notes and his bank so attractive and powerful that only the foolish or destitute would ignore them. He began by allying himself to the Regent's most trusted friend, Saint-Simon. Once a week Law visited Saint-Simon to let him know how business was progressing. This, he hoped, would gain him credibility, as well as useful snippets of inside information. But Saint-Simon was no fool: 'I soon knew that if Law desired these regular interviews it was not that he expected to make me an able financier; but as a man of intelligence, and he had plenty of it, he wanted access to a servitor of the Regent who was more than all others truly in his confidence.' But exposed to Law's mesmeric charm even Saint-Simon capitulated: 'We soon began to talk with a confidence which I never had reason to regret.'

At the bank's offices Law adopted a more straightforward approach to boost business. Rather like the incentives dangled before students today by high-street banks, he offered a tempting range of free or inexpensive banking services. At the Banque Générale, he proclaimed, you could transfer money from Paris to the provinces, discount bills and exchange foreign currency for little or no charge. Even the hostile *Gazette de la Régence* was beguiled when one of the author's friends with 1,800 livres to transfer from Marseille to Paris paid a visit to Monsieur Law's office. Here, according to the report in the *Gazette*, a Swiss footman, magnificently uniformed in green, introduced him to the bank's officials. They told him that if someone in Marseille handed his coins to the local director of the mint he would be given the 1,800 livres at the bank in Paris. There would be no charge for a transaction of this small size.

The Regent helped by making his well-publicized deposits and ensured that everyone knew he was using the bank for foreign transactions. Foreigners followed his lead, and at last found somewhere in Paris to discount their bills of exchange with ease and at reasonable prices. The influx of foreign currency alleviated the shortage of coins and, with the slow trickle of banknotes Law printed and issued to depositors, boosted the money supply sufficiently for commerce to begin to pick up. Traders liked the banknotes because the guarantee of being paid in coin of fixed value meant that they knew exactly what something would cost or what price they would receive. The notes began to command a premium, like those issued by the Bank of Amsterdam.

The small shoots of recovery were nurtured by the Regent's continuing sponsorship of the bank. In October 1716 he ordered tax collectors to remit payments to the Treasury in Law's banknotes. A few months later another edict declared that the public could pay their taxes in notes. Eighteen months after opening there were profits enough to pay shareholders a six-monthly dividend of 7 per cent, and Law's inconspicuous white notes, engraved with the legend, 'The bank promises to pay the bearer at sight, the sum of — livres, in coin of the weight and standard of this day, value received', were circulating throughout France and had begun to effect the revival he had promised.

But profit brought obstacles as well as dividends. Law was damaging the business of the private bankers of Paris: his offer of cut-price services to the public encroached on business they regarded as their domain. According to some accounts, mounting resentment inspired a group of anonymous opponents to combine their resources with the express intention of bringing him down. When their hoard reached 5 million livres in notes, they presented them at the bank for immediate payment. Law knew that his promise to 'pay on demand' underpinned the public's confidence, on which every bank depends. Without it the dream would crumble. He also knew that the bank reserves did not contain 5 million livres' worth of coins.

Chapter Nine

King of Half America

But the bank is not the only nor the greatest of my ideas. I will produce a work that will surprise Europe by the changes it will bring in France's favour, greater changes than those brought by the discovery of the Indies or by the introduction of credit. By this work Your Royal Highness will be in a position to relieve the kingdom of the sad condition into which it has fallen, and to make it more powerful than it has ever been, to establish order in finances, to replace, support and increase agriculture, manufacturing and commerce, to increase the population and the revenues of the kingdom, to reimburse useless and onerous charges, to increase the revenues of the King while helping the people, and to reduce the state debt without doing wrong to the creditors . . .

Letter from John Law to the Regent, December 1715

LAW SAVED HIMSELF BY STALLING. HE TOLD THE MEN HE would need twenty-four hours to raise such an unusually large sum and appealed to the finance ministry for support. Law's influence with the Regent still irked Noailles, the finance minister, but the bank's success had relieved the pressure on his ministry and, although he must have hated to admit it, he knew it was in his interest as much as Law's that the bank should be sustained. Thus, when Law outlined his predicament, Noailles ordered the mint to provide Law with the coins he required. One can scarcely imagine the incredulity of the men returning next day, expecting to find the bank in disarray; instead piles of coins were counted out before them. When they departed, along with their swollen bags of écus and louis d'or, they took with them the unwelcome news that John Law had unequivocally trounced them.

However, while the bank inched precariously towards success, Law was looking over his shoulder for more daring ventures. Two years after the bank had opened an opportunity to reveal his wider talents arose, unexpectedly, in the form of a diamond. The jewel came from India where, according to Saint-Simon, an employee at the Great Mogul's diamond mines smuggled out a 140-carat stone in his rectum. It was usual at the time for anyone dealing with precious stones to be closely searched and given a purgative before they were allowed to leave their place of employment but somehow the man evaded the usual checks and escaped with his jewel. Eventually, after changing hands several times, it was sold for the substantial sum of £20,000 to Thomas Pitt, governor of the English East India Company's Fort Madras settlement, immortalized ever after as Diamond Pitt. A stone of such prodigious size had never before been seen and Pitt, in high hopes that his purchase would prove a canny investment, sent it back to London for cutting. The jewel that emerged was 'the size of a Reine Claude plum, almost round in shape, of a thickness equal to its width, perfectly white, free from all blemish, cloud, or speck', enthused Saint-Simon. Naturally Pitt was anxious to recoup his considerable outlay as quickly as possible, but found that in times of war and climates of financial uncertainty, diamonds on such a scale are no one's friend. Even the quintessentially self-indulgent Louis XIV, when offered the stone the year before he died, refused it. In 1717, as Law was casting about for ways to impress the Regent, Pitt came back to Paris with his diamond, which was still for sale. He called on Law and showed him a crystal replica of the jewel that 'eclipsed all others in Europe'. At this pivotal moment in his career, the gem encapsulated Law's personal and patriotic aspirations. If he could bring about its royal acquisition, he would endorse his own influence at court as well as highlighting the Regent's pre-eminence in Europe. He encouraged Orléans to buy.

Orléans saw it differently; though tempted he was terrified. To make such an acquisition while widespread hardship continued would court controversy and criticism. But to Law, as to most men of his age, scruples were a selective luxury. Idealism could be put on hold when necessary and ambition now demanded a different rationale. With the help of Saint-Simon, he argued persuasively that the 'greatest king in Europe' should not apply the same rules as everyone else and that, in any case, the amount in question would have little real effect on the populace. The jewel's splendour would reinforce France's status in the world, and thus the greatness of the regency.

Orléans capitulated and authorized Law to make the final negotiations. A price of 2 million livres was agreed, but since there was no money to buy the diamond outright, a loan was secured against other jewels. Ever since, the Regent Diamond has adorned the regalia of France. Stolen during the Revolution, it was recovered in time to sparkle on the ceremonial sword of the first Consul in 1801, and remains in the Galerie d'Apollon in the Louvre, a gleaming testimony to Law's determination to make his mark and the Regent's irresolution in the face of temptation.

The spectacular diamond was a mere diversion compared with the mammoth drama to which Law had hinted in letters to the Regent: '. . . the bank is not the only nor the greatest of my ideas. I will produce a work that will surprise Europe by the changes which it will produce in France's favour,' he wrote, a few months before the bank was inaugurated.

The idea that would rock the world and immortalize its inventor seemed innocuous enough. Law's rapacious eye had focused on the wealth promised by the Indies, Africa and the Americas and he wanted to form an overseas trading company to exploit it. The Italians, the Spanish, the Portuguese, the Dutch and the English had all reaped immense fortunes from their fleets laden with silk, ebony, ivory, lacquer, coffee, tea, chocolate, spices, gold, silver, porcelain, and myriad other luxurious and lucrative cargoes. Now, said Law, France should share the harvest.

So far the French had enjoyed little success overseas. Cardinal de Richelieu, Louis XIII's great minister, had set up East and West Indian companies a little less than a century earlier. Under Colbert, in Louis XIV's reign, further ventures had been tried in Canada, the Caribbean, Newfoundland, the French Americas and the coast of Senegal. None had flourished, and overseas trade had been handed over to private enterprise. Among those who grasped the colonial baton was Robert Cavalier de la Salle, a native of Rouen, who in 1682 set out from Montreal, found and navigated the Mississippi and was murdered while trying to establish a colony in Louisiana. The Canadian-born captain of a naval frigate, Pierre le Moyne d'Iberville, continued the quest, and when he died, Robert Crozat, a wealthy Parisian financier, took over. Crozat had come closer than anyone before him to succeeding, ploughing 1.5 million livres into his enterprise. But when he came under the beady eye of the chamber of justice – and found he owed taxes of 6.6 million livres, he decided, with some reluctance, to relinquish his Mississippi concession in part payment of his dues.

Here was Law's great chance. The trading privilege that had reverted to the Crown was for the French colony of Louisiana, a territory many times larger than France, stretching from the mouth of the Mississippi for three thousand miles north, encompassing what is now Louisiana, Mississippi, Arkansas, Missouri, Illinois, Iowa, Wisconsin, Minnesota and parts of Canada. This vast tract was uncultivated, largely unexplored, and inhabited only by tribes of Indians. No one knew what riches lay beneath its soil or within its forests, most of France did not even know where the colony was, but it was whispered that this new Eldorado was copiously endowed with seams of gold and silver and with emerald mountains.

The ingenious scheme was baited to entice both the Regent and the private investor. The reason most other overseas ventures had failed, Law said, was because they were under-capitalized and badly directed. His venture would be amply funded, inspirationally managed, and would earn such huge revenues that France would again become the most powerful nation in the world. He would raise the necessary capital of 100 million livres by selling 200,000 shares, each valued at 500 livres. By forming a stock company and selling shares to the general public, everyone who wanted to could share in his company's success and grow rich. The draw for the Crown was that investors would partly pay for shares in Crown debt – the state bonds or billets that had been circulating in some form since the reign of Louis XIV. The company would charge a lower rate of interest for the *billets*, thus effectively doing the Crown a favour by saving precious money. The bargain for brave investors was that Law offered to accept the devalued billets *at face value* in return for company shares.

But when the scheme was discussed the Parlement (the sovereign law court of Paris with some political functions including registering all laws and state loans) voiced strong resistance. Suspicions remained of Law's motives; jealousy of his influence with the Regent rankled. Law was an outsider and, no matter how successful, ingenious and persuasive, always would be.

The Regent, however, viewed things differently. His affection and admiration for Law had grown with the bank's profits. Law tendered the promise of untold wealth, adventure, uncertainty, excitement. The Parlement represented the small-mindedness of judges. For a man who always craved the frisson of novelty, who had spent long years feeling frustrated under the reactionary Louis, there was little contest. He overruled the critics and Law was granted his privilege. In August 1717, the Company of the West, known popularly ever since as the Mississippi Company, was founded. It was given the right to all trade between France and its Louisiana colony for twenty-five years and to maintain its own army and navy, to mine and to farm. As managing director of the company Law held sway, ruling half of America in all but name.

But in these early days the company, like the bank, struggled to survive. The enticements Law had used to secure the concession had been costly and hindered progress. The fact that the shares were largely bought in devalued government bonds meant that the only capital available to build fleets and pay for crews, captains, stores, seeds, stock, tools, manual labour and all the other needs of the settlers was the 4 per cent interest payable on the bonds. If all the shares were subscribed, the most that would be raised would be 4 million livres a year (£275,000) – a modest sum, even then, on which to found a new Eldorado.

The reality was worse. While temptation to rid themselves of *billets* was great, the public, like the Parlement, were still distrustful of Law. Although joint-stock companies were familiar to English and Dutch investors, to the French they were not. The pleasures of share-dealing were as yet undis-covered, the profits unimaginable, the pitfalls worrisome. By the end of October, fewer than 30 million shares had been taken up and many of those subscribed for had not been paid in full. Racking his brain for ways to boost sales, Law announced that investors could pay for shares in five instalments, and might sell them at any point after the first instalment had been made. But even with this incentive shares still floundered below par.

Meanwhile, Law's enemies within the establishment were gathering. Noailles' animosity had grown with the launch of the Mississippi Company and he was 'setting all the machines at work to overthrow him', stirring up the councils and Parlement against him. Law grumbled to Saint-Simon, knowing full well that his complaints would reach the Regent and carry more weight than if he made the criticisms directly. In January 1718, the enmity between Noailles and Law had reached such a pitch that the Regent was forced to act. He hosted a supper party at Noailles' residence, La Raquette, at which he asked both men to present their ideas for the future. Noailles opted for the tried and tested tax and monetary manipulations. Law talked of nationalizing the bank, of expanding his trading company into a vast conglomerate, larger and more powerful than anything the world had ever seen, even of making the outstanding national debt disappear. Orléans' 'natural love of indirect ways, and the attraction of those mines of gold which Law made him foresee' made Law's innovative vision infinitely more appealing than Noailles' irreconcilable traditional approach. The finance minister was ushered expediently to a new post in which he would have nothing to do with John Law.

His place was filled by the gimlet-eyed d'Argenson. Many questioned the appointment. Some said that d'Argenson knew little of finance, that he would take the role and its perks and let Law run things behind the scenes. Others felt that he was a hard-liner who had been brought in to keep a stronger control of the Parlement. Certainly it seemed that he was not going to let Law run his show and take all his glory. As if trying to outmanoeuvre him, d'Argenson swiftly proposed his own remedy for the country's financial problems: he would slash government debt by calling in old coins and state bonds for revaluation. The livre would be devalued by a sixth but a substantial tranche of debt would be absorbed.

If Law had had anything to do with the scheme he did not show it. His main worry was to prevent the public losing trust in his banknotes although, since they were guaranteed at value on date of issue, they would be unaffected – or, if anything, more desirable. Thus, he reasoned, he could lie low while d'Argenson played at finance. He was wrong.

In the Parlement there was outcry. Unlike in England, members of the French Parlement were non-elected and had little real influence over the absolute monarchy; their role was no more than that of a judicial high court with administrative and legal duties. To bolster his own position in the early days of his regency, Orléans, however, had restored to them the right of 'remonstrance' before registration, which Louis XIV had removed in 1673. It was a decision he now regretted, since it gave them a lever – albeit a flimsy one – with which to challenge his authority. Law had not been overtly involved in the devaluation of the currency and later said he had opposed it. But the scheme presented the Parlement with a two-fold opportunity: to assert its power and to dispose of Law, against whom distrust festered. 'The Parlement are still doing all they can to pick a hole in Mr Law's coat, striking at the Regent through his sides,' reported Fanny Oglethorpe – a Jacobite exile and friend of Law – of the mounting tensions. The English ambassador, the Earl of Stair, also marked the mood: 'What makes it dangerous to employ Law is that everyone is against him, and that the Duke of Orléans, in the present situation of his affairs, would run a great risk in putting the administration of the finances into the hands of a stranger so generally hated, even if his system were good.'

The turning point came when the Parlement audaciously demanded that the Regent revoke the devaluation. When he refused, the judges retaliated by publishing an edict that outlawed the link between the bank and the government. No longer would taxes be payable in banknotes, it said – and, moreover, it was 'forbidden to all foreigners, even naturalized, to meddle directly or indirectly, or to participate under assumed names, in the handling or the administration of the royal funds.' The reference to Law could not have been clearer.

The crisis deepened. Word reached Saint-Simon that the Parlement intended to send bailiffs 'some morning with a warrant to arrest Law and hang him within three hours in the prison-yard'. At this, according to the Jacobite exile General Dillon, the Regent 'sent immediate orders to the foot and horse guards to be ready at a call and had powder and ball distributed to them. There are actually footguards at Law's house to secure his person from insult.' It must all have been a frightening reminder to Law of his trial and imprisonment. During an emergency meeting hastily convened by Saint-Simon, the strain of the past days took their toll and Law's self-possession crumbled: he broke down, according to Saint-Simon, 'more dead than alive, [he] knew not what to say, still less what to do'. Saint-Simon calmed him, and suggested that Law and Katherine take refuge in vacant apartments at the Palais Royal. Here, said Saint-Simon, he would be able to 'make more noise and bind the Regent more and . . . talk with him at all hours and urge him up to the mark'. In fact the Regent was too preoccupied to keep Law briefed with the unfolding events and Law, already unsettled, became increasingly isolated and insecure.

Orléans had decided to surprise the Parlement with a meeting known as a *lit de justice*, in which the young King would assert his regent's authority and override the Parlement's remonstrance. Saint-Simon helped lay plans to crush the

Parlement and only perceived Law's anxiety when he was accosted by one of Law's servants, who begged him to visit his master. He found Law in distress with Katherine. It may have been the first time she had seen Law's vulnerability, and to judge from Saint-Simon's account of this meeting, she had failed to allay his fears. Law was taut with the fear that the Regent was abandoning him to his enemies and it was only when Saint-Simon reassured him that there was nothing sinister in the Regent's behaviour that he seemed 'to breathe again'.

On 26 August, the day of the *lit de justice*, Paris awoke to find Swiss guards, musketeers, cavalry and household troops posted around the Palais Royal, the Tuileries, Law's bank and other strategic landmarks. The meeting began at ten in the Palais de Justice. Before the regency council, the Parlement, officers of the bodyguard and a contingent of spectators 'of consideration and mark', the eight-year-old King mounted the small staircase to his throne beneath a tapestry baldachin. D'Argenson, as Keeper of the Seals, made the announcement on the boy's behalf: 'The King chooses to be obeyed, and obeyed on the spot.' Thus, with more than a dash of melo-drama, the royal authority of the Regent was upheld, and the sixty-nine rebellious magistrates of the Parlement quashed. Three refused to fall into line and were arrested. The rest sweated profusely into their powdered wigs and robes of ceremonial velvet and conceded, reluctantly, that their moment had passed. The challenge had failed: once again Law, the outsider, had eluded them.

Chapter Ten

Finding the Philosopher's Stone

There appears nothing but new clothes, new figures and an infi-
nite number of families raised to new fortunes. They see 800
new coaches set up in Paris, and the families enriched purchase
new plate, new furniture, new clothes and new equipage, so
that there is a most prodigious trade there.

Daniel Defoe, 12 September 1719

THE PARLEMENT'S THREAT TO HANG HIM SHOOK LAW PRO-
foundly but did not alter his resolve to set his master plan, the
so-called 'system', in train. He was still fired by the gambler's
will to win, a philanthropic desire to improve and the urge to
experiment. Also, he was still obsessed with the rejection of his
appeal for a pardon for the death of Wilson, and craved redemp-
tion. But Law's sense of isolation at the Palais Royal seems also
to have awakened a more profound, barely acknowledged need
for social acceptance and belonging. Law the opportunist, once
happy to live outside the conventions of society and to make
use of his *haut monde* connections for his own ends, now longed
to be properly part of them. As with many successful businessmen today, he was consumed by political ambition. Perhaps

Katherine had something to do with this shift in his thinking: the death threat and the rapid turns in political events must have disturbed her and underlined the vulnerability of their position. Perhaps behind Law's increasing desire for public office lay not only his ambition but concern that the family's future should be made more secure. It is possible, too, that Katherine felt she had an important role to play: as a doyenne of society, she could forge alliances that would help to stabilize Law's political career. One fundamental belief, however, she could not change: in money, he was convinced, lay the key to salvation and the answer to his aims.

As France's premier banker, he was ideally poised to become a man of repute. The following autumn, when Lady Mary Wortley Montagu was passing through Paris, she noted the change in his fortunes: 'I must say I saw nothing in France that delighted me so much as to see an Englishman (at least a Briton) absolute at Paris. I mean Mr Law, who treats their Dukes and Peers extremely *de haut en bas* and is treated by them with the utmost submission and respect.' Always an enthusiastic patron of the arts, Law sat for his portrait, probably to the artist Alexis Simon Belle, at around this time. The painting shows a man in his mid-forties, of refinement, charm and still youthful appearance, wearing a full-length brown periwig, embroidered velvet robe and lace cravat – grand clothes befitting his already elevated status. His face is thin and rather angular, his mouth, though half-smiling, has an air of determination, and the expression is distant – the piercing grey-eyed gaze avoids the viewer, as if his mind is elsewhere, perhaps with his system's next phase: his bank's takeover by the state. The bank's assets now included over 9 million livres in coins and 1.6 million in bills of exchange. Against these were fewer than 40 million livres in outstanding notes. Law had remembered the warnings of Saint-Simon and the lessons of the Bank of Amsterdam and restricted the issue of notes.

In December 1718, the Banque Générale became the Banque Royale, the equivalent of a nationalized industry today. Law continued to direct it and, under his leadership over the next months, the finances of France leaned more heavily on it. New branches opened in Lyon, La Rochelle, Tours, Orléans and Amiens. To ensure that everyone made use of paper money, any transactions of more than 600 livres were ordered to be made in paper notes or gold. Since gold was in short supply, this obliged nearly everyone to use paper for all major transactions. Meanwhile, for the leap of confidence they had shown in purchasing shares in the bank in its early uncertain days, and perhaps to buy his way into their world, Law rewarded investors lavishly. Shares that they had partly bought with devalued government bonds were paid out in coins. Both he and the Regent had been major shareholders and were among those who profited greatly from the bank's takeover.

Few recognized the dangers signalled by the bank's new royal status. Hitherto Law had kept careful control of the numbers of notes issued. There had always been coin reserves of around 25 per cent against circulating paper notes. Now, with royal ownership and no shareholders to ask awkward questions, the bank became less controllable. The issuing and quantity of printed notes, the size of reserves would all be decided by the Regent and his advisers. The temptation to print too much paper money too quickly would thus be virtually unchecked.

Within five months of its royal takeover the writer Buvat noted in his journal, with more than a touch of irony, that eight printers, each of whom earned only 500 livres a year, were employed around the clock printing 100-, 50- and 10-livre notes. A further ominous change followed: notes were no longer redeemable by value at date of issue but according to the face value, which would change along with coins if the currency was devalued: the principle that underpinned public confidence in paper had been discarded and one of Law's most basic tenets breached. But, as the eminent eighteenth-century economist Sir James Steuart later incredulously remarked, 'Nobody seemed dissatisfied: the nation was rather pleased; so familiar were the variations of the coin in those days, that nobody ever considered anything with regard to coin or money, but its denomination . . . this appears wonderful; and yet it is a fact.'

If Law was unhappy he gave no sign of it. Apparently he was busy re-investing profits from his bank shares. He began to build a vast property portfolio, buying the Duchy of Mercoeur from the Dowager Princess of Condé for the sum of 100,000 livres and the Hôtel de Soissons from the Prince of Carignan for 750,000 livres. The Hôtel became the headquarters of the Mississippi Company, but the beautiful gardens were retained by the shrewd Prince, who later profited by letting them as a marketplace for share-dealing.

At around this time, Law was joined in Paris by his brother William, who was four years his junior, had trained in Edinburgh as a goldsmith, and was, Law believed, one of his most trusted allies. William was a founding director of the Banque Générale and had worked for some time as Law's agent in London. Among his friends was George Middleton, one of London's leading bankers, whose services the Laws used to undertake their investments in diamonds, Scottish property and South Sea and East India stock. Shortly before settling in France, William married Rebecca Dives, the strikingly beautiful daughter of a London coal merchant. In Paris the couple took up residence in a suitably imposing mansion, employed a retinue of liveried servants, acquired several carriages and, thanks to Law and Katherine's influence, were introduced to court circles.

Meanwhile, Law was casting his net ever wider. He was anxious to encourage local industry, having always seen it as fundamental to national prosperity. An agent in England was employed under his brother's direction to find clock- and watchmakers, weavers, metal-workers and other specialist craftsmen and tempt them with various financial enticements to move to France. According to Buvat around 900 workers settled at Versailles, where they were given lodgings in a converted stable block belonging to the Duchesse de Berry, the Regent's daughter, and in the nearby Parc aux Cerfs. Each received a salary of thirty livres per month plus thirty sous a day for food. It was a move few immigrants can have regretted: a huge demand for luxury goods was one of the immediate effects of the incredible economic boom France was about to experience.

Chiefly, though, the price of Mississippi shares, which was still struggling disappointingly below par, engrossed Law. The way to turn the ailing Mississippi Company into Europe's most successful conglomerate and to return France to a state of prosperity, Law concluded, was to monopolize French trade and state finances. This audacious idea was, in a sense, the lesson of youth reapplied: as a young man he had learned that the way to win was to ensure that the odds of winning were always in his favour. Now the same principle was utilized in corporate enterprise. Law was dealing his company an unbeatable hand.

The first acquisitions targeted overseas trade: the right to tobacco farming in the colonies, to slaves and other lucrative products in Senegal. Tobacco-smoking had yet to become entrenched in polite circles but snuff was the height of fashion – the Princess Palatine tartly criticized ladies for 'arriving here with their noses dirty as if they had rubbed them in mud', although a year later she remarked perceptively, 'They call it the magic plant, because those who begin to use it can no longer give it up.' The profits from such a monopoly, as many investors quickly realized, were therefore likely only to grow.

Then came the most crucial coup so far: the acquisition of trade to the East Indies. Law had noted that the French East

India and China Company had been badly managed and was making huge losses. He contended that if it was merged with the Mississippi Company it would form an enterprise with global trading rights from which each company would benefit. The idea was grandiose, daring, risky, but he made it sound plausible. The acquisitions would be paid for by a second issue of 50,000 shares, nicknamed *filles*, daughters (the first issue was known as *mères*, mothers), priced at 550 livres each (with a nominal value of 500 livres). Unlike the *mères* issue, which investors had bought with state bonds, the *filles* would be paid for in cash. This, Law explained, was because the first move he would make to revive French overseas trade would be to invest in two dozen ships of 500 tons each and the capital from the shares would be necessary to finance them.

The establishment sneered. As usual d'Argenson, who – according to Law – was 'jealous of the credit that I had acquired with His Royal Highness and the public by the direction of the bank and the Western company', was a vociferous opponent, claiming that the plan was doomed and casting doubt on public willingness to invest, given that the first issue of shares was still trading below par. Egged on by d'Argenson, even the Regent was anxious about the scheme's viability and stalled Law's request for royal sanction. Realizing that the doubters would only be silenced if he demonstrated, irrefutably, that the idea was fail-safe, Law conferred with several key friends and potential investors. They agreed easy terms of payment for the new issue of shares: ten monthly instalments (later made even more tempting by being increased to twenty). Ships would be slow to prepare and fit, Law said, so the company would not need its full working capital immediately. With this incentive dangling before them, five supporters were keen enough to pledge to buy a million livres' worth of shares each. Law's gambling instincts now surfaced: he guaranteed to put up 2.5 million livres as a first down-payment on the par price. This effectively obliged him to buy over 90 per cent of the entire issue and invest a total of 25 million livres. To the Regent, self-assurance on such a scale was irresistible: on Sunday 23 May he overruled d'Argenson's misgivings and authorized the deal. The new enterprise was named the Company of the Indies, although most still used the old sobriquet, Mississippi Company.

Beneath his surface bravado, Law fretted over the wisdom of his move: 'On Monday night I did not sleep; I had gained a great confidence with the public and I feared losing it by the action that I had taken,' he later owned. In fact, his gamble paid off. In the goldfish-bowl society in which he moved, under-writing an issue on such a scale could scarcely fail to attract attention. Everyone assumed that to do so Law, with his inside knowledge, had to have been certain of success. The growing profits of his acquisitions, particularly of the tobacco monopoly and the distant Louisiana colony seemed assured. The shrewdest began to follow suit.

Rapidly, amid a flurry of rumour, the herd instinct took hold. The price of the old shares broke through their par price and rose to 600 livres, and subscriptions for the new issue streamed in. By mid-June shares were changing hands at 650 livres, and 50 million paper notes poured off the bank's presses to enable people to purchase the next issue of shares, which would be offered at the end of the month. Slowly, the sceptical French public, who had burned their fingers with state bonds, were learning that paper investments could rise as well as fall in value. Law was about to compound the lesson with manoeuvres that laid bare his grasp of consumer psychology: the elementary concept that reducing supply increases demand.

New issue restrictions were imposed: in order to buy one new share investors had to own four old ones. Thus, those who had bought the original issue enjoyed the pleasure of watching the value of their investment rise as, over the summer of 1719, France savoured her first taste of a bull market. By the time the second instalment was due on the new issue, the share price had doubled to 1,000 livres. Meanwhile, Law gilded the lily still further by stating that the company would pay a generous 12 per cent dividend of 60 livres in the following year. As the bank printed more notes and issued more loans to allow greater numbers of people to buy and deal in shares, prices continued to rise.

Law's summer spending spree was still incomplete. At the end of July 1719 he bought the rights to the Royal Mint for 50 million livres. To cover the cost a third issue of 50,000 shares was offered. These were nicknamed *petites filles*, granddaughters, and as before were linked to earlier issues. To buy one granddaughter you had to own four mothers and a daughter.

Outside the Mississippi Company office, throughout the summer of 1719, Paris was rapidly engulfed in unprecedented speculation madness. By mid-August the shares that three months earlier had languished at 490 livres were being snapped up at 3,500. A carnival atmosphere descended on the city, and on the evening before St Louis Day, 25 August, thousands gathered in the Jardin des Tuileries to enjoy a firework and musical extravaganza. At the end of the evening the fashionable crowd funnelled towards an exit at one end of the gardens but found their way partially barred because a steward had forgotten to open one of the gates. Impatience became a surge of panic when word spread that pickpockets were capitalizing on the wealthy captive audience. A dozen or so thieves were later arrested, pockets crammed with gold and silver snuff-boxes, watches, diamond crosses, embroidered shawls, handkerchiefs, lace headdresses, pieces of men's waistcoats, and panels of expensive ladies' coats that had been subtly cut from their backs. Amid the pandemonium, eleven women fell and were suffocated or trampled to death. Hundreds more suffered broken limbs, heat exhaustion, the after-effects of crushing. Paris mourned.

News of the disaster reached the rest of Europe along with reports of Law's most daring manoeuvre. He had offered to take over the burden that had weighed so heavily on the nation since Louis' final failing years, and lend the state enough to repay the national debt – 1.2 billion livres at an interest rate of 3 per cent. The proposal was intertwined with a highly contentious pledge to pay 52 million livres for the right to take over tax collection. At the time France leased this right to private enterprise in the shape of the General Receivers, who were responsible for direct taxation, and to the Farmers General, a syndicate of forty private financiers, who were responsible for collecting indirect tax, such as customs duty and levies on salt and alcohol. The Farmers General were also the largest creditors of the state and profiteers from government indebtedness. The owner of a so-called 'tax farm' lease had to estimate the sum of revenue he would raise and advance it to the state. If the revenue was below this amount he himself was obliged to pay the state, while any revenue above it he could keep. In fact, research has recently shown that the forty financiers were not actually rich enough to advance the whole sum to be collected. They acted as 'names', or front men, for numerous anonymous investors and courtiers. It was a system that lay open to huge profits, corruption and inefficiency, and one that was dominated by the Pâris brothers, the four most powerful financiers of France. Law's fascination for finance had always been entwined with concern for moral economic issues. He saw injustice in the huge advantages the tax system gave to an established élite. Now he grasped the chance to eliminate them, little realizing how fiercely they would respond.

The massive sum needed to cover the government loan would be raised by a further issue of Mississippi shares. Existing bond-holders would be given a choice of converting into shares or company annuities, which offered a return of 3 per cent – at least 1 per cent less than they currently received. The intention was to make shares a far more attractive proposition than annuities. The scheme was by far the most grandiose yet: Law was aiming to raise seventeen times more than the sum of all the previous issues and again he made it sound entirely plausible.

Thus on 13 September a fourth issue of 100,000 shares, known as *cinq-cents*, was launched, priced at 5,000 livres with a nominal value of 500. As before the issue was consumed hungrily by the Mississippi-mad public. Two more identical issues followed, then a final one of 24,000. Unlike earlier subscriptions there were no restrictions on purchase – you did not need to own shares already, anyone might grow rich by buying into the Mississippi dream. The Earl of Stair noted, 'The public had run upon this new subscription with that fury, that near the double of that sum is subscribed for: and there have been the greatest brigues [intrigues] and quarrels to have place in the subscription, to that degree that the new submissions are not yet delivered out, nor is the first payment received. Mr Law's door is shut, and all the people of quality in France are on foot, in hundreds, before his door in the Place Vendôme.'

Canny and ambitious though the scheme undoubtedly was, Law seems to have naïvely ignored the effect of his plans on the tax farmers and financiers, and the court nobility who backed them. The double blow – denying their lucrative tax profits, and significantly reducing their income from their government bonds – was bound to spark an angry response and make them determined to undermine his reforms. He disregarded the danger at his peril.

The shares were traded in the company's new offices in Paris's ancient commercial heartland, the rue Quincampoix, a street that today crouches under the shadow of the Centre Pompidou, in the Les Halles district. The rue Quincampoix is a long thin thoroughfare, terminating at the rue aux Ours to the north and the rue Aubry le Boucher to the south. The road had long been a centre for money-changers, businessmen raising capital to start new ventures and, during the reign of

Louis XIV, traders in the unpopular *billets* – its tongue-twisting name comes from one of its twelfth-century money-dealing residents, Nicolas de Kiquenpoit.

In volatile markets news is an essential tool that helps traders anticipate where prices might move next. Today's brokers have at their disposal data vendors such as Reuters and Bloomberg offering a mass of up-to-date analysis, research, prices and charts. The eighteenth-century equivalent was gossip. News of the colonies, government policy and Law's next move was end-lessly anticipated and assessed in the rue Quincampoix. So many gravitated here to talk and trade that the surrounding streets were paralysed by horses and carriages. D'Argenson, the finance minister, whose official residence was also in the street, was infuriated when one day in November he spent more than an hour stuck in a traffic jam. Eventually carriages were banned, gates erected to control the crowds and guards posted to prevent night dealings which disturbed residents. In another futile attempt to restore some semblance of order, one entrance was reserved for speculators of quality, the other for everyone else.

At the sound of a morning bell, the gates opened and convention vanished. Aristocrats jostled with their footmen and maids; bishops and priests vied with courtesans, opera singers and actresses; magistrates did business with pickpockets; Italians, Dutch and English mingled with the French. Daniel Defoe described the extraordinary scenes: 'Nothing can be more diverting than to see the hurry and clutter of the stock-jobbers in Quincampoix street; a place so scandalously dirty, as if it had been not the sink of the city only, but of the whole kingdom . . . The inconvenience of the darkest and nastiest street in Paris does not prevent the crowds of people of all qualities . . . coming to buy and sell their stocks in the open place; where, without distinction, they go up to the ankles in dirt, every step they take.' Even the nine-year-old King

Louis XV was caught up in the frenzied mood. When a plan of Paris was laid before him he was said to have demanded that Quincampoix be highlighted in gilding.

The Parisian élite was startled by the extraordinary number of people from the lower orders who prospered spectacularly from Mississippi speculation. Money was easy to borrow and, since you only needed put down a 10 per cent deposit to play the market, people from all walks of life rushed to sell their châteaux, their diamonds, their cows and their crops to join in. The privileged greeted the new social mobility with diffidence, worried that the hierarchy that for centuries had underpinned their superior status had vanished along with financial gloom. Even Voltaire was bemused. Writing to the Parlement councillor Nicolas de Genonville he commented:

> It is good to come to the country when Plutus is turning all heads in the city. Have you really all gone mad in Paris? I only hear talk of millions. They say that everyone who was comfortably off is now in misery and everyone who was impoverished revels in opulence. Is this reality? Is this a chimera? Has half the nation found the philosopher's stone in the paper mills? Is Law a god, a rogue or a charlatan who is poisoning himself with the drug he is distributing to everyone?

Journals and memoirs of the time recount scores of tales of Mississippians propelled from poverty to wealth overnight. As with today's lottery winners, writers of the rags-to-riches stories revelled in the difficulties of those who found the transition hard to make, often ridiculing them for daring to aspire to luxurious living. There are tales of a footman who earned so much that he was able to buy himself a fine carriage, but when it was delivered forgot his changed circumstances and found himself taking up his old position at the rear. A baker's son from Toulouse was said to have bought an entire shop full of silver plate for 400,000 livres, and sent it home to his wife with orders to invite the local gentry for dinner and use the silver. The woman was unused to such luxurious objects but did as instructed. When her guests arrived they collapsed in mirth to see soup served in a church offertory basin, the sugar dispensed from an incense burner and the salt from chalices.

Of the fabled Mississippi investors who came from modest backgrounds the most spectacular success was that of the Widow Chaumont from Namur who came to Paris to collect a debt, which was paid to her in *billets d'états*. She invested them in Mississippi stock and swiftly made several million livres. She spent part of the proceeds buying the Château d'Ivry, and every week held legendary banquets where guests consumed 'an oxen, two calves, six sheep and numerous fowls'.

Law's own coachman was said to have made such profits that he tendered his resignation, having employed two drivers, one for himself and one for Law – he offered his ex-employer first choice. Another much-recorded incident relates the story of an exquisitely dressed woman who was observed descending from an immaculate carriage. When the aristocratic spectators asked who she was they were told 'a woman who has tumbled from a garret into a carriage'.

Many of the servants who grew wealthy did so when their employers commissioned them to sell on their behalf at a certain sum. Often they arrived at the rue Quincampoix to find the price far higher than expected, in which case they could pocket the difference and use it as capital to trade. One of the many diarists of the time tells of a gentleman who sent his servant with 250 shares and instructions to sell at 8,000 livres. The servant sold them for 10,000, making a profit of half a million livres in a morning, then reinvested and a few days later found himself worth 2 million.

By October the share price was 6,500 livres. The rise was not, however, without vacillation. In the tumult of rue

Quincampoix, traders operated independently and un-regulated; prices at one end of the street varied dramatically from those at the other, and fortunes made in one hour could be reversed during the next. The Princess Palatine, the Regent's mother, recalled wryly that when the royal physician, Monsieur Chirac, heard that his stock had fallen dramatically he muttered, while taking a patient's pulse, 'Good Lord, it's going down, it's going down.' Fearing she was about to die the lady began to sob. Chirac hastily consoled her: 'Your pulse is splendid and you are quite well. I was thinking of the Mississippi shares on which I am losing because they are going down'.

Along with the share-trading frenzy came an orgy of property speculation. Houses in the rue Quincampoix were bought or let by the shrewdest businessmen 'foreseeing from the commencement that the ground of the street would rise in value to such an extent, that ten square feet might bring in the income of a lordly estate'. Property previously let at up to 800 livres per annum could be divided into twenty or thirty tiny offices and each sub-let at up to 400 livres a month, a sum equivalent to an average craftsman's annual salary.

Lean-to shacks were erected in alleyways and on rooftops and rented out for vast sums. As the throng continued to swell, local innkeepers, confectioners and chefs charged huge prices for their services. Cafés opened nearby where aristocratic ladies and gentlemen could sip their *tasse* of coffee or chocolate and play quadrille while their brokers made them rich. All usual constraints of value were lost: a single chicken was said to change hands for 200 livres and, in one of the most bizarre and often repeated legends of the time, a hunchback was said to have earned 150,000 livres in a few days by leaning against a mulberry tree and hiring his hump as a writing desk on which to sign contracts.

A golden key, so the saying goes, opens any door, and many craved social acceptance along with their new-found wealth.

Saint-Simon recorded the desperate lengths to which some would go to improve their status. The wealthy Mississippian d'André who 'had made mounds of gold' used some of it to betroth his three-year-old daughter to the thirty-three-year-old Marquis d'Oyse, paying 600,000 livres and undertaking to make further annual payments of 20,000 livres until the child reached twelve, when an enormous estate would be made over as a final payment and the wedding would take place. The deal so amazed the *haut monde* that the lawyer Marais wrote in his diary, 'The babies of Mississippians now cry for marquis instead of dolls.' D'André was one of many who subsequently lost his fortune and the contract ended in an acrimonious lawsuit that was still dragging on fifteen years later.

Predictably Mississippians were drawn to unbridled luxury: a fine carriage trimmed with crimson velvet and gold fringing became the badge of success in the same way that a Rolls Royce, Mercedes or Ferrari broadcasts prosperity today. The age-old symbols of wealth – jewels, expensive clothing, gold, silver, property and prestigious furnishing – were avidly sought. A window into this world of unabashed materialism is revealed in the paintings of Watteau, in which flamboyant figures in shimmering pastel silks pose in stagey *fêtes champêtres* or, as in the famous painting *L'Enseigne de Gersaint*, shop for works of art. The diplomat Daniel Pulteney gasped at the excess: 'It is certain that the commerce of people here increases every day and that all manner of luxury does too; the Hollanders have drawn several millions from hence for jewels, lace and linen; I was told yesterday that one shop had sold in less than three weeks lace and linen for 800 thousand livres and this chiefly to people who never wore any lace before.' Defoe was similarly staggered by Parisian consumer frenzy: 'Money,' he said, 'flows like the waters of the Seine.'

Gold- and silversmiths, whose business had languished in the wake of Louis XIV's financial crisis, now found themselves inundated with orders. Within three months, 120,000 silver plates and matching dishes to a total value of more than £7 million had been cast, chased, engraved and sold. The weavers at tapestry workshops in the Gobelins, in the provincial town of Aubusson and the Savonnerie carpet factory were deluged with commissions. Porcelain, another eye-catching, luxurious status symbol, was imported in vast quantity to fill the table-tops, cabinets and walls of the elegant salons of the newly rich. The ateliers of furniture-makers such as Charles Cressent and the Boulle brothers, sons of the great Charles André, pandered to the burgeoning craving for articles of unrivalled ostentation and intricacy. Showpiece commodes, *bureaux plats* and cabinets were expensively veneered in exotic tropical timbers such as amaranth, kingwood and satinwood – imported in Mississippi Company vessels – and further embellished with gilded nymphs and goddesses writhing among lush foliage. Such objects embodied prestige, bounty, status – the universal message of wealth both old and new. Summing up the prevailing mood the Regent's doughty mother wrote, with a note of apprehension, 'It is inconceivable what immense wealth there is in France now. Everybody speaks in millions. I don't understand it at all, but I see clearly that the god Mammon reigns an absolute monarch in Paris.'

Chapter Eleven

The First Millionaire

'. . . he was civil, and his fortune did not seem to have puff'd him up. He was a fine handsome man, of a fair complexion as the English generally are, and had a very noble past'.

Baron de Pollnitz, *Memoirs* (1738)

WHILE PARIS WAS TRANSMUTING INTO AN ENCHANTED city, John Law, the enigmatic outsider who had effected the magical transformation, was recast as an international superstar. The Law residence in the Place Vendôme drew the eminent like pilgrims to some sacred shrine. Once-scornful princes, prelates and grandees scurried to ingratiate themselves, waiting for hours in his antechamber which, said du Hautchamp, was 'never empty of noblemen and ladies, whose sole occupation seemed to be a desire to pay court to him'.

Most came with the intention of asking for a few extra shares at a preferential rate. Many had their requests granted – Law's generosity was almost as legendary as the economic miracles he wrought. Saint-Simon, however, was sickened by the mass cupidity: 'Law . . . saw his door forced, his windows entered from the garden, while some of them came tumbling down the chimney of his cabinet.' Like royalty, Law restricted most callers to formal audiences, and gaining entry was no easy feat. 'The Swiss must be fed for entrance at his gate, the *lacqueys* for admittance to his antechamber, and the *valets de chambre* for the privilege of access to his presence chamber or closet,' grumbled the Baron de Pollnitz.

Ladies had always found Law attractive; now that he had celebrity and vast wealth, they openly adored him. Haughty duchesses and elegant *mesdames* prostrated themselves before him, overturned their carriages in front of his house, inveigled their way into his home – anything to get themselves noticed. 'If Law wanted it, the French ladies would kiss his backside,' grumbled the Regent's mother, aghast at their shamelessness. She related one incident in which Law had granted an audience to several ladies then begged to be excused because he needed to relieve himself. The women refused, saying, 'Oh, if it's only that, it doesn't matter, go ahead, piss, and listen to us.' In sheer desperation, he took them at their word; they were unabashed. Madame de Bouchu was another audacious lady whom Law was eager to avoid. Undeterred by his rebuffs she followed him to a dinner given by an aristocratic rival, who had pointedly excluded her, and ordered her coachman to drive in front of the house and shout, 'Fire.' On hearing the alarm, the guests, including Law, left the table and ran into the street. Madame de Bouchu spotted her quarry and pounced on him but he managed to make a speedy escape.

As a man who had always cherished his privacy, and lived much of his life ignoring convention, Law must have found the constant fuss, formality and fawning hard to bear. In later years he would remember how 'Every day I had a hundred impertinent demands.' He remained, for the most part, gracious, affable and irrepressibly witty. When an elderly lady stumbled over her words in her eagerness to ask him for shares and said, 'Give me, I beg you, a conception' instead of 'a concession', Law hid a smile and replied kindly, 'It is not possible at the moment.'

According to the gossips, he was not always immune to the charms of those who offered themselves to him. Through his royal connections he was introduced to Claudine de Tencin, a renowned hostess whose salon was famed for attracting leading intellectuals and beauties. She was a vivacious, glamorous adventuress, who had run away from a convent and given birth to a son, whose presence was so inconvenient that she abandoned him on a church doorstep. She had been the mistress of the Regent, who had told her when pressed that he 'never discussed politics with a whore between the sheets', and later of his foreign minister Dubois. There were many rumours that Law also shared her favours, along with those of others: Fanny Oglethorpe let slip in a letter, 'Law is in love with Mlle de Nail [possibly Madame de Nesle] and gives her 10,000 livres a month to visit her when Prince Soubise is not there.' There were whispers, too, of an improbable romantic entanglement between Law and the Princess Palatine who, at sixty-eight, clearly found him attractive. Her letters mention that he 'was worthy of praise on account of his cleverness', and that she was 'greatly taken with him and he does all he can do to please me'.

Keeping a mistress was a common enough practice among the élite of Paris. Nevertheless it is likely that there was little substance to most such stories, and that the majority were no more than scurrilous gossip. Yet, true or not, Katherine, who can hardly fail to have been aware of what was said, must have been pained. She could do little, however, but turn a blind eye. Later events revealed that her affection for Law survived. At the time she distracted herself by falling into the role of society wife, and became one of the most celebrated hostesses in Paris. 'If you want your choice of duchesses,' one courtier reportedly told the Regent, 'go to Madame Law's house, and you will find them all gathered there.' Few realized that she and Law were not married. Perhaps those who suspected the alliance was illicit dared not mention it, bearing in mind her social clout and the desirability of an invitation to her salon.

Her children were propelled into an equally elevated social orbit. The thirteen-year-old John learned to hunt and to dance with the young Louis XV, and was invited to perform in a ballet with him — although at the final moment an attack of measles prevented him from taking part. He was educated, as befitted nobility, by a private tutor, one Charles Chesneau, by all accounts a kindly and gifted man. Mary Katherine received numerous offers of marriage from noble families — among them the Prince de Tarente, all of which Law, a devoted and protective father, turned down. When Law gave a party in his daughter's honour, the papal nuncio Cardinal Bentivoglio was among the first to arrive and amazed everyone by kissing the child's hand and playing with her doll.

Along with the invasion of his family life came a sprinkling of public accolades. Law was elected an honorary member of the Academy of Sciences, and as he passed through the streets for the inauguration ceremony the crowds shouted, 'God save the King and Monsieur Law.' Scotland bestowed on him the freedom of the city of Edinburgh; the document was delivered to his door in a gold box valued at £300 and obsequiously engraved with the legend: 'The Corporation of Edinburgh, having done themselves the honour to enrol in the liberties of their city, John Law, Earl of Tankerville etc., a gentleman of a graceful person, fine parts, the first of all the bankers in Europe, a happy contriver and manager of societies for trade in the remotest parts of the world . . .'

At heart, in the beginning, Law was little changed. Though now a man of inordinate wealth — he owned at least 100 million livres' worth of shares — with stereotypical Scottish canniness, he spent his money carefully. Property continued to be a major investment. Along with a dozen or so French country estates, he bought vast areas of Paris, including a third of the houses in the Place Vendôme where he lived. He also acquired land in the area surrounding the Boulevard St Honoré, and the Palais Mazarin (which today houses the manuscript department of the Bibliothèque Nationale with his memoirs and documents). The balustrade from this building now adorns the Wallace Collection and features a cornucopia out of which gushes a torrent of gold coins. Law invested in diamonds, both cut and uncut, through his London banker George Middleton; paid 180,000 livres for the Abbé Bignon's extensive library of 45,000 books; and acquired further properties in Scotland.

Art was another passion. He collected Italian and Dutch masters and commissioned works from contemporary artists. The pastellist Rosalba Carriera became a family friend, who made portraits of Law, Katherine and the children (her portrait of Kate entitled *La Jeune Fille au Singe* survives in the Louvre). He commissioned Carriera's brother-in-law, the artist Antonio Pellegrini, who had just failed to secure the contract to decorate the dome of St Paul's Cathedral in London, to decorate the ceilings of the offices of the Banque Royale. Pellegrini's master-piece was every bit as ambitious as Law's system, measuring a spectacular 130 feet by 27 feet. The design, an apotheosis of all that was dearest to Law, showed the child King Louis XV and the Regent surrounded by personifications of Commerce, Riches, Credit, Security, Invention, Arithmetic, Book-keeping, Navigation, and, naturally, the Mississippi. (The ceiling's fate echoed Law's: it fell in 1724.)

But, compared with the excesses of the day, Law eschewed overt materialism: 'Inordinate influence and fortune never spoiled [him], and . . . behaviour, equipments, table and furni-ture could never shock anyone,' Saint-Simon affirmed. Perhaps the stalwart Katherine and his children kept his feet firmly on the ground. His house was simply furnished, he dressed relatively plainly, and still relished an evening with friends over a hand or two of cards. An old friend, Archibald, Earl of Ilay, remembered visiting Law's house at around this time. On arrival he was shown into an antechamber crowded with visitors. When word reached Law that Ilay was waiting the Earl was ushered swiftly into Law's private study, where he found the great man writing to the gardener at Lauriston – according to some accounts, about the cabbages he wanted planted in the garden. Law was delighted to see him, and the two sat and played piquet for some time before joining the assembled throng.

Law's old obsession with improving public prosperity still preoccupied him. The effect of his policy proved beneficial throughout the nation. Du Tot, deputy treasurer at the bank, commented: 'Plenty immediately displayed herself through all the towns, and all the country. She there relieved our citizens and labourers from the oppression of debts . . . she revived industry.' As the economy burgeoned Law zealously effected reform. He set in train a dynamic programme of public building, funded by the abundant supply of paper money. Bridges were constructed, canals dug, roads improved, new barracks built. In Paris a generous endowment was given to the university, and a bequest made to the Scots College where his father was buried. More controversially, he set about stream-lining a tax system riddled with corruption and unnecessary complexity. As one English visitor to France in the late seventeenth century observed: 'The people being generally so oppressed with taxes, which increase every day, their estates are worth very little more than what they pay to the King; so that they are, as it were, tenants to the Crown, and at such a rack rent that they find great difficulty to get their own bread.' The mass of offices sold to raise money had caused one of Louis XIV's ministers to comment, 'When it pleases Your Majesty to create an office, God creates a fool to purchase it.' There were officials for inspecting the measuring of cloth and candles, hay trussers, coal measurers, inspectors of wood piles, paper and bridges, examiners of meat, fish and fowl. There was even an inspector of pigs' tongues.

This did nothing for efficiency, Law deemed, and served only to make necessities more expensive and to encourage the holders of the offices 'to live in idleness and deprive the state of the service they might have done it in some useful profession, had they been obliged to work'. In place of the hundreds of old levies he swept away (over forty in one edict alone), Law introduced a new national taxation system called the *denier royal*, based on income. The move caused an outcry among the holders of offices, many of whom were wealthy financiers and members of the Parlement, but delight among the public. 'The people went dancing and jumping about the streets,' wrote Defoe. 'They now pay not one farthing tax for wood, coal, hay, oats, oil, wine, beer, bread, cards, soap, cattle, fish.'

Elsewhere a similar sense of well-being came from share-dealing. The Regent's family and favourites were given preferential allocations and prospered spectacularly. His mother reported that the King had millions for his household and that 'My son has given me 2 million in shares which I have distributed among my household.' The Marquis de Lassay, the Maréchal d'Estrées, the Duc de la Force and the royal princes of Conti and Bourbon made millions. Bourbon spent part of his colossal windfall in starting his own porcelain factory and re-decorating his château at Chantilly. An avid equine enthusiast, he was convinced that he would come back in the after-life as a horse, and had luxurious stables, the so-called Grandes Écuries, designed by the architect Jean Aubert. Arcaded, domed and studded with sculpture, the palatial building could house 500 horses and survives as an equestrian museum.

So numerous were the private fortunes gained that a new word was invented to describe them. The word 'millionaire' was coined at this time to describe the rich Mississippians, first appearing in print in the lawyer Marais' journal in 1720:

> *Espérons que la dividende*
> *En sera plus sûre et plus grande*
> *Sur le rapport qu'il en fera,*
> *Et que l'on communiquera*
> *Aux calotins actionnaires,*
> *Lesquels n'ont point realisé*
> *Comme certains millionnaires*
> *Peuple avare et mal avisé.*

> *Let's hope that the dividend*
> *Will be more certain and larger*
> *On the return that it will bring*
> *And one will inform*
> *The smug investors*
> *Who have realized nothing*
> *Like certain millionaires*
> *A greedy and ill-advised breed.*

The term 'millionaire' exerted a seductive appeal. Drawn by stories of unbelievable gains that echoed throughout Europe, foreigners flocked to Paris. Estimates vary but around 200,000 (some put it as high as 500,000) people from Venice, Genoa, Geneva, Germany, England, Holland and Spain, as well as vast numbers from the provinces, gravitated to the city to play the markets. The streets were choked with carriages; all modes of public transport from the major cities of Lyon, Aix, Bordeaux, Strasbourg and Brussels were booked up months in advance; people gambled or bid outrageous sums for a place on a coach. The lucky ones arrived in Paris to find every room occupied, and even stables let as accommodation. Journalists revelled in the frenzied get-rich-quick ambience. In one periodical Defoe commented, 'Beau Gage has gained three hundred thousand pounds sterling by the stocks. The Lord Londonderry also . . . being the same that sold the great diamond to the King of France is there, and they say has likewise gotten very great sums of money.' Gage was later nicknamed Croesus and, with his winnings, attempted to buy the island of Sardinia and the crown of Poland. He was trounced in Poland, equally dishonestly, by Augustus the Strong of Saxony, prompting Alexander Pope to write in his 'Epistle to Bathurst':

> *The Crown of Poland, venal twice an age,*
> *To just three millions stinted modest Gage.*

But in certain Parisian salons the flourishing fortunes of countless overseas investors met with a chilly reception. Why, many asked, should foreigners profit when many French were unable to buy as many shares as they would have liked? What right had Law to help English investors at their expense? 'Some of the French have endeavoured to represent to Mr Law's prejudice the great gains they pretend his countrymen have made', the diplomat Daniel Pulteney observed. Law ignored the fault-finders. In reality, nostalgia for the land of his birth had nothing to do with it: he encouraged outside investors because he recognized that to play the markets they brought with them silver and gold currency without which the system of paper money could not survive.

While the holiday mood continued, the foundation of the fabulous gains remained unquestioned. Shrouded in the mists of inexperience, speculators of the rue Quincampoix had no yardstick against which to measure their experience. Almost a century earlier, in the 1630s, speculation fever had descended on Holland when the price of tulips and futures contracts for bulbs had bubbled and burst – the now notorious Tulipmania. But, though shares had long been available, investors had been largely confined to small, select groups. The wider general public had never before taken part, nor had such rapid rises on such a scale ever been witnessed. Like gluttons at a Mississippi banquet, most investors ingenuously accepted the opportunity to gorge themselves and never considered the consequence. The fact that the huge increase in share prices was founded on little more than hype and the hugely expanded money supply was unthinkingly brushed aside.

The quantities of notes that had been circulated were vast indeed. Estimates differ – there are no precise figures because all records were burned in the aftermath of the Mississippi – but one assessment generally accepted by scholars puts the figure at over 1.2 billion livres' worth by the end of 1719. Added to this, the 624,000 shares that had been issued at 221 million livres were, on current market valuations at the end of November 1719, worth 4.8 billion livres. Of these the Crown and the company probably owned a third. France, thanks to Law's magic system, was now richer to the tune of 5.2 billion livres. The Regent himself had earned a fortune, which he circulated liberally to his paramours and favourites, and Law believed himself 'the richest subject in Europe'. But the question of what underpinned these paper fortunes had been dangerously ignored.

The share price had been boosted on its upward path by the ease with which money could be borrowed from the bank. Loans at 2 per cent interest were readily available and shares could be used as collateral. The eighteenth-century economist Du Tot summed it up: 'Law,' he said, 'had built a seven-storey building on foundations that would support only three.' Now we would call it a bubble. As the autumn of 1719 yielded to winter, share prices scaled ever more precarious heights: shares that in August had traded for 3,000 livres tripled in value by December and by the new year reached a peak of 10,000, a twenty-fold increase on the original par price of 500 livres, for which Law had been so hard pressed to find subscribers seven months earlier.

As the year drew to a close there were signs, however, that he was beginning to succumb to the pressures of his own success. In November the journalist Buvat noted that the Duc d'Antin, the Marquis de Lassay, Law and several unnamed ladies had travelled by carriage to the rue Quincampoix – where carriages were banned to everyone else – to visit a banker by the name of Bergerie. Law was at the carriage window and, to amuse the ladies, threw several fistfuls of coins into the street. They watched as 'The rabble and courtiers tumbled over one another in the mud to pick them up [and] someone threw from a neighbouring window several buckets of water on the opportunists, one can imagine as a result the state they were in.' The incident's unsavoury undertone raised questions as well as eyebrows. Had Law's concern for public well-being been blunted by his success? Was ego blinding his moral sensibility to the extent that he now saw avarice as a form of entertainment?

One key long-standing supporter feared the worst: the Earl of Stair, Law's old friend, became increasingly antagonistic. An inveterate and often unlucky gambler, Stair was distrustful of Mississippi speculation and scoffed at every price rise. In August, as share prices zoomed upwards, he had commented venomously that the frenzied market was 'more extravagant and more ridiculous than anything that ever happened in any other country'. Law had then offered him a large number of shares and was offended when he refused them with the pompous rejoinder that, 'He did not think it became the King's ambassador to give countenance to such a thing.'

This version of the argument conflicts, however, with the Princess Palatine's account of their dealings. Stair, she said, 'cannot conceal his hatred of Law, nevertheless he has made three good millions through him'. Stair's animosity, detectable by his ever more alarmist dispatches, was sparked by his worries about Law's emerging anti-British sentiments. Law, he said, was interfering in diplomatic matters that were no concern of his, and threatening the British economy: 'He . . . pretends he will set France much higher than ever she was before and put her in a condition to give the law to all Europe; that he can ruin the trade and credit of England and Holland whenever he pleases; that he can break our bank whenever he has a mind, and our East India Company.' Law, who had three times been refused a pardon, was now exacting painful revenge. Ironically, the pardon had been granted by George I two years earlier, but Law responded with typical impetuosity by handing over the document to the Regent as proof of his unstinting loyalty.

Stair, however, ignored this detail. According to him, by the year's end the Regent was losing faith in Law: '[The Regent] heard daily that Law used very extraordinary language upon all kinds of things . . . he assured me he had recently spoken to him of this in a manner which ought to have restrained his insolence.' A few days later, Stair averred, Orléans was again denouncing Law for 'his vanity, presumption and insolence. He said he knew him to be a man whose head had been turned by his vanity and unbounded ambition; that nothing would satisfy him but to be absolute master; that he had such an opinion of his own talents and contempt for the talents of others as to be quite impracticable with any other person'.

Stair's assessment did not tally with other diplomatic intelligence, which suggested that Law's authority was substantial. The Paris-based diplomat Martin Bladen appraised the situation in a revealing letter to Lord Stanhope. 'The Regent has already reaped many solid advantages from the establishment of this company, he is resolved to throw all the revenues of France under their management, which cannot fail of raising the actions to a much higher price.' Of Law's part in all this Bladen was in no doubt: 'Mr Law is become the idol of the people, the

Regent has gained many new friends, the public debts of the government are all discharged, and the revenues of France very considerably increased.' He drew the inevitable conclusion: 'Your Lordship knows better than I how precarious our friendship is with this kingdom, and consequently how necessary it will be that some speedy methods should be thought on for payment of the public debts without which His Majesty cannot long continue the arbiter of Europe.'

The growing anxiety was not only that France's economic renaissance would increase her political aspirations but also that the flurry of tourists investing in Mississippi stock would drain England of her coinage. Concerns were amplified by Law's overt jingoism. Openly contemptuous of the English economy, 'He spared no occasion of declaring without reserve, even without decency that we are bankrupt and shall be forced to shelter our country under the protection of France,' wrote Daniel Pulteney to the Secretary of State James Craggs. Stair told a similar story: 'He [Law] said publicly the other day at his own table, when Lord Londonderry was present, that there was but one great kingdom in Europe . . . He told Pitt that he would bring down our East India stock, and entered into articles with him to sell him at 12 months hence, a hundred thousand pounds of stock at eleven per cent under the current price.'

Law was convinced that the price of East India stock would fall and was therefore, in modern parlance, taking a bear futures position. The stance was most likely more of a propaganda exercise, meant to bolster confidence in French investments by running down English ones, than a considered opinion – and later it turned horribly wrong. But, faced with this nose-thumbing, England could do nothing but squirm. Despite what Stair said, Law was far too powerful to risk offending and, ever the arch manipulator, he played mercilessly on the anxiety, even complaining to Pulteney about comments in the English press calling his company 'a chimera', at which he professed to take umbrage. Meanwhile, the career of Stair, the weakling who had picked an argument with a prizefighter, was doomed. When Lord Stanhope visited Paris in early 1720 his predictable conclusion that Law should not be provoked heralded the end of a brilliant diplomatic career for Ambassador Stair. The following spring he was recalled.

For all the carefully calculated bravado and insults bandied over the dinner-table, success had not turned Law into an ego-maniac. Nor had it silenced his driving demon: his need for acceptance and his desire for political advancement. He might relish behaving high-handedly towards the English establish-ment and his role of bad-boy-made-good but part of him craved acknowledgement of his achievement and wanted to be recognized for his honourable intentions, as well as respected for the money he could bestow. Success offered the chance to anchor himself to the country he had served so well by seeking a position within its government. The Regent welcomed the idea but there was a constitutional dilemma: Law still followed the Protestant faith of his forebears and in Catholic France a Protestant could have no legal role in government. For Law to hold public office he would have to convert.

Oddly for the descendant of a family whose livelihood had once depended on and been doomed by its faith, religion seems to have been of little significance to John Law. His choice of English friends bears this out: among them were several leading Jacobites although he was also close to the duke of Argyll and Earl of Ilay, who were staunch anti-Jacobites. If he felt any qualms about his conversion there are no records of it. There are, however, signs that Katherine did not share his feelings: she refused to follow suit, and was said to be 'very much upset about it', according to the Regent's mother, especially when Law insisted that both children should adopt the Catholic faith. But Law, at the zenith of his career, blinkered by ambition, ignored Katherine's opposition. The ceremony of his acceptance into the Roman Catholic Church took place in Melun in December 1719, presided over by the Abbé de Tencin, the brother of the infamous nun turned courtesan Claudine de Tencin, whose numerous lovers were said to include Law. The association must have been a double blow for Katherine. Like his sister, Tencin was renowned for his venality and corruption and agreed to Law's conversion largely because he knew he would profit from it. Later he received shares worth 200,000 livres. A few days later, on Christmas Day, Law participated in his first mass at his local church of St Roche and marked the occasion with a sumptuous ball and dinner.

Uplifted by his conversion and anxious to secure public affection, Law donated vast sums to good causes. 'He gives away lots of alms that are never talked about . . . and helps many poor people,' wrote the Princess Palatine. 'It is impossible to express the bounty and munificence of Mr Law; and what a world of money he gives away on charitable and generous occasions.' Daniel Defoe agreed: 'The other day he gave 100,000 livres to the rebuilding of the church of St Roche in Paris, being the parish church in which he lives and where he received his first communion, after the renunciation of his religion, he gave the same day a hundred thousand crowns to the relief of his country men at St Germain . . . he had given very considerable sums to the Hospital la Charité.'

Law's critics were unmoved by his generosity. They were forced to pay him lip service, but many secretly regarded him as a parvenu, whose reforms had seriously damaged their financial muscle. However well they had profited as a result of the escalating price of Mississippi shares, they still felt they would be better off with the old order, in which their preeminence was unrivalled. Moreover, they must have known his reward was imminent.

It came on 5 January 1720, with the announcement that Law

had received the ultimate accolade: he had been appointed Controller General of Finance. The position surprised few. Law had been the nation's 'first minister' in all but name for many months, but the title underlined his ascendancy. The world could no longer ignore the fact that he held the purse strings and therefore held sway over the most powerful and populous nation in Europe.

To commemorate his new office, a portrait was made of France's new Controller General, probably painted by the fashionable artist Hyacinthe Rigaud (the painting was feared lost but appeared recently at a Sotheby's house sale). Something of the dandy lingers: in it Law wears a gold-buttoned velvet coat and showy turquoise waistcoat embroidered with gold leaves and bunches of brilliantly coloured fruit, and sports a powdered grey periwig. The once angular face is now softened with the jowls and ruddy complexion of good living. But it is a grandiose portrait, which forces you to acknowledge a man of exceptional stature and achievement. Gone is the dreaminess: the eyes, brooding beneath luxuriant black brows, focus directly on the viewer, while behind, the emblem of his empire – a Mississippi ship at full sail – powers towards the horizon.

*After the death of Louis XIV, Law, a Scotchman, a very extra-
ordinary person, many of whose schemes had proved useless,
and others hurtful to the nation, made the government and the
people believe that Louisiana produced as much gold as Peru,
and that it would soon be able to supply as great a quantity of
silk as China. . . . The settlers almost all perished from want;
and the city was confined to a few paltry houses. Perhaps one
day, when France shall have a million or two of inhabitants
more than she may know what to do with, it may be of some
advantage to her to people Louisiana.*

Voltaire, *Short Studies: The French Islands*

EVER SINCE LAW HAD TAKEN CONTROL OF THE LOUISIANA
colony, tantalizing reports of it had appeared in France's official
newspaper, the *Nouveau Mercure*: correspondents described a
land of milk and honey in which the climate was temperate,
the soil fertile, the woods replete with trees suited to building
and export, and the countryside populated with wild yet benign
'horses, buffaloes, and cows, which however do no harm but
run away at the sight of men'. In this wonderland, said an article

published in September 1717, the soil bulged with seams of gold and silver ore; other valuable minerals – copper, lead and mercury – also awaited exploitation, and the natives had spoken of an enormous rock near the Arkansas river made of a type of rock that was 'dark green, very hard and very beautiful, resembling emeralds'. In short, said the endlessly imaginative Mississippi journalists, 'Nothing almost is wanting . . . but industrious people, and numbers of hands to work.' The optimistic dispatches continued to circulate Paris for three more years. 'The most solid foundation for the hopes of the Mississippians,' wrote the captain of the *Valette*, a vessel that had recently returned from the region, 'are the silver mines discovered in the country of the Illinois [the local Indian tribe]'. Elsewhere, in the fairs, markets and taverns of provincial towns and villages, catchy songs advertised the colony's charms:

> *Aujourd'hui il n'est plus question*
> *De parler de Constitution,*
> *Ni de la guerre avec l'Espagne;*
> *Un nouveau pays de cocagne,*
> *Que l'on nomme Mississippi,*
> *Roule a présent sur le tapis.*

> *Today there is no longer any question*
> *Of talking of the constitution*
> *Nor of the war with Spain;*
> *A new wonder land*
> *That they call Mississippi*
> *Has appeared on the scene.*

By 1719, the showpiece settlement of New Orleans, founded a year earlier and strategically placed at the mouth of the Mississippi to control the trade on the Mississippi–Missouri rivers, was said to be a prosperous town of 'nearly 800 very comfortable and well appointed houses, each one of which has attached 120 acres of land for the upkeep of the families'. Furthermore, mineral finds exceeded all expectation, said the *Mercure* of April 1720: samples sent for testing had proved astonishingly pure – 'One scarcely finds the same quantity in the richest mines of Potosi.'

It was all an illusion. The reality, concealed beneath the veils of beguiling disinformation, was that the colony was struggling to stay alive. Between 1717 and 1720, of the thousands that made the arduous journey to Louisiana, over half perished *en route* or returned exhausted and disenchanted with what they found. Hundreds more perished from disease or starvation. No sizeable deposits of silver or gold, let alone emeralds, had been found and, according to the report of de Bienville, the colony's governor, to the company in 1719, New Orleans consisted only of four modest houses, where the immigrants survived entirely by trading with the natives.

The glossy reports and alluring songs had been masterminded by Law more as a marketing ploy than a deliberate deception. He was adamant that, given enough time and money, the colony would become the valuable territory everyone believed it to be. But he was hampered by innate French reluctance to emigrate: there were too few willing pioneers. Yet having realized that, along with the predictable profits of the other rights acquired, much of the pyramid of speculation depended on public belief in the colony's prosperity and their expectation that this was sure to increase, he had no alternative but to conceal the facts until more potential settlers came forward.

To tempt them he offered attractive incentives. Colonists' expenses would be met by the company from the time they took up residence until they were established, and they would be provided with land, livestock and thirty pounds of flour a head until their first harvest. But however successfully in the past he had manipulated the public's opinion, he could not persuade them willingly to leave France for an unknown, undeveloped wilderness, even though much of the nation's money was staked on it.

Undaunted, and in the expectation that where he led others would follow, Law acquired a concession of his own in 1719. In partnership with the Irish émigré Richard Cantillon, one of Paris's most successful private bankers, and the English speculator Joseph Gage, he acquired the rights to a plot of 16 square leagues bordering the Ouachita river to the west of the Mississippi, in what is now the state of Arkansas. While Law and his partners observed operations from the comfortable security of their Paris mansions, around a hundred settlers, including carpenters, mine-workers and gardeners, were enlisted to prospect for minerals and to grow tobacco. The party, supervised by Cantillon's brother Bernard, left La Rochelle on the slave ship *St Louis*, in March 1719. Three months later it dropped anchor in the brave new world of Louisiana. By one account, Law's expedition was unusually well equipped, with 'such a large quantity of merchandise and other effects that they filled three boats to get to their concession'.

As he had hoped, his example inspired similar partnerships. A handful of aristocrats, several successful speculators in Mississippi stock, including the Widow Chaumont, and several of his English, Irish and Scottish émigré friends, including the glamorous Fanny Oglethorpe, joined in ventures aimed at farming tobacco, rice and silk or prospecting for minerals.

Within months of hearing of his expedition's safe arrival Law was trumpeting its success. Rumours eddied through salon society of the silver deposits discovered on his land, and of a mine already yielding five ounces of silver for every hundredweight of ore. Few suspected that the whispers emanated from Law's imagination rather than the correspondence of his settlers, for the mission, despite its ample resources, was far from triumphant.

Bernard Cantillon and his team had found themselves in a

dismal, hostile territory in which the struggle for survival over-shadowed any attempt to farm or prospect. The immigrants were racked with scurvy, dysentery, malaria and yellow fever. There was the ever-present danger of hostile Indians, who needed constant bribes to remain friendly. According to Buvat, in one attack that took place in March 1719 and was never publicized, 1,500 French colonists were ambushed in their homes and slaughtered. There was also danger from the Spanish settlements to the west – with whom war was waged between 1719 and 1720 – and English settlements to the east, between which the French colony was sandwiched. Cantillon and his party, like others before them, realized the extent of the exaggeration only when they arrived but by then it was too late to go back. Within four years, desertion, disease and other hazards had culled the expedition's numbers until only a quarter remained. Law and his partners found little in the way of quick profit. In a letter to one partner two years later, when his own fortunes were in decline, he was forced to relinquish his investment: 'With regard to my Louisiana colony, I thank you for your offers. As I am not in a state to continue to take on the necessary expenditure to support it, don't hesitate to take the party that suits your interests best. Wishing you success in what you undertake.' Another two centuries would pass before the true wealth beneath the soil was found, not in silver, gold or emeralds but in oil.

In Paris, conscious that the rising share market depended on public confidence that large-scale revenue would come sooner rather than later, Law moved to speed things up. The stumbling block as he saw it was still the dearth of settlers and an inadequate support system. He responded first with orders for new shipping, making so massive an investment that even the pragmatic Daniel Pulteney was astounded: 'Besides the ships the company had already bespoke in England, which I think were 8 or 9 orders, are lately sent for building there

8 more . . . 4 ships are now fitting out at port Louis,' he wrote, in early 1720, by which time the company fleet had already swelled to some thirty ships, more than the rival English East India Company.

Meanwhile, the problem of where to find settlers had been dramatically addressed: new legislation was passed whereby every criminal, vagabond, prostitute and any servant unemployed for more than four days was listed and liable for transportation. An army of mercenary soldiers, known as 'archers', was employed by the company to trace, apprehend and escort them to the nearest port for transportation. In Paris, with the blessing of the authorities, Law rounded up orphans and young people from the so-called 'hospitals', many of which served also as detention centres and poor-houses. Thus, in Paris alone it was estimated that some 4,000 people – among them society's most defenceless, disreputable and dangerous citizens – taken from Bicêtre, l'Hôpital Général and Salpêtrière, would swell the numbers of settlers and provide the necessary unskilled labour. According to the reports, the first cargo of female deportees arrived to the warmest of welcomes from the male settlers and quickly found marriage partners. Problems arose, however, when two men claimed the last woman and the matter had to be decided by hand-to-hand combat.

In Paris, at a comfortable distance from wrestling matches on the dockside, few at first opposed the transportations. Echoing the general mood, Saint-Simon commented, 'If this had been done with wisdom, discernment and necessary caution the object they proposed would have been accomplished, and Paris and the provinces relieved of a heavy, useless and sometimes dangerous burthen.' But public approval was short-lived. The journalist Buvat sternly noted the problems caused in Louisiana by certain categories of female immigrants: 'The debauched girls that had been transported to the Mississippi and other French colonies had been the cause of much disorder by their libertine actions and by the venereal disease that they had spread.'

But increasing displeasure was voiced over the brutality of the archers. Poorly supervised, ill-disciplined and corrupt, they were soon universally detested and feared. If too few people from the designated categories were captured they were known to arrest anyone unfortunate enough to stumble into their path. According to Pulteney, their fiendishness was exacerbated by financial temptation. They were paid commission for every captive and the system was widely abused. With a word in the ear of an archer and few sous slipped in his hand, it was all too easy for an unwanted relative, awkward son, inconvenient competitor or demanding spouse to be dispatched to the swamps of Louisiana – there was even a popular song to warn husbands of the danger:

> O vous tous, messieurs les maris,
> Si vos femmes ont des favoris,
> Ne vous mettez martel en tête;
> Vous auriez fort méchante fête.
> Si vous vous en fachez, tant pis:
> Vous irez a Mississippi.

> O all you husbands
> If your wives have favourites
> Don't get worried;
> You will have a terrible celebration.
> If you get angry, too bad:
> You will go to Mississippi.

Despite growing public concern, archer chicanery showed no sign of diminishing. Even infants were reported to have fallen prey: 'I have heard that they have taken children out of houses; some they release again for money, those who cannot or will not pay a ransom are carried to a prison whence they are to be sent to the Mississippi,' Pulteney lamented. Those who could not escape were abysmally mistreated: 'Not the slightest pains were taken to provide for the subsistence of these unfortunates on their journey, or at the places where they disembarked; they were shut up at night in barns without food, or in cellars from which they could not issue. Their cries excited both pity and indignation,' recorded an outraged Saint-Simon. The injustice of impressment would find most famous literary expression in the novel *Manon Lescaut* published in 1731 by Abbé Prévost. The story charts the life of a young girl, Manon, during the Regency era, who is diverted from life as a nun by the appeal of money. Manon betrays her first suitor, who loves and wants to marry her, takes numerous lovers, and is eventually arrested and deported to Louisiana, where she dies from the hardship she encounters.

The groundswell of disapproval did not diminish Law's quest for settlers but, conscious of the problems created by deportations, he concentrated his efforts on enticing volunteers – especially young married couples – to the colony. On visits to Paris hospitals he offered generous dowries to couples who would marry and emigrate. 'They took 500 boys and girls from the hospitals of Bicêtre and de Salpêtrière . . . the girls were in wagons and the boys on foot escorted by 32 guards,' noted Buvat. But the most bizarre event Law engineered took place in September 1719 when the pealing bells of the St Martin *quartier* of Paris proclaimed the mass nuptials of eighty young girls of doubtful repute and eighty specially pardoned criminals. While the marriage took place the couples stood shackled together in heavy iron chains. Afterwards, under the watchful eye of a company of archers, they were paraded, still in chains, through the streets of Paris before being sent to La Rochelle for transportation to Louisiana. The chains caused consternation among the public, and a similar mass wedding, in which couples were linked with flowers – presumably to symbolize the fecundity that awaited them – took place soon after in a blaze of publicity.

Publicity stunts and propaganda fuelled much gossip, and filled pages in the journals, but had little impact. Inevitably, rumours of the sufferings of colonists penetrated even the institutions from which many were culled. The promise of freedom could not overcome the mounting terror of trans-portees – some became so reluctant to emigrate that they were willing to risk life and limb to avoid it. Riots and skirmishes escalated in ports and prisons. On 20 January 1720 it was reported that nineteen married couples placed in gaol awaiting departure had ambushed their guard, grabbed his keys and succeeded in setting themselves free. At La Rochelle, 150 girls about to embark sprang at the archers guarding them and attacked them with nails and teeth. The affray was only brought under control when the archers fired at the transportees, killing twelve and forcing the rest to embark at gunpoint.

By early 1720, numbers of emigrants had dwindled to the point at which Law was having to recruit large numbers of foreigners: 'A great many Scotch rebels are to be employed there and I am told they have got people from Ireland and will endeavour to get more,' observed Daniel Pulteney. But although Irish, Scottish, Swiss, German and other non-French settlers were more easily lured aboard the new Mississippi Company vessels with financial incentives, the press-gangs and atrocities continued. Some attempt was made to control the worst excesses of the archers by forcing them to operate in groups rather than individually. To highlight the improvement they were given smart new uniforms – blue coats and silver-banded tricorn hats – but such token measures did nothing to diminish their brutality. Inevitably, Law was seen as condoning their activities, and public opinion erupted against him. 'One could wonder that Mr Law who cannot but be extremely sensible how very obnoxious he is already to the generality of people here should yet provoke them more and more every day by some fresh hardship,' wrote Daniel Pulteney, of public consternation at some new archer savagery.

To be great, said Ralph Waldo Emerson, is to be misunderstood. In Law's case, no one comprehended that his apparent indifference to public criticism over transportations was not a signal of inhumanity but rather that he was preoccupied with far more pressing concerns. Weeks after his promotion to the position of controller general he faced the most challenging dilemma of his career. Unfettered speculation fever still spiralled. His enemies – the financiers, tax inspectors and councillors of the parlement whose livelihoods he had damaged – had regrouped. The very survival of the system he had created was endangered by the combined perils of still rising share prices and burgeoning conspiracies. In such a climate, Law was understandably slow to respond to public outrage. Eventually, however, the message seems to have filtered through and the deportations were halted in May 1720.

By then, though, Paris and the world at large had awakened to the perils of paper and to the struggle that confronted him. To save the bank, the Mississippi Company and the fortunes of thousands of investors, Law unleashed a cataclysmic financial storm.

Chapter Thirteen

Descent

As long as the credit of this bank subsisted, it appeared to the French to be perfectly solid. The bubble no sooner burst, than the whole nation was thrown into astonishment and conster-nation. Nobody could conceive from whence the credit had sprung; what had created such mountains of wealth in so short a time; and by what witchcraft and fascination it had been made to disappear in an instant, in the short period of one day.

Sir James Steuart, *An Inquiry into the Principles of Political Oeconomy*, Book IV (1770)

ON 30 DECEMBER 1719, IMPECCABLY CLAD AND BEWIGGED AS always, Law entered the cabinet of the Mississippi Company and addressed the annual general meeting. The sense of expec-tation was almost palpable. Within the past month share prices had dropped from a high of over 10,000 livres to 7,500, only to recover eleven days later and reach 9,400. Even among this informed circle of co-directors few fully understood why. Was the company the thriving enterprise that the world at large believed it to be? If so, why had the price fallen? If not, how long could recovery be sustained? Law appeared oblivious to the anxieties. With his customary charm and self-assurance, he reassured them that the company was flourishing. Overseas trade was expanding and the outlook so favourable that he would pay shareholders a dividend of 200 livres. For all those present this was festive tidings of the best kind.

We do not know if anyone at the meeting had enough direct contact with the colony to have an inkling of the true situation. Nor can we tell how many, even without such knowledge, sensed that this was a smokescreen or that Law had decided the dividend not according to company profits but according to the market share price to sustain the public's confidence in their investment – another ingenious marketing ploy. But behind closed doors, in assorted cabinets and boudoirs, a handful of cannier investors were questioning what Saint-Simon later scathingly termed 'the chimera of the Mississippi, its shares, its lingo, its science . . . its hocus pocus for taking money from some and giving it to others'. Rumours relating to Louisiana added to the ripples of disquiet. 'I have spoken to a Frenchman who is lately come from the Mississippi . . . The account he gives of the French settlement in that country would not encourage me to put my money into that stock,' Pulteney reported to Whitehall. Law's charm and the dividend announcement were not enough to staunch the niggling insinuations. Even Saint-Simon could read the writing on the wall. 'As the company possessed neither mines nor philosopher's stone it was obvious that its shares, in the long run, must decline in value.'

The climbing share price had been nourished by the injection of vast sums of paper money into the economy. Law realized the pitfalls of continuing on this route: the bank's reserves of coins could not keep pace with such expansion. If faith in paper wavered supplies would run out. Everything rested on the willing suspension of disbelief. The system would self-destruct if people began to doubt it. Confidence –

or credulousness – was all. But confidence was increasingly fragile.

Meanwhile, in the dingy alleyways and offices of the rue Quincampoix, the bonanza continued. Dealers taking advantage of the unregulated market became greedier and more daringly unscrupulous. Shady practices proliferated and futures trades – contracts whereby an investor agreed a share price and made a down payment for delivery at some future date – were, as far as Law was concerned, a particular problem. During the autumn of 1719, shares officially trading for around 10,000 livres were being sold in various forms of forward contracts for 15,000. Law saw that investors believed that share prices would rise still further. He knew that they would have to be controlled. He himself had caused the great dip and upward turn in the market in December 1719 by refusing loans, in an attempt to curb the money supply, then realizing how quickly the tide could turn and revoking the instruction.

To curtail the dubious dealings in the rue Quincampoix, company sales offices were opened in the new year to buy and sell shares at fixed prices. To satisfy the public hunger for shares and restrict the trade in futures, a new investment opportunity, called primes, was launched. The equivalent of what traders would today term a 'call option', a prime allowed investors to pay a deposit of 1,000 livres for the right to buy a share priced at 10,000 livres for delivery within the next six months.

Most investors still thought that shares would go above 10,000 livres. Lured by the leverage opportunity, they scrambled to sell their *mères, filles, petites filles* and *cinq-cents* to increase their gearing. One share sold for 10,000 livres enabled them to multiply their future holding tenfold. Within four days of the launch of the primes, the shares plummeted from 10,000 to 7,000 livres, as people sold out to reinvest in primes. Law was forced into a position where he had to pay out large sums to buy up shares for which demand had evaporated.

Aside from vacillating share prices, Law was beset with another dilemma. Silver and gold were draining from the bank's coffers. Anticipating that an end to the boom was near, numerous shareholders were selling out and converting to coins. One of the first to sense the instability of the market was Law's close friend and possibly the only person to comprehend the precariousness of his policies: the Irish banker Richard Cantillon. Whether in currencies, shares, futures, wine or art, Cantillon had an unerring eye for a good deal and a ruthlessness that prevented personal loyalty from standing in the way of profit.

Perhaps with the benefit of inside information gleaned over several good bottles of burgundy shared with Law, he was one of the few to anticipate the sudden upturn in share prices, and begin buying Mississippi stock at the low of 150 livres. By August, when the share price rose to over 2,000 livres, remembering what his brother in Arkansas had told him, Cantillon realized that the bull market was based on little more than smoke and mirrors and ever-increasing quantities of paper money. Feeling that a crash was both inevitable and imminent he cashed in. His profit from these few weeks' exposure was reputed to be £50,000. Leaving Paris with his winnings he went on a tour of Italy to enjoy the sights and invest in art.

Cantillon was the first to turn his back on Law but he was not alone. Several more major shareholders followed his example throughout the autumn and by December the trickle had become a stream that seriously threatened the bank's reserves. Most investors converted banknotes from share sales into coins and either hoarded or exported them. The stock-dealers Bourdon and La Richardière did it quietly, changing notes for coins and jewels and dispatching them abroad. The most notorious seller was the Prince de Conti. Furious with Law for refusing him further handouts, Conti took some 4.5

million livres in notes to the bank and demanded coins. As in the bank's earliest days, Law had no alternative but to comply. Conti needed three wagons to carry away the coins.

By the end of 1720 some 500 million livres in silver and gold had been taken out of the country, and the trend showed no sign of diminishing. Market vendors and merchants, aware of mounting unease, took paper with marked reluctance, often only at a discount, or spurned it altogether. In February, live-stock sellers bringing their animals to market at Poissy refused to accept anything but gold and silver. Their customers, the butchers of Paris, were forced to hire a carriage to return to the city and collect the required coins.

Much of the money taken out by investors was dispatched to London where the South Sea Company was now starting to gather its own momentum. It was one of several British chartered stock companies and, like the East India Company and the Bank of England, had been granted a privilege in return for lending the government money. In 1711 the company lent £9.5 million to the government to pay off its floating debt and was granted a monopoly of trade with the south seas and South America. Unlike Law's Mississippi Company, however, revenue was not expected from the profits of colonization. The vast income generated by the company, investors were told, would be made by an agreement with Spain that allowed the company's ships free trade with ports in Peru, Chile and Mexico. In reality the only rights the company held with Spain enabled them to supply slaves and allowed for one ship a year to trade with the region.

Those who wisely chose to ignore British South Sea stock looked for more tangible repositories for their wealth in France. Many, including the wily widow Chaumont, invested in property, and within a few months the vast pool of paper money available multiplied the price of land three- or fourfold. Inflation in other areas also escalated. The recently arrived

British diplomat Daniel Pulteney found difficulty in making ends meet and had to ask for an increase in his allowance. 'I am told that most things are considerably dearer than they were when Mr Bladen [his predecessor] came here. I find it so in the instance of a berlin [a carriage]. He paid 34 pistoles a month for his and I cannot have one under 50; the prices of things seem to rise as fast as the clocks do.' More serious than this was the fact that the cost of staples was rising similarly and causing the poor increasing hardship. In the two months between December and January alone prices rose by 25 per cent. The cost of some foods rose even more steeply; a loaf of bread costing one sou before the boom cost four or five times that by December, noted the diarist Buvat.

Law had always held that markets should be allowed to develop freely, with a minimum of bureaucratic intervention. 'Constraint is contrary to the principles upon which credit must be built,' he had once written. Now the tune changed. 'Despotic power, to which we are beholden for it [the system], will also sustain it,' he decided. Turning to strong-arm legislation, he moved swiftly and devastatingly.

To curtail the export of coins and to discourage hoarders, on 28 January, a little over three weeks after assuming his office, he passed an edict banning the export of coins and bullion. But again the theory was flawed: faced with unpopular regulations, humankind tends to seek an escape route. Prevented from salting away coins in Amsterdam or England the public looked for alternatives or defied the ruling altogether. The wiliest turned to diamonds and other jewels, which they hastily sent abroad. Others, more daringly, smuggled money over the border. Vermalet, a prosperous stock-dealer, was said to have placed his stash of a million livres in coins in a farmer's cart and covered it with manure. Then he donned a peasant's smock and drove himself to Belgium from where he sent his money on to Amsterdam.

Law retaliated even more dramatically than anyone expected.

On 4 February, the purchase and wearing of diamonds, pearls and other precious gems, emblem of every Mississippi millionaire, were prohibited. But the ban did not succeed in halting the stampede away from paper. In place of diamonds, pearls and rubies, investors turned instead to silver and gold: candelabra, tureens, dishes, plates, even furniture made from precious metal, were hunted out and bought for vastly inflated sums. Two weeks later this escape route was also blocked: a new law prohibited the production and sale of all gold or silver artefacts with the exception of religious paraphernalia. Within days the price of crosses and chalices soared.

The bloated share price and over-expanded money supply still awaited Law's remedial scalpel. He called an extraordinary meeting of shareholders. Some 200 of the wealthiest Mississippi millionaires attended, clad, according to one account, in such finery that they completely outshone the Regent, the Duc de Bourbon and the Prince de Conti, who were also there. Law announced that the royal bank was being taken over by the Mississippi Company. This apparent formality – he already directed both institutions – facilitated a further significant change. The royal holding of 100,000 Mississippi shares would be bought back by the company for 300 million livres – the entire sum recently raised from the sale of primes – with a guaranteed additional payment of 5 million livres a month over the next ten years.

Law justified this acquisition by arguing that reducing the number of shares on which he would have to pay a dividend would help the company's balance sheet and curb the money supply. But some wondered whether in attempting to stop the flood of departing investors Law was not quietly encouraging the Crown to follow suit. Having paid the equivalent of 9,000 livres a share into the royal coffers, Law closed down the company sales offices and withdrew official support of the share price.

This was bad news for investors. Within a week shares plunged 26 per cent from around 9,500 to 7,800 livres. The public was incandescent with fury. 'The rage of the people is so violent and so universal against Law that I think it is above twenty to one, that, in the course of one month, he will be pulled to pieces; or that his master will deliver him up to the rage of the people,' Stair wrote gleefully.

Cornered between public distress and inexorably ebbing reserves, Law could see no alternative but to take even more despotic action. On 27 February he issued an edict that outlawed the possession of more than 500 livres' worth of silver or gold and stipulated that in future all payments of more than 100 livres were to be made in banknotes. All surplus gold was to be brought to the bank and exchanged for paper. Transgressors could expect to be severely punished, and informers were encouraged with the promise of generous rewards. The slightest suspicion that gold was being concealed illegally would be enough for any house, whether palace or hovel, to be searched. The dreaded methods of the Visa, which Law had once scorned, now returned at his instigation. Servants were tempted to turn on their employers, children on their parents. Seething distrust made the crowds who took their silver and gold to the bank feel relieved of a burden when they returned with paper.

Predictably, however, not all complied. The most notable transgressor was the horse-loving Duc de Bourbon who, getting wind of the new regulation, exchanged a reported 25 million livres for coins just before it came into effect. He was summoned by the Regent to explain why he had 'destroyed in a moment what we have struggled to establish over several days'. Both Bourbon and Conti, who had cashed in earlier, were ordered to comply with the recent measures immediately, and return the gold, or risk having their property searched by the authorities and the gold confiscated. When both refused, investigators, who had doubtless been bribed, made cursory searches of their châteaux and, predictably, discovered nothing.

Law was condemned mercilessly for his actions. Ambassador Stair commented sarcastically that it was impossible now to doubt his sincerity in converting to Catholicism since he had established the Inquisition after having revealed his faith in transubstantiation by turning so much gold to paper. Public opprobrium extended also to his supporters. Bourbon was heckled in the street, and his manservant was pelted with stones when he attempted to remonstrate. Even the usually aloof Saint-Simon was aghast: 'Never was sovereign power so violently attempted; never did it meddle with any matter so sensitively felt or so vitally connected with the temporal well-being of the community.'

At the Palais Royal the unfolding turmoil was monitored anxiously by the Regent. Always inclined to take the route of least resistance, Orléans feared that widespread hatred of Law would affect his own standing. When he sensed that his mentor's faith was wavering, Law's self-confidence slipped. Humiliating tales circulated by his opponents added to his distress. According to Stair, when Law arrived at the Palais Royal for an audience, the Regent admitted him while relieving himself 'upon his close stool'. Orléans was, said Stair, 'in such a passion, that he run to Law with his breeches about his heels' and threatened him with the Bastille if matters did not quickly improve. Even if Stair fabricated this crude incident, it seems certain that the worry of losing Orléans' favour, upon which Law's political survival and his family's future depended, had a profoundly adverse effect on Law. Under the barrage of reproach his nerve failed, and the combined reports of servants, enemies and friends suggest that he had a nervous breakdown. His servants reported that he suffered from insomnia and anxiety attacks, was prone to sudden angry outbursts and his mood, even with his close family, became volatile and unreasonable. 'He gets out of bed almost every night, and runs, stark staring mad, about the room making a terrible noise, sometimes singing and dancing, at other times swearing, staring and stamping, quite out of himself,' said Stair, who had heard the account from one of Law's footmen. 'Some nights ago, his wife, who had come into the room upon the noise he made, was forced to ring the bell for people to come to her assistance. The officer of Law's guard was the first that came, who found Law in his shirt, who had set two chairs in the middle of the room and was dancing round them, quite out of his wits.' The usually poised Katherine must have been alarmed.

The burdens on Law's shoulders were great indeed. Pressured by the Regent and debilitated by his failing stamina, his resolve faltered. He backtracked.

Chapter Fourteen

The Storms of Fate

At length corruption, like a general flood,
Shall deluge all, and av'rice creeping on
(So long by watchful ministers withstood)
Spread, like a low-born mist, and blot the sun.
Statesman and patriot ply alike the stocks,
Peeress and butler share alike the box;
The judge shall job, the bishops bite the town,
And mighty Dukes pack cards for half-a-crown:
See Britain sunk in Lucre's sordid charms.
Alexander Pope, *Epistle to Lord Bathurst*

A FORTNIGHT AFTER WITHDRAWING SUPPORT FOR THE
shares, Law reversed the decision. He announced that the
share–sales office would reopen and pegged the share price at
9,000 livres. The gesture temporarily appeased his critics but in
reality made an already dire situation worse. Crowds frightened
by the sudden changes in policy and sensing the precariousness
of the financial situation, rushed to the bank to cash in their
shares, and the printing presses went into overdrive to pay
for them.

As the crush at the bank exceeded all expectation, Law reached the most radical decision of his career thus far. If the balance between paper and coins could not be redressed, he concluded, his only alternative was to abolish gold and silver coins entirely. While paper notes would remain invariable, coin made from precious metals would be gradually reduced in value against the livre then phased out. Within two months in the case of gold, and nine months in the case of silver, they would cease to exist as currency within France. France would depend entirely upon paper.

It was a step too far. In a country noted for its financial conservatism a monetary system based on anything other than gold and silver was inconceivable. Law was suspected of tampering with the foundations on which society was built and depended for its stability. As Saint-Simon ranted,

> *They tried to convince the nation that from the days when Abraham paid four hundred shekels of silver, current coin, for Sarah's sepulchre to the present day, the wisest nations of the earth had been under the grossest error and delusion as to money and the metals of which it was made; that paper was the only profitable and necessary medium, and that we could not do a greater harm to foreign nations, jealous of our grandeur and our advantages, than to pass over all our silver and gold and precious stones to them.*

Even the Regent's mother, who until now had admired Law, was averse to the move: 'I think it hard lines that there is no more gold to be seen, because for forty-eight years now I have never been without some beautiful gold pieces in my pocket . . . Monsieur Law is certainly terribly hated.'

Others interpreted a more sinister reason for Law's apparent madness: 'The silver is to be employed in such foreign trades as cannot be carried on without it, or as Mr Law may propose to beat us and the Dutch out of it by that means . . . Mr Law has said he will drain us of all our silver,' mused Daniel Pulteney. Opinion was divided then, and still is, over what Law was trying to achieve. Pulteney believed he was reducing the value of gold and silver to draw it into the bank, and that he would use the gold to buy up Europe's silver, and bring it back to France. 'I am told that Mr Middleton, the goldsmith in the Strand who is Mr Law's agent and banker, has already heaped up in his house very considerable quantities of silver,' he affirmed. Law's enemies believed he was forming silver caches for his personal use rather than for the national good. Later biographers, bearing in mind his fragile mental state, felt he had lost his way and saw this as a drowning man grasping a straw.

The unfurling financial maelstrom had a further insidious consequence for which Law was also held responsible. Paris was engulfed in a crime wave. The unprecedented epidemic of hold-ups, kidnappings, violent robberies and grisly murders was widely blamed on the avarice, envy, uncertainty, big wins and big losses that Law had generated. In one particularly horrific incident the watch discovered the body of a woman hacked into small pieces inside an overturned carriage. It was said that she had been murdered after being robbed of 300,000 livres in banknotes. Even Daniel Defoe was astounded by the scale of the villainy, reporting in early April, 'No less than 25 bodies have been taken out of the filets of St Cloud in about ten days. This is a net that's put across a narrow part of the river Seine, from one side to the other . . . into which the murther'd bodies are carried by the stream that are thrown over the bridges in the city.'

By far the most notorious of all the horror stories to send shivers through Europe was that of a dissipated and unprincipled young aristocrat, Count Antoine Joseph de Horn. Greedy for money to gamble on shares, de Horn, in league with two others – Laurent de Mille, a Piedmontese soldier, and a courtier named d'Étampes – plotted to rob a rich stockholder called Lacroix, who was known to carry quantities of shares and large sums of money about with him. On the pretext of buying his shares de Horn agreed to meet Lacroix in the Épée de Bois, a tavern famed for its musical entertainment, on the corner of the rue de Venise and the rue Quincampoix. D'Étampes stood guard while the others lured the broker into a back room, threw a tablecloth over his head and stabbed him several times in the chest. But, hearing his cries, one of the tavern staff realized what was taking place and locked the attackers in the room. Despite his efforts, however, the assailants jumped from a window and escaped. D'Étampes ran to a nearby street where horses were waiting and got away. De Mille headed for the crowds of the rue Quincampoix but was quickly arrested. De Horn, who had sprained an ankle in his flight, tried to bluff his way out of trouble saying that he was one of the victims, but when de Mille was brought to the tavern he was identified and arrested. The next day both men were tried, found guilty and condemned to death by being broken on the wheel.

This particularly gruesome method of execution (later immortalized by Hogarth in his satirical engraving of the South Sea Company, which shows Self-interest breaking Honesty on the wheel), usually reserved for common criminals, involved being spreadeagled on a wooden wheel and bludgeoned to death, limb by limb. A seventeenth-century visitor to France described the spectacle: 'A place of execution made of timber, at the top whereof there is a wheel, whereon the bodies of murderers only are tormented and broken to pieces with certain iron instruments, with which they break their arms first, then their legs and thighs, and after their breast. That blow on their breast is called the blow of mercy because it does quickly bereave them of their life.'

Understandably distraught at the thought of their kinsman suffering such a death, de Horn's noble family pleaded with the

Regent for leniency. As a distant relation of the Royal Family, they claimed, he should be spared or at least executed in a more fitting way. Unusually, the Regent remained resolute and, according to several accounts, replied, with the words of Corneille, 'Le crime fait la honte, et non pas l'échafaud' – 'It is the crime that is the dishonour, not the scaffold'. There was no reprieve.

Four days after the murder, on 26 March 1720, at four in the afternoon, a ghoulish crowd gathered in the Place de Grève to witness the spectacle of de Horn and his accomplice being broken on the wheel as sentenced. De Horn, the first to be executed, took three-quarters of an hour to die after receiving the executioner's blows.

Law capitalized rapidly on the publicity surrounding the crime. He had always detested the seediness, hysteria and double-dealing stirred up in the frenetic atmosphere of the rue Quincampoix. Now he had cause to eliminate it. Shortly after de Horn's execution a ruling was issued prohibiting crowds from congregating in the rue Quincampoix and outlawing any dealing in shares or primes other than through official company offices.

Amid the ongoing financial malaise, the printing presses rolled on. By May 1720, more than 2.6 billion livres in banknotes had been issued, doubling the amount circulating since January. The country was awash with paper. Fearing that his system was on the brink of disintegration, Law made his most desperate, and, many would later argue, most drastically misguided move.

On 21 May, a holiday weekend, when most of his opponents were conveniently out of town, he announced that by December shares presently pegged at 9,000 livres would be worth only 5,000. The value of banknotes would also be reduced gradually until they were worth 50 per cent of their present value. The moves, he argued, were for the national good, to redress the balance between paper and the coin reserves on which France relied for foreign trade. Nobody would suffer. The same share dividend would be paid, and the balance between the value of paper notes and silver would return to what it had been before the devaluations announced in March.

No one believed him. In the last five months the long-suffering public had witnessed multiple changes in the value of their currency; their coinage had been outlawed; wearing jewellery had been prohibited, even crucifixes were banned. He had left them only with paper. Throughout every vacillation, every turn and twist of financial policy, he had maintained, adamantly, its immunity to change. As far as the public was concerned, by casting aside this fundamental tenet he had revealed himself as a charlatan. Distress ripened to civil unrest as the almost unbelievable news spread. Everyone felt they were about to be robbed of half of what they had and, as Pulteney put it, Law had effected 'the most notorious cheat that ever was committed, and it is very plain now that Mr Law has as little capacity as integrity'.

The day after the announcement a disaffected mob gravitated to the bank. When they found it closed they began to pelt it with stones. For three days riots erupted in the streets of Paris. Crowds gathered each day outside the bank, throwing missiles, shattering windows, chanting their dissent, while inside officials struggled to cope with the throng of investors exchanging banknotes at the new rate.

The widespread hatred with which Law was regarded inevitably spilled over to jeopardize his family. On an outing with her daughter, with only her maid and a footman for protection, Katherine found herself in the midst of the menacing rabble and was forced to take refuge in a nearby house. The burden of realizing that his actions were gravely endangering his family's safety can only have added to Law's misery. From now on the children spent much time exiled to the country homes of their father's supporters, such as the Duc de Bourbon. Katherine, who was increasingly concerned for his mental resilience, remained staunchly in Paris.

At the Palais Royal, the Regent tried to remain calm and wait for the storm to pass. He had failed to anticipate the fury unleashed by the edict of 21 May and now regretted his decision to agree to it. Sensing his unease, Law's enemies grasped the chance to promote their own interests. On the following Monday an emergency session of the Parlement was called and 'in one moment the nation was carried from extreme trust to extreme distrust'. Denouncing Law and his fellow directors as corrupt, bankrupt and deserving of the death sentence, the Parlement demanded that the Regent revoke the edict. Orléans had never felt so intimidated. Terrified that his rule might be terminated, he privately admitted to feeling 'very sorry he had ever engaged in any of Mr Law's schemes' and capitulated. Law was duly summoned before a meeting of the regency council to explain himself. He faced the members with dignity while both his erstwhile ally, the Duc de Bourbon, and his long-standing adversary d'Argenson attacked him. The Regent merely commented, 'A single pillar can not withstand a torrent.'

The betrayal struck Law to his heart. Years later he wrote of this moment:

> When M. le D [Bourbon] demanded the revocation of the arrêt of 21 May with such rage, he believed he was acting for the public good. When M. le D harangued me in the council, he did not believe that he was acting against his own interests. When the different parties joined together to rid themselves of me, the old court, the keeper of seals etc., each believed their own business would benefit. They were wrong. The Regent, who knew the situation better than anyone and who in his heart wanted to be fair to me, yielded out of fear of a greater ill. But he was wrong.

The battle was lost. Conscious that if he remained in office, the Parlement's defiance would escalate, Law tendered his resignation. The Regent did not accept it. A week later, however, yielding to the anti-Law cabal, Orléans ordered that the legislation reducing the value of paper and shares be revoked and both were restored to their former worth. Law knew such a reversal would destroy public confidence even further. 'Happy for France if those who forced the revocation of this *arrêt* had given the same time as the Regent and to themselves to reflect on the consequences of what they asked,' he wrote despairingly. A few days later all the earlier limits on owning silver and gold were lifted. But, as one wag wryly commented, 'The permission comes when nobody has any left.'

Terrified by the seesawing developments, investors scrambled to sell Mississippi shares and put their money somewhere safer, even if it meant sustaining hefty losses to do so. Prices went into free-fall, plunging within a week to 4,000 livres. Defoe reported from Paris that 'Country people run with as much precipitancy from Paris as ever they flocked to it.'

France's ruin was England's gain. Numerous bruised Mississippi shareholders chose to reinvest in English South Sea shares. The previous month, with a weather eye to developments in France, the South Sea Company managed to beat its rival the Bank of England and secure a second lucrative deal with the government whereby it took over a further £30 million of national debt and launched a new issue of shares. A multitude of English and foreign investors were now descending on London as they had flocked less than a year earlier to Paris 'with as much as they can carry and subscribing for or buying shares'. In Exchange Alley – London's rue Quincampoix – the sudden surge of new money also bubbled a plethora of alternative companies launched to capitalize on the new fashion for financial fluttering. Many of them, like the 'company for carrying on an undertaking of great advantage, but nobody to know what it is', were as fictitious as the emerald mountain of Mississippi.

In Paris, euphoria vanished and the atmosphere was sinister. By the end of the month, the Regent's Secretary of State, Claude Le Blanc, accompanied by sixteen Swiss Guards, informed Law that the Regent had decided to dismiss him from his position as France's controller general. Law was ordered not to leave his house. The guards were to remain outside the Place Vendôme mansion for his own protection. Or so Le Blanc said. It was clear, however, that to all intents and purposes Law was under house arrest.

Sensing the net drawing closer, Law blanched but retained his composure. Privately, though, he was immobilized by the real fear that his enemies' next move would be to demand his execution – and that should they do so the Regent would not stand in their way.

Chapter Fifteen

Reprieve

Lundi j'achetai des actions;
Mardi je gagnai des millions;
Mercredi j'arrangeai mon ménage;
Jeudi je pris un équipage;
Vendredi je m'en fus au bal;
Et samedi à l'Hôpital.

My shares which on Monday I bought
Were worth millions on Tuesday, I thought.
So on Wednesday I chose my abode;
In my carriage on Thursday I rode;
To the ball-room on Friday I went;
To the workhouse next day I was sent.

LARGELY THROUGH DRAWING ON THE OLD GAMBLING standbys – masking emotion, following a set strategy – Law overcame his dread and resisted the challenge. His victory was typically audacious. The morning after his dismissal from office, with a contingent of guards camped outside his door and sundry investigators nosing through his private papers at the bank, he had sent word via Lord Peterborough requesting an urgent audience with the Regent. The response was swift: the Duc de la Force had been sent to escort him to the Palais Royal, where he was left to wait in a small gallery. Eventually, after several hours, an equerry informed him that the Regent was unable to see him. Law returned to his house, aware that the public humiliation had been intentional – and that his critics were exultant.

Yet the Regent, despite appearances to the contrary, had not forsaken him. Public unrest had allowed Law's enemies – most notably d'Argenson, whom Law had so spectacularly trounced on numerous occasions, and the Pâris brothers, deprived by Law of their lucrative tax farms – to pressure him to abandon Law and his system. Only three years of his regency remained to Orléans before Louis XV came of age and the Parlement was whispering that they might try to oust him sooner. Fearful for his own survival, he had decided to play them along, give them rope and watch them become ensnared in it. His rejection of Law, even though Law failed to realize it, was part of the charade. He had invested too much in his protégé's ideas to abandon them without a fight. Only if all else failed would Orléans sacrifice Law.

For Law a resurgence of hope, and an inkling of the Regent's underlying regard for him, came late that night when he was summoned clandestinely to the Palais Royal where Orléans greeted him warmly, according to Law with '*mille amitiés*', and listened approvingly to a torrent of ideas for resolving the problems of the bank and company.

Next day, the guards were withdrawn and Law's allies felt bold enough to champion him as 'the only man capable of getting them out of the maze they were in'. Law, under secret instruction to return to duty, worked continuously for the next forty-eight hours, returning to his original idea of maintaining credit but placing it under firm control. At a council meeting two days later, much to the astonishment of those assembled, Law entered as if the drama of the past days had never happened. His strategy, he announced, was ready.

Law's adversaries were flabbergasted. Somehow he had evaded confinement, emerged from disgrace and, moreover, the Regent airily informed them, was about to return to high office – as Intendant Général du Commerce and managing director of the bank and the Mississippi Company. The Duc d'Antin testified to the general astonishment of such a turn-around: his diary entry for 2 June reads, 'We saw this day a rare thing: a minister deposed for several days, who had been placed under arrest by a major of the Swiss Guards, returned on Sunday to council to propose a policy and to be approved by the entire assembly.'

But return to royal favour, though welcome, did not mean that Law's worries were over. Loyalties ebbed and flowed daily amid shifting tides of political ascendancy. Bourbon, Conti and de la Force, aware of how much they had gained, fearful of how much they could lose, usually rallied round him, but their support vacillated according to their appraisal of the current political situation. No one wanted to be associated with failure and thus jeopardize their own position.

Law's return to grace was bad news for his enemies. D'Argenson, who had done most to undermine the Regent's trust in Law, and whom one critic famously described as having 'a soul as black as his peruke', was dismissed as Keeper of the Seals and sent into retirement. The Pâris brothers were banished to the provinces. But the changes in Law's favour were limited: the Parlement was still hostile and most of his critics in the council retained their posts.

Meanwhile, within the grandiose offices of the bank, an investigation into the accounts was drawing to a close amid murmurings that it was no more than a token gesture, intended to endorse the Regent's support of Law. 'It is thought he [the

Regent] will influence the commissaries a point to take Mr Law's accounts to make a report in his favour,' Pulteney observed perceptively. A week later, when the commissioners reported that they had found no evidence of irregularities, few believed them. Their scepticism was later justified: the inquiry had discovered that large unauthorized issues of notes had been circulated but to save the Regent embarrassment the matter was glossed over.

Elsewhere in Europe the speculative boom was still gathering pace. By the summer of 1720, in the fetid passages of London's Exchange Alley, the skin on the South Sea Bubble was perilously overstretched. Shares that in January had traded for £130 were changing hands for £1050 at the end of June. As in France, every echelon of society – country parsons, impoverished widows, kings, princes, courtesans, yeoman farmers, eminent scientists, philosophers, writers, artists – caught the contagion and, with loans easily available, joined the multitude, though few fully comprehended its shady complexities. Even Isaac Newton blindly took part and when asked for advice on the subject is said to have responded that while he could calculate the motions of the heavenly bodies, he could not do the same for the madness of the people. 'Our South Sea Equipages increase every day,' wrote Daniel Defoe in early August. 'The city ladies buy South Sea jewels, hire South Sea maids, and take new country South Sea houses; the gentlemen set up South Sea coaches, and buy South Sea estates.' The boom in London's other bubble companies continued equally frenziedly. 'The hurry of our stock-jobbing bubblers has been so great this week that it has exceeded all that was ever known. There has been nothing but running about from one coffee-house to another and from one tavern to another, to subscribe without examining what the proposals were. The general cry has been, "For God's sake, let us subscribe to something, we don't care what it is,"' reported the *London Journal* on 11 June 1720. Mainland Europe was similarly sucked into the craving for effortless fortune. The stock markets of Amsterdam and Hamburg boomed as never before. Dealers jostled for Dutch West India stock, which by midsummer had doubled in price since the beginning of the year; Dutch East India was similarly coveted and rose from £800 to £1000; prices of insurance shares in at least half a dozen Dutch cities also rose.

In Paris, the story was very different. Law returned to the bank's offices in early June to find himself confronted by the pitiful sight of hordes congregating outside in the sweltering summer heat in the hope of exchanging their banknotes for coins. Such visible evidence of vanished confidence – a run on the bank – represented, and represents still, every banker's worst fear. Law had always been a man of high ideals. The desire to do good, to bring happiness and prosperity had, he always claimed, spurred him more than the desire for personal wealth or status. Now, witnessing people's suffering, he must have been stung more profoundly than by any criticisms from his peers. He *had* to find an answer.

Only about 2 per cent of the money now in circulation was in silver and gold. To eke out the dwindling supply as fairly as possible and to ensure that the neediest had access to coin, he decided on a system of rationing. From early June, only a single 10-livre note per person could be exchanged, and the bank opened twice a week for the conversion of 100-livre notes into smaller denominations. Financial stability could return, he decided, if the numbers of shares and banknotes were reduced, and the value of coins boosted. Immersed in redressing this balance, Law failed to spot his enemies' quiet resolution that he was to be tolerated but manipulated. Once enough paper was withdrawn and the system was sufficiently weakened, they would step in. Law was hammering nails into his own scaffold.

The withdrawal of banknotes and shares from circulation began with more than a touch of melodrama, with vast public bonfires witnessed by thousands of astonished onlookers. The first burning of 100,000 shares owned by the Crown and 300,000 belonging to the company took place outside the Hôtel de Ville. In the following weeks thousands of livres' worth of notes and shares were crammed into iron cages and similarly ignited, as an array of ingenious schemes, each aimed at pruning the paper system and partially restoring the metallic one, was set in train. The Regent's mother shook her head over the irony of it all: while no one in France had a *sou*, she quipped, they had toilet paper in plenty.

But confidence once lost is hard to regain and burning vast quantities of money and shares was not the way to restore it. Every smouldering bonfire further sapped the credibility of paper and the press for coins grew more insistent. The poor could only scour the street for coins, or barter to feed themselves. The most basic necessities of life were affected by the crisis. Coins had to be specially dispatched to the bakers of Gonesse, who supplied Paris with bread, so that they could buy wheat: corn merchants refused any form of payment in paper.

While the poor scavenged, the privileged inhabitants of the grand *hôtels* and *palais* danced on. Cocooned by credit, which no supplier dared deny them, they revelled in ever more conspicuous excess, as if by an orgy of spending they could hold the menace at bay. Just as during the 1930s depression the Waldorf Astoria was fully booked, in 1720 ten times more was spent at the opera than in the previous year; theatrical productions were more lavish than ever; people dressed with ever more extravagant ostentation and gorged themselves at banquets with scores of exotic courses. 'There is still a great deal of money in France,' wrote the Princess Palatine in August 1720. 'They are very fond of luxury, which has never been indulged in to such an extent as it is at present.'

For foreign investors who held French banknotes the situation was particularly dire. Their losses were amplified when the French exchange rate plummeted even more dramatically than the share price. A pound sterling, worth 39 livres in May, was fetching 92 livres by September, and was unquoted for the next three months. One expatriate who managed to profit from the falling value of French currency was Law's friend and sometime business partner Richard Cantillon, who had returned to Paris in search of further investment opportunities. With a foresight that sets him apart from every other financial pundit of the day, he anticipated the downward slide in French currency and by various currency dealings – advancing loans in one currency while taking deposits in another, fixing French currency loans in sterling then waiting for the livre's value to fall – made a second fortune. The size of some of these deals, sufficient further to depress the livre and worsen the shortage of coins, inevitably drew Law's attention. Legend has it that he paid a visit to Cantillon's office and presented him with a curt ultimatum: 'If we were in England we would be able to talk and reach an agreement, but in France, as you know, I can tell you that you will be in the Bastille this evening if you do not give me your word to leave the country in forty-eight hours.' Cantillon, who understood the importance of quitting while ahead, left Paris for London, where he turned his attention to South Sea shares – and a similarly spectacular fortune.

At the bank, the bonfires and rationings had done nothing to improve matters. Coin supplies could not keep pace even after the restrictions were imposed. Reserves ran so low that vast quantities of copper coins were minted, but there was still a hopeless insufficiency. Bank openings became briefer and more sporadic and the queues continued to grow. When the doors did open, the competition to get to the front of the line was frenzied. 'The demand is so prodigiously great for the money, and the notion that everyone has in their heads that they will stop payment again in a few days, is such as makes people even mad to get their money, and hazard their lives to come at it,' wrote Defoe, referring to an incident in which armed guards were forced to fire on the crowd, killing three people, to preserve order. It was just a prelude.

On 17 July, at 3 a.m. a crowd of around 15,000 had gravitated from distant suburbs to congregate in the streets outside the bank. Word had spread that for the first time in over a week 10-livre notes would be converted into coins between nine and one that morning. Wooden barricades had been erected in anticipation of a throng, but a multitude this size was unexpected, unprecedented and, it turned out, uncontrollable. At five o'clock several workmen, exasperated by the wait and fired up by alcohol, vaulted the barricades and launched themselves into the crowd on the other side. At the entrance in rue Vivienne there were similar scenes. Men picked their way over the ruins of the houses Law had demolished to make way for the new exchange, mounted the garden wall and swung themselves through the chestnut trees to jump the queue. From every direction a hysterical multitude funnelled towards the bank and those at the front found themselves defenceless against panicked surges from the throng behind.

By dawn a dozen or more people had perished, crushed to death against the barricades, trampled under foot by the stampede, their cries pitifully audible above the rabble's roar. Buvat, the diarist, who left one of the most gripping accounts of the day, found himself caught in the mêlée when five or six men hurled themselves off a barricade and only narrowly escaped being crushed or stifled to death. Defoe was moved by witnesses' accounts: 'It is impossible to describe the pressing and thronging for money at the bank, the outcries of those who were almost killed were most affrighting.'

A large mob carried three bodies in angry procession to the

Palais Royal and demanded the Regent's attention from outside the locked gates. While the Regent sent for military reinforcements – some 6,000 uniformed troops were presently camped on the outskirts of Paris – Le Blanc, the Secretary of State, and the Duc de Tresmes, the governor of Paris, arrived outside the forecourt. As the gates opened to admit them, a crowd of four or five thousand flooded in. Still in his carriage, the Duc threw handfuls of silver and gold into the crowd to appease them. Minutes later his sleeves were torn to shreds. Le Blanc needed an armed escort to reach the steps of the *palais* and face the tumult. Eventually, having secured a promise that money would be distributed throughout the city, the crowd began slowly to drift away.

But the mood in the streets remained ugly. A second mob directed their attentions to Law and marched to the Place Vendôme to lynch him. Having failed to force the gates they hurled missiles at his house, shattering most of the windows before guards arrived and arrested the ringleaders. Law had heard the furore and wisely escaped to the Palais Royal. Had he not, there was little doubt in anyone's minds what would have happened. 'The rabble, who take things as they understand them, be they right or be they wrong, threw it all upon Mr Law; and, had he returned into his coach, there had certainly been an end of all his designs and projects at once,' Defoe affirmed.

Later that morning Law's empty carriage was spotted in the rue Richelieu, leaving a side entrance of the Palais Royal. A group barred its path and attacked. Law's driver suffered cuts and bruises and a broken leg before he escaped; the carriage was reduced to a splintered wreck.

For his own protection Law moved into the Palais Royal. He was deeply shaken by the violence and, as before, the symptoms of acute distress were apparent. According to the Regent's mother, he remained 'as white as a sheet' for several weeks after the incident. Even when he returned to his own residence the risk of assault still lingered. Youths said to have been employed by Law's growing band of opponents kept watch on his every move, in the hope that a chance for vengeance would present itself. The children were still at Bourbon's country estate, but Katherine was now a virtual prisoner in her home and the hostility with which Law and she were regarded must have seemed terrifying. From now on, according to Buvat, a watch on foot and horseback patrolled the house and the bank's offices day and night. Law ventured out only with guards and careful precautions were always taken. 'When he removes,' wrote Daniel Pulteney, 'it is not in his own équipage, and it is observed that the Swiss guards are dispersed about the streets he is to pass through.'

Throughout the riots, the Parlement was deep in session. Their president, hearing of the attack on Law's carriage and driver, with a sudden (if improbable) burgeoning of poetic wit, is said to have told fellow members:

> *Messieurs! Messieurs! Bonne nouvelle!*
> *Le carrosse de Lass est reduit en cannelle!*

> *Sirs! Sirs! Good news!*
> *Law's carriage has been reduced to splinters!*

The Parlement was supposedly pondering an edict to extend the trading privileges of the Mississippi in return for a substantial payment, which would allow further notes to be withdrawn. Swift to blame the disruptions on Law's system, the members pushed home the advantage, refusing to register the edict, in the hope that their dissension, added to civil unrest, would finally topple Law. But the Regent struck back, banishing them to Pontoise, a village forty miles from Paris. This was perceived by shareholders as a move in Law's favour and share prices rallied modestly. But the recovery was fleeting, soon overshadowed by frightening news: France faced an epidemic of plague.

The outbreak had begun in Marseille when crew members of a merchant ship from Syria, where the disease was rampant, evaded the usual rigorous quarantine restrictions and docked in port. Only after the cargo of silk and wool had been unloaded was the crew found to be infected. Eight people suddenly succumbed in the insanitary shanties surrounding the port. Slowly and insidiously the disease spread through the crowded dockside slums to the spacious villas of the well-to-do. 'The fury of this distemper can't be described,' wrote a terrified Defoe. 'It begins with a light pain in the head, and is followed with a cold shivering, which ends in convulsions and death; and (which is more terrible) we are informed that not one person, no not one . . . touched with it, has been known to recover, and they seldom live above six hours after they are first taken.' At the end of July, an epidemic was formally acknowledged and a *cordon sanitaire* placed around the city, preventing people from leaving the infected area but also hindering supplies of food from reaching the inhabitants who desperately needed it. As the disease ran rife, piles of rotting corpses were heaped so high that galley slaves were brought in to bury them and, since they were poorly supervised, looting broke out. By August, a third of the city's inhabitants – around 15,000 people – had perished from famine or disease and the *cordon sanitaire* had failed. The disease, like some exotic creeper, had spread its tendrils through Provence. In Toulon some 9,000 perished; a further 7,500 lives were claimed in Aix, a city, Defoe said, that was 'utterly abandoned; the inhabitants poor and rich are fled to the mountains of the upper Provence, in hopes that the sharpness of the air, those hills being always covered with snow, may preserve them from the infection'. A month later the lawyer Marais recorded the harrowing descriptions of a doctor who had recently visited the affected area: 'A town desolate and moaning, entire families destroyed, doctors and surgeons nearly all dead . . . the outskirts of the town full of looters and robbers who ransack the country houses of the bourgeois, who themselves don't know how they will escape either the plague or the thieves.'

Europe looked on compassionately but amid growing fears that the epidemic's grasp would reach Paris, the Netherlands and even London. 'Large collections have been made and are making in the cities of France for the relief of the distressed people at Marseille and other places,' reported Defoe, who singled out for special mention the city of Genoa, which sent both money and a ship laden with food and medical supplies. Law and the Regent also sent large sums to help.

To stop the spread, draconian quarantine restrictions were imposed. Ships were liable to weeks of delay: in one particularly extreme example in Holland, three ships arriving from the Levant were burned while their crews were forced to wade ashore naked and spend a period of quarantine on an island. Private travellers were also hampered by the inconvenience of being obliged to have health certificates stamped in every town through which they passed, and in certain areas such as Tyrol were still liable to be held in quarantine for weeks if they were known to have passed through France.

In the minds of many the plague became a metaphor for economic malaise, and Law, whose schemes had sparked the speculation contagion, was blamed. For his system the disease proved fatal. The key ports of Marseille and Toulon shut down, trade with Africa and the rest of the Mediterranean, until now flourishing, drew to a standstill. 'Not a ship comes in to Marseille from any place that has heard of it,' remarked Defoe. 'Commerce is universally stopped.' He could also have added that so had much of the income of the Mississippi Company. As a general slump in trade took hold, manufacturing dwindled, taxes on imports and exports diminished, holders of state investments could not be paid and thus had to sell Mississippi shares. 'One cannot say what effect the demand for silver had but every prudent man sold some of his shares to have enough to feed his family during this public calamity,' Law later wrote. By the time the epidemic was over it had claimed over 100,000 lives and, as Law had feared, the system he had created.

Chapter Sixteen

The Whirligig of Time

Cy git cet Ecossais célèbre,
Ce calculateur sans égal,
Qui par les règles de l'algèbre,
A mis la France à l'hôpital.

Here lies this famous Scot,
This peerless calculator,
Who by the rules of algebra
Has put France in the poorhouse.

Anon, Paris (1720)

AMID THE MURKY INTERIOR OF JONATHAN'S COFFEE-HOUSE in London's Royal Exchange people gather to gossip, intrigue, bargain, or perhaps to gape at a new print strung on the wall before them. The image is profoundly disturbing. A billowing curtain is drawn back by Harlequin and Scaramouch – two well known figures from the *commedia dell'arte* – to reveal hell on earth, the rue Quincampoix, in which a heaving tangle of anxious investors, arms flailing, eyes wild, mouths beseeching, wave serpentine banknotes overhead. Amid the mêlée, oblivious to the madness, three men, representing English, French and German investors, stand complacently on a dais of paper. A supplicant figure – John Law – squats obscenely at their feet and allows them to pour coins in his gaping mouth, while from bared buttocks he excretes paper notes that are snatched by one of the frenzied figures in the mire below. In the foreground a caged figure of Mercury – symbolic of commercial prosperity and, in this case, of ruined speculators – weeps as a man in front performs various gambling tricks. The message, of venality, folly, degradation, chaos, is explicit and sickening – deliberately so. But by the time this engraving, from a famous series published in Holland in 1720, entitled *The Mirror of Folly*, was printed, disseminated, grasped and gawped at in scores of similarly unsavoury interiors, it was far from unique.

Anti-Law venom enveloped Europe. There were scores more equally scathing compositions, mostly dwelling on the imagery of windmills, whirligigs, bubbles, bladders, cabbages, corruption, folly and cruelty. Elsewhere satire surfaced in hundreds of ferocious poems, medals, pamphlets, plays, novels and playing-cards that circulated in the cabarets, taverns, coffee-houses and meeting-places of every town and city in Europe. Ironically, a series of silver coins were produced in Gotha, immortalizing Law in the very substance he had tried so hard to banish.

Law could avert his gaze from such vitriol, but he could not ignore its existence, nor that it sprang from a crystallization of public hatred. For a man whose intentions had always been benevolent, who had cherished dreams of bringing contentment to all, mass condemnation was deeply wounding. His behaviour became increasingly erratic. One day he was full of the old bravura, attending a concert at the home of the financier Crozat with the Regent and Katherine, convincing others, and himself, that the economy was improving, that was in control, and telling friends that 'what has been his is still, and that he would always be the master of all the money in Europe'. The next he was beset with doubt, unusually short-tempered and high-handed with members of the council, introducing ever harsher legislation to bring the system back on course. Occasionally, as if overburdened by responsibility, he withdrew totally. Remembering such a day spent in solitude in his apartment at the Palais Royal, when members of the Royal Family were out of town and staff had been instructed to admit no one, he wrote, 'The idea came to me then, that one would be less unhappy to be enclosed in a town infested, like Marseille, than to be in Paris overwhelmed with people – as I usually was.'

He threw himself frenetically into work. Six hundred workmen were employed to build a new mint – presumably in the expectation that by the time it was complete there would be metal enough to make coin. The share market, which had reopened in the Place Vendôme, was now moved to the gardens of the Hôtel de Soissons, which was renamed the Bourse. The official opening took place on 1 August, to a musical accompaniment of kettle drums and trumpets. As at some latterday Field of the Cloth of Gold, the dealers, food-sellers, jugglers, fire-eaters, tricksters, prostitutes, pickpockets and throngs of investors glided through a forest of streamered pavilions, embodying not royal puissance but the waning power of paper.

To bolster his reputation he published an anonymous defence of his system. When he came to France, he said, the country had been 2 billion livres in debt. Now thanks to the Mississippi Company and other reforms France was far stronger financially. But readers of this slickly argued pamphlet were infuriated by the fact that it skirted the current economic problems. Inflation, the fall in value of banknotes and shares, the shortage of coin and the damage to investors were completely ignored. In short, said Pulteney, it was 'very ill-timed as it pretends to show that people are richer and happier, while they complain with reason of want and ruin.'

Law meanwhile turned quietly for help to the one man whose financial acumen he deeply respected: his old friend Richard Cantillon. Since Cantillon had been banished from France under threat of incarceration in the Bastille the two men had patched up their differences, and Law had been using Cantillon's broking services in Amsterdam to buy copper, probably with the intention of minting it into coins to help the ailing French economy. Now, with his system crumbling, Law tempted Cantillon, 'with great offers of preferment', to come and help him sort out the financial morass. The precise nature of the carrot Law tendered remains mysterious, but it was alluring enough for Cantillon to weigh it up carefully and ask his friends' advice. Eventually, realizing the precariousness of Law's situation, he refused. Law was not at first put off by the rebuff. More persuasive letters were dispatched to Holland, but when Cantillon declined to change his mind, Law's amiability changed to an overtly threatening tone: 'If he [Cantillon] does not comply with the offers they will not pay some bills to the value of £20,000 which he had drawn for copper he bought in Holland by commission for the company and has sent here,' reported Pulteney. It is a measure of the pressure Law was under in France that he felt impelled to act with such uncustomary lack of scruple. In fact, menacing a wily bird like Cantillon was self-defeating – if anything, it only made him even more determined to keep well away.

Law was rapidly becoming an embarrassment Orléans could ill-afford. He too was tainted by Law's bad press and he felt uncharacteristically sensitive to the deluge of criticism and malice. Death threats, accusations of incest and of murder had been directed against him; his mother had been threatened and advised to poison her own son. In the past he had shrugged off the slanders. Now they began to hit home. The anonymous publication of one particularly vicious play riled him so much that he offered a reward of 100,000 livres for the name of the culprit. The only response this elicited was another cheeky couplet:

> *Tu promets beaucoup, O Régent.*
> *Est-ce en papier ou en argent?*

> *You promise much, O Regent.*
> *Is it in paper or in silver?*

Real economic recovery, the Regent now felt, would never take place while the people were determined that Law and his paper system were untrustworthy, and while the Parlement, the financiers and the wealthy élite were so determined to oppose him. Behind the scenes he began to make discreet overtures for assistance, appealing to private bankers and financiers in the hope they would offer his stranded regime hard money. Their response was not what he hoped. Though keen to ingratiate themselves with the Crown, they were aware that any loan might help save Law. They volunteered no tangible assistance, only the well-worn advice that all the problems would be swiftly solved with a return to the old metallic system of money, and the abandonment of paper credit. The seed that had been scattered many times before, now began to take root.

On 15 September Law's career plunged to new depths with the publication of one of his most detested edicts. 'The pen falls from one's hands and words fail to explain the measures of this decree, which withdrew all the horrors of the dying system. Poison was in its tail,' wrote the lawyer Marais as he mulled over the new regulations, which stipulated that high-denomination notes would soon cease to be legal currency; that, with immediate effect, all banknotes could only be used if 50 per cent of the payment was in coin; that bank accounts, compulsory since August, were to be reduced to a quarter of their present value; and shares pegged at 2,000 livres. In sum, said Marais, painfully picking over each clause, it was a bankruptcy of three-quarters of the bank and five-sixths of the Mississippi Company.

Economic historians still quibble over whether the edict was in fact the brainchild of Law or whether, as seems likely, it was the outcome of the Regent's consultations with the private financiers. What is not in doubt is that the public perceived the ideas as Law's and blamed him for their suffering. 'The desolation,' wrote Marais, 'is in every family. They have to pay for half of everything in coins and there aren't any; and moreover everything is going up in price instead of coming down.'

Soaring inflation was worsened by profiteering merchants and members of the aristocracy who formed cartels, stockpiled staples and then charged extortionate rates for them. Some of the worst offenders were Law's supporters: 'The distress people are under by the excessive prices of all things is very much increased by certain monopolies which some of the great favourites of the system have got; the Maréchal d'Estrées has the coffee, Mr William Law the lead, others have the sugars, the Duc de la Force has the wax and tallow,' wrote Pulteney. Law must have known that racketeering was going on but, terrified to risk losing his few remaining allies, turned a blind eye. The Regent was similarly partisan, volubly intolerant of outsiders' scams, mute when it came to his favourites' ruses. When a deputation of merchants came to grumble about the reduction of their bank accounts, the Regent denounced them coldly as charlatans who had charged exorbitant sums for the past year. He told one scornfully, 'My friend, are you so stupid as not to understand that this quarter you have is worth more than the total?' The man replied that his business would be destroyed, to which Orléans answered, 'So much the better, I am delighted.'

The edict was painful not only to French citizens but also to countless foreigners who traded with France. There were deputations from merchants of Savoy, Piedmont and Brussels, who supplied vast quantities of silk and lace and, having been paid in French banknotes of diminishing value and desirability, were particularly badly affected. For English investors, developments were even more tragic. London was by now reeling from the effects of the collapse in South Sea shares which, from a June high of £1,050, had plummeted at the end of August, and by mid-September were trading at £380. Investors who had borrowed heavily to invest in South Sea stock at high prices, expecting that the value would continue to rise, were now forced to sell other investments to repay outstanding loans. European markets in France, Holland and elsewhere buckled from the effect of the London stock-market collapse.

Throughout the tangle of confusion, anger and distress, Law and his family were viewed ever more stonily. The once-fêted celebrities who had danced at Versailles and had their hands kissed by international dignitaries now lived in the perpetual shadow of danger. The lawyer Barbier, strolling in the Étoile, saw Law's wife and ten-year-old daughter Kate returning from the fair in Bezons in a carriage drawn by six horses. Law's livery was recognized and the carriage was surrounded by a mob screeching obscenities at Law's refusal to pay out for banknotes and pelting the women with manure and stones. Before the coachman could whip up the terrified horses and drive away Kate was struck by a missile and injured.

In the malicious ferment anyone who vaguely resembled a member of the Law family could find themselves in grave peril. Madame de Torcy, wife of the foreign secretary, was mistaken for Katherine and half drowned in a pond before she convinced her assailants that she was not the person they believed her to be. During an argument between two coachmen over right of way in the rue St Antoine, one untruthfully alleged that the passenger inside the other's coach was Law, knowing that this would cause a distraction in which he might triumph. Within minutes a mob had descended and attacked the innocent passenger, who escaped with his life by sprinting for sanctuary to a nearby church.

There is frustratingly little to tell us of how Katherine reacted to the dramatic reversal in Law's fortune. We can only surmise, from the affectionate reassurances that Law later wrote to her, that she remained supportive but increasingly frightened by the volatile political situation that threatened her family's safety. After the scare with her daughter she rarely went out, and then often disguised as a pregnant woman – a significant come-down for a woman who had always been noted for her elegance. Social calls were not only hazardous but could often be humiliating. Growing numbers of doors closed in her face. When she visited the Duchesse de Lauzun, an ageing courtesan famed for her sarcasm, she was callously mocked. 'My God, Madame, you have done us a great favour with this visit. We know the risks you run exposing yourself to a populace who is mutinying against you *for no reason*.' A few friends remained steadfast. The Duc de Bourbon continued to offer the family refuge at his country residence in St Maur when it was feared the mob might invade their home. The artist Rosalba Carriera still visited long after most fashionable callers had left and, unlike her relative Pellegrini, who had been part paid for the ceiling of the bank but wanted more, Rosalba never hounded the Laws for money.

The final decisive blow to Law's debilitated empire came on 10 October with another stinging, but by this stage predictable, ruling. In view of the still depreciated paper-money system, in which no one any longer had faith, from 1 November France would depend once again entirely upon metal coins. Holders of banknotes were obliged to convert them into annuities. Law's rivals had finally won round the Regent. On hearing the news Voltaire remarked sardonically that paper was now back to its intrinsic value, but Marais' response was more emotional: 'Thus ends the system of paper money, which has enriched a thousand beggars and impoverished a hundred thousand honest men,' he wrote. When the bank finally closed its doors on 27 November few mourned its passing.

Mississippi shareholders shuddered at news of the bank's impending closure, and Law's newly ascendant rivals were swift to exact vengeance against those who had earlier triumphed. Profit as a result of speculation was now deemed suspect. The sea change was heralded in mid-October with a menacing new ruling that warned of an investigation to root out anyone who had not 'acted in good faith', or enjoyed an opulence that was 'odious to the public and contrary to the good of the State'. Especially offensive to the new law-makers were less privileged investors who had prospered – the 'thousand beggars' to whom Marais had referred. The balance would now be redressed: the victors would be victimized.

So that the profiteers could be identified, investors were ordered to bring their shares to the offices of the now defunct bank to register them; any unregistered certificates would be worthless. If no evidence of misdealing was discovered, shares would be returned after a week. Those deemed guilty of illicit moneymaking would be penalized by confiscation of large portions of their property. The process was little more than an arbitrary witch-hunt.

While nemesis was thus zealously pursued, the Bourse, scathingly condemned as 'a riotous assembly', was shut down. When news of the impending closure broke Marais visited the market. The reaction, he recalled, was one of bewilderment and utter devastation. 'Faces changed. It seemed a defeat, as if a battle had been lost.' Along with thousands of others he took his shares to the bank and was alarmed at the lengthy and apparently chaotic tangle of red tape. After endless form filling and rubber stamping, he wrote, 'You take away only a small unsigned slip, on which is your name, the number of your shares and the page in the register . . . There was much outcry at this procedure, which was not mentioned in the decree, but finally all the shareholders had to go through it; it was suffocating in there and no one knows what will happen.'

Many were so fearful of investigation that they packed their bags with as much portable wealth as they could cram in and made immediate preparations to leave. At least four senior members of Law's staff absconded, doubtless fearing that they would be subjected to extra-rigorous scrutiny. Vernezobre, one of the head clerks of the bank, fled to Holland, taking several millions belonging to him and others. Angelini, Law's Italian secretary, appeared in mourning and informed Law that his father had died and begged leave to go to Italy to collect his inheritance. He never returned, spending his remaining years living in comfort on the income from money he had invested in buying property in the Roman *campagna*.

Though precipitous, this descent did not mark the end of the Mississippi Company. The anti-Law cabal that had striven for months to demolish Law's conglomerate clamoured to cherry-pick its prime assets. The lucrative rights to revenues from the mint and taxes were their first targets. Meanwhile the company, in common with every other business in the land, was short of cash. To repay various loans and continue to trade, money was urgently required and further drastic action was deemed necessary. At the end of November a new order ruled that every shareholder would be required compulsorily to lend the company 150 livres per share, two-thirds of this amount to be paid in coin, one-third in paper, which were still in limited circulation, despite legislation, because of the shortage of coin. The shares of anyone failing to pay the levy would be annulled. Again, this was news of the worst kind for investors. 'It is believed that very many will not be able to pay the sums charged on them by this *arrêt*, having their whole subsistence in actions; and that many who are able to pay, will choose rather to sacrifice their actions,' wrote Pulteney gloomily.

Swamped by suspicion and blame, Law remained isolated and melancholy in his home, with only Katherine to alleviate his distress. Even she, however, could not distract him from the fact that, now the bank had closed and the Mississippi Company was foundering, his position was no longer tenable. He tendered his resignation and asked for permission to leave the country. The Regent, playing for time, ignored him. Once again Law was a man condemned, waiting for sentence to be pronounced.

With Katherine's help he passed his time in trying to regulate his personal financial affairs. During the past weeks these had become hopelessly entwined with those of the company. Law was still a soft touch, and whenever an investor confronted him with a hard-luck story he invariably offered to help. Many of the financial problems that haunted him in years to come arose from the personal bills he issued at this time to impoverished investors to reimburse them for their losses.

Outwardly he could still, where necessary, summon something of his old *élan*. When told of his enemies' rapprochement with the Regent he responded, 'The Regent only follows this course to amuse himself, he takes pleasure from it.' Marais watched when Law ventured out to oversee the registration of shares. He arrived at the Company's offices on 21 November amid the crowds who were depositing their shares. The front seemed convincing: 'He was called a thief, a charlatan, a rascal. He carried his head as high as possible, and everyone wanted him to hang it low.' But ten days later, in early December, his spirit was crushed again. There were signs that the Parlement's return loomed closer and that, as Law had feared, their agreement to co-operate was based on the understanding that he would be hunted down. Yielding to pressure from those who wanted to see Law punished, the Regent continued to ignore his repeated, and increasingly urgent, requests to be allowed to leave the country. By 10 December it was murmured that Law had been arrested, or dismissed and banished to his estate at Effiat. Marais, keeping closer watch, knew that he had still not been given permission to leave the capital but saw the strain becoming clearly visible: 'He is in a state of great despondency and dismay. A tremendous storm is brewing, and we will soon see the results. Everyone is getting ready to torture him, and even in the bank there is much scandalous talk against him and the Regent.'

With tensions escalating hourly, Law again asked for an audience with the Regent, only to be told that he was too ill to see him, an excuse he read as meaning that dismissal and arrest were imminent. A day later the movement to bring down Law gathered still deadlier momentum: 'There is no doubt that this time he will succumb, the party is well made,' said Marais, numbering not only the usual confection of the Parlement, financiers and courtiers against Law, but also Madame de Parabère, the Regent's estranged mistress, who had said she would only return to his bed if Law was ousted. According to Marais, the Regent, unable to resist such a challenge, was running after her 'like a child'. Faced with such massed opposition, even Law's most staunch supporter, the Duc de Bourbon, conceded that Law would have to go. The only remaining question was how he should be disposed of and, more crucially, whether his life could be saved.

Pressed by the Duc, Orléans acknowledged at last that he would have to move, and quickly. Law was finally granted his audience and suggested that Councillor Le Pelletier de la Houssaye should be promoted to the position of controller general of finance, to help steer the country out of the economic doldrums. The Regent was unconvinced, reportedly telling the council, 'He did not see among the French anyone who had enough intelligence and insight to succeed him [Law] in the position with a better chance of success.' De la Houssaye agreed, reluctantly, to take office but not while Law remained in Paris, and recommended that he be sent to the Bastille. Orléans ignored this suggestion and instructed Law to prepare to leave. The British diplomat Sutton noted the sudden flurry of activity: 'He [Law] goes to see those with whom he has business, he receives people at his home with as much if not more freedom than before. He works on settling his accounts, he gives all the explanations asked of him.'

When the new production of Lully's opera *Thésée* opened on 12 December, there was general astonishment as the assembled *beau monde* realized that the Duc de la Force's party included John Law, Katherine and their children (the children, one writer conceded, were 'fairly handsomely made'). As far as observers were concerned, to appear so brazenly in public at such a moment of crisis exemplified 'English impudence playing his game'. Law the suave, cocksure gambler had apparently returned.

In fact, this was Law's farewell to Paris. Earlier that day he had had a final audience with the Regent. The meeting had been highly charged. 'I confess,' Law said, 'I have committed many faults. I committed them because I am a man, and all men are liable to error; but I declare to you most solemnly that none of them proceeded from wicked or dishonest motives.' He left Paris with his son John on 14 December, heading for his country estate Guermande, near Brie, one of the string of magnificent properties he had acquired but had rarely had time to visit. He planned to wait here for a few days until passports arrived allowing him to leave the country. Katherine and Kate stayed on in Paris, to settle outstanding debts, but he expected them to follow soon. Two days later the Parlement was recalled and the hounding of Law and his family began in earnest.

Chapter Seventeen

The Prodigal's Return

The Regent desires that I retire to Rome, that has made up my mind. The enemies of the system take offence at seeing me prepared to return to France, and try to trouble me even outside the kingdom.

It costs me nothing to please them, I have always hated work, a well-meant intention to do good to a nation, and be useful to a prince who gave me his confidence; these ideas made me proud and supported me in a disagreeable business, I have come back to myself.

from a letter to the Duc de Bourbon from Law,
December 1720

AT GUERMANDE, LAW'S INITIAL SENSE OF RELIEF AT LEAVING Paris was shadowed with sorrow and disquiet. His attachment to the Regent was unaltered. A letter sent shortly after he left underlines his affection: 'It is difficult to decide between the desire that I have to retire from public life to avoid the jealousies of those who Your Royal Highness has charged with finances, and the desire I will always have to contribute to your glory . . . I had lost all vanity before deciding to ask Your Royal

Highness's permission to retire but I shall always retain my affection for the state, and my attachment for Your RH. Thus when you believe that my opinions could be useful, I will give them freely.'

Law's royal friends seemed to respond with equal sadness at his departure. Bourbon sent an emotional letter of farewell. 'I cannot sufficiently express my grief on your departure. I hope that you do not doubt it and that you rest assured that I will never abandon you. I will never allow any attack on your freedom or your property. I have the Regent's word on this and I will never allow him to go back on it.' Law was both flattered and relieved by the outpouring – Bourbon and the Regent's support represented his only defence against those straining to see him arrested. 'My enemies act with passion but in working against me they work against the interests of the King and people – but I count on the goodness and the protection of the Regent and your lordship – be united, sir. On your union depends the good of the state and my safety in retirement,' he replied.

In reality there was more to Bourbon's fretting than met the eye. Both he and the Regent were keen to protect Law from his adversaries because Law alone knew exactly how much money had been printed and where it had all gone. If he were arrested and tortured into confession they would be incriminated. Ensuring Law's safe exile, and preferably his disappearance from France, was thus as much in their interests as his. As Guermande was within easy reach of the capital, Law, also conscious of the danger, pressed Bourbon for his passport. His departure would be in the national interest, he argued: 'Perhaps my distance will soften them [his enemies], and time will make them realize the purity of my intentions.'

On the morning of his first day in exile the inquisitive English diplomat Crawford arrived unannounced. The English, always riveted by Law's dazzling career, were gripped by his sudden decline in fortune and the press was full of tales of the fall of 'that blazing meteor, which, for two years, had kept so many spectators at a gaze . . . a minister far above all that the past age has known, that the present can conceive, or that the future will believe'. Crawford found Law in reasonable spirits, in the company of Lord Mar, a Jacobite friend who in earlier, happier days had persuaded him to lend money to the Pretender and other impecunious exiled Stuart supporters. Law's links with the Jacobites were now proving an embarrassment to him, implying subversive designs towards England that might damage his reputation on both sides of the Channel: since the signing of the Triple Alliance in 1716, France had undertaken to recognize the Hanoverian George I as England's rightful ruler. Law hastily refuted the imputations. 'I have learned today that I have been accused of having aided the Pretender and been in liaison with Spain. I helped some poor people who needed bread. Among them were some who in earlier times rendered service to me: the Duke of Ormond saved my life,' he wrote hastily to the Regent.

Crawford was as captivated as the rest of the English establishment by Law, and hankered to find out as much as he could about his downfall. On the pretext of discussing an outstanding debt, he invited himself to stay for a few days. Law welcomed his visit – talking was therapeutic and, more importantly, allowed him to ensure that the British authorities heard his version of events at first hand.

In lengthy conversations over the next two days he mulled over his career in France. He was still full of swagger, unapologetic for his actions, intensely proud that the Regent had already told him that, 'He did not need to distance himself too far, and that he could count on his friendship and on his protection against enemies.' He poured scorn on the cabals and conspiracies that had toppled him and defiantly maintained that, thanks to his actions, France was 'the best and most flourishing state in the world, and that this is how they are still'. When Crawford grilled him about future plans Law hinted that he did not see himself staying in France much longer. He said he had asked the Regent's permission to have returned to him the 500,000 livres he had originally brought with him from Holland and to settle in Rome.

Soon after Crawford had gone back to Paris to scrawl a detailed account of all he had learned, the Marquis de Lassay and Bourbon's secretary, de la Faye, arrived, bringing with them, on the orders of the Duc de Bourbon, the passports Law had requested and a substantial sum of money he had not expected. Law was thankful for the passports but refused the money, saying he already had enough for his journey and the immediate future. Later he recalled that he had with him 800 louis d'or, dispatched by one of his staff at the bank because 'I didn't have the value of ten pistoles in my house'. This, together with a diamond or two, were the only valuables he would take. He expected that, as Bourbon and the Regent had pledged, the rest of his money would be sent once his accounts were settled. There seemed no reason to doubt their integrity. It was a misjudgement he would regret for the rest of his life.

Preparations for leaving France were made hurriedly. With enemies clamouring for his arrest he had to travel incognito and it was impossible therefore to use his own liveried coaches. Bourbon placed two carriages at his disposal – one of his own, the other belonging to his mistress, the seductive and vivacious Madame de Prie, a woman said to have had 'as many graces in spirit as in her face'.

The party left Guermande on the evening of 17 December. Law was accompanied by his son, three valets and several of the Duc's guards, who wore long grey coats over their livery to avoid being recognized. He had two passports, one in the name of du Jardin, the other in his real name, and several letters from friends, including one from the Duc pledging his safe passage.

The escape route, planned by Bourbon so that fresh horses were waiting where necessary, passed north of Paris towards St Quentin, Valenciennes and across the border with Flanders to Mons and Brussels.

When news broke the next day that Law had vanished, Parisian gossips aired many imaginative theories as to his whereabouts. Some said he had secretly met the Regent at St Denis, others that he had entered Paris and spent an evening at the Palais Royal or gone into hiding at Chantilly.

In fact, despite the painstaking precautions, the plan had gone awry. The party had been stopped at the border in Valenciennes by the bullying local official who, unfortunately for Law, happened to be the eldest son of Law's old adversary, the Marquis d'Argenson. The *intendant*'s initial confusion at the false passports gave way to relish when he realized the true identity of the passengers. To exact revenge for his father's fall, he 'refused absolutely' to allow Law to pass and pretended that the passports could have been fraudulently acquired. Having confiscated Law's money and the Duc's letter, he held them while word was sent to Paris. 'I made Law very frightened, I arrested him and held him for twenty-four hours, only releasing him when I received formal orders from the court,' he reminisced. In fact, Law recounted later that he was released before the courier returned, but only after 'much arguing' and on the understanding that d'Argenson would keep his passport, the letters and the gold. The gold was never returned. When he asked for it, d'Argenson is said to have pointed out that exporting gold was illegal – according to a regulation introduced by Law.

He arrived in Brussels exhausted, shaken, but relieved to have escaped. Still anxious to remain incognito, he registered in the Hôtel du Grand Miroir in the name of Monsieur du Jardin. But with the whole of Europe on the lookout, the identity of the party was impossible to keep secret. 'I had hoped to be able to pass through here without being known, and I sent the name of du Jardin to the gate; but to no avail, they already knew I was arriving, and I have just received visits from the principal people here – a fact which makes me determined to make the shortest possible stay here,' he wrote wearily to Bourbon.

Brussels rolled out the red carpet. He spent the first morning in conference with the French ambassador, the Marquis de Prie, husband of Bourbon's glamorous mistress, and attended a banquet that evening at which the élite of Brussels was present; the next night he went to the theatre, and on entering the auditorium was honoured with a standing ovation. 'This conduct,' the English diplomat Sutton remarked ominously, 'attracts attention.'

In Paris, meanwhile, scandalmongers worked overtime to spread rumours of 'an astonishing quantity of wagons filled with gold and silver' that had also been sent across the border to Flanders. Numerous theories were mooted as to what the money was for: buying political support; part of the marriage settlement between an archduchess and the Duc de Chartres; a private fund with which the Regent would retire when the King reached his majority. On one thing everyone agreed: 'It is certain that Law is part of the agreement with the Regent and as his negotiator he wants for nothing.' In England similar accusations appeared in the press. The *State of Europe* reported, 'The general opinion is still that he goes for Rome, where he has remitted part of the booty he has plundered in France, and bought a magnificent palace. He has carried his son with him and left his wife and daughter in France. Letters from Paris told us thereupon that he designed to be divorced in hopes to be made a cardinal. I don't know whether the red cap is so easily purchased, but there are certain marriages which can be easily dissolved.'

The accusations of misappropriation of French money lingered for years and caused Law great heartache. His letters to Bourbon, Orléans and de Lassay are filled with countless explanations and protestations of innocence: 'What could have given rise to this rumour were the dispatches of silver that were made by order and for the service of the state or the India Company . . . The dispatches were registered in ledgers in Paris and at the frontier . . . I declare to Your Royal Highness that I have never sent any carriage in secret, nor any remittance apart from those that were publicly made,' he told the Duc de Bourbon. 'As far as diamonds are concerned, I had four that together were worth £4,000 and before the ban on exporting diamonds I gave them to my brother to send for sale in England with his, but he gave me one back because it was not of good quality. This was the sole and only diamond, the treasure that I took with me on leaving France.'

The furore he aroused in Brussels made Law uncomfortable and he decided to move on as quickly as he could. The intention had always been that he would travel south and settle in Italy, either in Venice or Rome. But since his money had been confiscated at the border he spent the next two days raising two hundred pistoles, presumably either through loans or by gaming, before continuing on the journey south, with new passports quickly organized by de Prie. Crossing the Alps in the middle of winter was fraught with peril. Another intrepid traveller, George Berkeley, who made the crossing in the new year of 1714, could have warned him of the terrors: 'We were carried in open chairs by men used to scale these rocks and precipices, which in this season are more slippery and dangerous than at other times, and at the best are high, craggy and steep enough to cause the heart of the most valiant man to melt within him. My life often depended on a single step. No one will think that I exaggerate, who considers what it is to pass the Alps on New Year's Day.'

Added to the hazards of appalling weather and treacherous roads were the perils of infamy and the pain of separation from

Katherine. Law continued to use his false passport, but he was frequently recognized, and in several cities disaffected investors in Mississippi shares and those who had held on to French banknotes held him personally responsible for their losses, and pestered him for compensation. According to one biographer, in Cologne the Elector would not allow further horses to be supplied unless Law agreed to exchange his banknotes for coins. Law had none to give and was eventually forced to hand over a personal guarantee that they would be reimbursed.

If anything, the affection Law and Katherine felt for one another had strengthened through the months of worry, and the uncertainty of their predicament and enforced separation was painful to both. From the tenderness he expressed in a letter written *en route* to Italy, it seems that while Katherine had been greatly distressed by his departure, Law was confident of her ability to endure and make decisions for herself:

> *I am sensible that you suffer extremely by the resolution I have taken of going to Italy, there was no choice in my situation, Holland is not proper. Your son and I are well, though much fatigued by the bad weather, and bad roads. I desire to have you and Kate with me, yet I can't well advise you to set out in this season; you will be better able to judge what you are to do, than I can. But I fear you will pass your time disagreeably in France, and I would rather suffer in my affaires; than want your company.*

By 21 January Law and his son had arrived in Venice. Law, ready to drop after the rigours of the journey, saw no one for a few days. 'I have suffered terribly from the voyage,' he admitted to Lassay, in one of the first letters he wrote after his arrival. While he recuperated, the British resident, Colonel Burges, who was an old friend, reported his arrival to London: 'He goes by the name of Gardiner, not caring to be publicly known till he resolves whether he shall continue here or no, which he cannot do till he receives his next letter from France ... if he leaves this place he talks of going to Rome but I believe would be much better pleased if he was well settled in England.'

Law felt he could make no firm decisions about the future until money was sent and Katherine and his daughter had joined him. Added to these personal worries were concerns about French financial affairs. For the time being, he was reasonably stoical about the collapse of the paper-money system: 'It is better to return to the old system of finance than to leave the system to survive in the midst of a spirit of opposition'. But he remained anxious that the Mississippi Company – his lasting legacy to France – should survive and thrive once more in the wake of the English stock-market collapse. 'I hope that the company being free will make progress. The return of South Sea will put it in a state to continue its expansion, and to distribute to its investors. I hope that . . . business will be re-established, so long as the plague does not progress; this is the greatest fear for the state.'

Over the following weeks, as he waited impatiently for news from France, he settled into city life. The *State of Europe* reported that Law 'partakes of all the pleasures this carnival affords' and recorded the closing entertainments for its readers:

> *On the 20 instant [of February 1721] the great square of St Mark was crowded with spectators of a grand bull feast, where many of those creatures were encountered and killed by dexterous cavaliers, as usual; several shows were acted, representing the Labours of Hercules; and a person flew down by a rope from the top of St Mark's steeple, to the great contentment of the spectators; the Doge himself was present at these diversions, seated in his gallery; adorned with crimson velvet; and to conclude the sports of the carnival a noble fireworks was played off, and several devices and figures artificially prepared*

with diverse kinds of burning matter continued blazing very agreeably for a good while.

The entertainments made Law miss Katherine and his daughter even more. He wrote poignantly to Kate: 'We often think of you, your brother and I, and wish that you were here with Madame, to enjoy the diversions of the carnival. I hope to see you again soon, until then your main duty must be to please Madame, and to soften the pain that she has in my affairs.' He had rented a palazzo, conveniently close to the Ridotto, from the Austrian ambassador, Count Colloredo, went every night to the opera and began to enjoy his life of seclusion. 'I find myself well, being alone without valet, horse and carriage, to be able to walk everywhere on foot without being noticed in any way, so that I would prefer a private life with moderate means, to all the employments and honours that the King of France could give me.'

Money had still not arrived, and he relied on friends such as Lassay, who lent him £30,000, and on gambling to provide enough money to live on and pay off the endless creditors, most of them losers in Mississippi shares, who came knocking. Law's financial débâcle in France made him deeply unpopular in certain circles: 'The chief bankers at Venice have represented to the Senate the great losses they have sustained are chiefly owing to the councils of that gentleman,' the *State of Europe* reported.

He was mortified at being unable to honour his commitments and struggled to come to terms with the sudden change in his fortunes. 'What has happened is very extraordinary, but doesn't surprise me. Last year I was the richest man there ever was and today I have nothing, not even enough to subsist – and what embarrasses me most, I owe and have nothing with which to pay.' The old gaming skills, based on his knowledge of probability, were quickly honed, but the opportunity for spectacular gain seems to have been lacking. Perhaps, given his impecunious circumstances, he was no longer allowed to play banker. A friend from Paris described him as playing 'from morning to night. He is always happy when gambling and each day proposes different games.' After one especially profitable foray he was said to have made 20,000 livres at cards. But on several other occasions he was less fortunate and there are references in his letters to losses that he could ill afford. Favourite moneymaking ploys included staking 10,000 to one that a punter could not throw sixes six times in a row – the odds against such a sequence are 46,656 to one (six to the power of six). Another game he loved was to offer a thousand pistoles to anyone who could throw six sixes with six dice, if the opponent paid him two pistoles whenever he threw four or five sixes. The odds against this are nearly 5,000 to one.

Away from the gaming tables, he wrote increasingly urgent letters to the Regent and Bourbon, imploring them to honour the agreement to send the 500,000 livres he had brought with him to France. All his other possessions, including shares, which he estimated still to be worth 100 million livres, and his properties, he willingly made over to the company to pay his debts and help those who had lost most during the system's downfall. 'I can only believe that you will agree to what I have the honour of proposing to ensure the security of my children. In the case of Your Highness refusing me this justice, I will be reduced to abandoning all I have to my creditors, who will grant me a modest pension of as much as pleases them.'

When it arrived, the news from Paris was alarming. In the wake of Law's departure, de la Houssaye had reported to a council meeting convened to discuss the economic situation that 2.7 billion livres in bank accounts, notes and other forms of debt guaranteed by the Crown were still outstanding. Much of this sum had been issued without authority and there was no hope, in view of the already depleted coin reserves, of repaying it.

Scrambling to distance themselves publicly from Law, the Regent and Bourbon each tried to blame the other for sanctioning his escape, and the meeting degenerated into an undignified squabble. Bourbon demanded to know how Orléans, who had been aware of the figures, could have let Law leave the country. The Regent replied shiftily, 'You know that I wanted to have him sent to the Bastille; it was you who stopped me, and sent him his passports to leave.' The Duc agreed that he *had* sent the passports, but only because the Regent had issued them and he did not think it in the Regent's interest to allow a man who had served him so well to be imprisoned. Had he known about the unauthorized issue of notes, though, he would have acted differently. By now thoroughly embarrassed, Orléans could only argue feebly that he had permitted Law's escape because he felt his presence harmful to public credit.

In view of the dire financial situation, the council agreed that the investigation into the bank, Law's private affairs and speculators who had made large gains should be hugely expanded, with a view to reducing the Crown's outstanding debt. Law's longstanding adversaries, the Pâris brothers, were recalled from exile to supervise. Crozat, another eminent private banker, from whom Law had snatched the colonization rights to Mississippi, was appointed to look into Law's private affairs. Eight hundred investigators were set to work in the old offices of the bank, at a cost of 9 million livres. Anyone holding shares, annuities or banknotes was ordered to deposit them and explain how they had acquired such sums. As before, if they were deemed to have acted illegally they were liable to severe fines and confiscation of much of their property. The scale of the impact of Law's schemes became clear when a total of more than half a million people – equivalent to two-thirds of the then entire population of London – came forward with claims for losses as a result of his shares and banknotes. Nearly two hundred investors were penalized to the tune of almost 200 million livres – the Widow Chaumont received the heaviest fine of 8 million livres, but remained rich because she had cannily put so much money into tangible assets. Other less fortunate, or less shrewd, investors found their gains dramatically reduced. 'Those who have lost are already ruined, and now they wish to ruin those who gained,' wrote one journalist, as the pruning was uncomfortably achieved. In England the *State of Europe* commented that 'Other ministers are now undoing what has been done by that projector [Law]', and went on to remark, 'The French court after so many trials and expedients to no purpose may be convinced that a public bank is one of those plants which cannot grow in all soils, and that people will never entrust with the keeping of their cash a company which may be dissolved by any sudden blast of an arbitrary wind.' In fact, as Law had pointed out, the State had benefited greatly from his system. Rising inflation, falling share prices and the reduction in the value of paper had bankrupted state creditors but reduced Crown debt by two thirds.

The Mississippi Company was also targeted by the investigators. The privilege of administering the tax system and mint was withdrawn, and the company retained only its maritime interests. Through a painful process of confiscations and contractions, shares were decreased in number from 135,000 to 56,000. In this depleted state the company survived its founder's downfall, and in one sense fulfilled his fervent hope, remaining in business until the end of the eighteenth century.

Amid the financial confusion Law, the convenient whipping boy, was accused of massive misappropriation and of leaving vast unsettled debts. According to one report, a week before his departure he had helped himself to 20,000 livres from the bank. A later document sent to the Duc de Bourbon showed that in fact Law's account was several millions in credit.

Conscious of ill-will mounting against him, and unable to defend himself, Law's concern grew for Katherine's safety. In mid-April, when travelling conditions had improved, he instructed her to arrange for the dispatch of their horses, carriages and furnishings by boat, settle outstanding debts – according to the Regent's mother, she owed 10,000 livres to the butcher alone – and prepare to leave: 'I want your company and to live as we used to before I engaged in public business . . . Though I determine you at present to come to Venice and though I like the place very well, I don't propose that we shall always stay here.' He was desperately worried at the thought of her making the hazardous journey across Europe without him, and sent detailed instructions of the route she should take and the documents she would need. Certificates of health would have to be stamped in every town they passed because of the travel restrictions caused by the plague; she should avoid crossing through the Tyrol in case she was held for quarantine; and she should travel incognito: 'Keep your journey private, there are malicious people . . . and though I received no insult on the road, yet I think you should shun being known, it may be thought that you have money or things of value with you.'

Katherine's preparations to leave must have been underway when the investigators swooped and she, unwittingly, became a pawn in their lust to hurt Law. Her request for passports was refused. All Law's assets, including the Hôtel de Langlée, where Katherine was living at the time, and a dozen or so other properties belonging to him, were confiscated. She was reduced to taking lodgings in a modest inn in St Germain, with only a valet and chambermaid to attend her. Then, on 8 May, William Law, suspected of planning an escape, was arrested and incarcerated in the Fort l'Évêque. Perhaps to spare him further worry, Katherine failed to tell Law what had happened, and he was still unaware of the situation – a letter from Paris to

Venice could take weeks to arrive – when he wrote disappointedly to her, 'I find you have no inclination to come to Italy, I agree that England or Holland would be better . . . you may go to Holland'.

When news of the situation in Paris eventually filtered through, he was outraged, even though she still had not told him the full truth of her own reduced circumstances. 'Mme Law writes that they find me a debtor of 7 million to the bank, and of five or six million to the company, and that the King has seized my effects, that my brother is in prison, and his effects seized, without being told the reason. You know that I paid no attention to my own interests, that I didn't know the exact state of my affairs; my time was entirely taken up with public service.' He was paying an unimaginable price for his idealism and failure to attend to his own affairs. Plainly if he were to exact justice, he realized, he had only two choices left: to return to France, or to move to England and put pressure on Bourbon and Orléans through his connections at the English court.

He pursued both avenues: he dispatched new reports for ways to improve French finances to Paris in the hope that they would clear the way for his return, and made overtures to friends in London. According to the English diplomat Crawford, the schemes were warmly received in Paris. 'Mr Law . . . has sent a new project for the re-establishment of finances to the Regent, which was very well liked, they infer from hence that gentleman will soon return into France.' But the Regent, though quietly keen to bring him back, was fearful of a public outcry if he did so. Still in the grip of Law's enemies, he refused to intervene. The stalemate persisted.

In London, Law's approaches to Lord Ilay and Lord Londonderry were greeted with only marginally less ambivalence. Four years earlier, through Londonderry's intervention, Law had been granted a pardon by George I and a discharge from the Wilsons. As a pledge of loyalty to France, he had given the royal pardon to the Regent – another impetuous gesture of steadfastness that was now a cause of regret – and had left the Wilsons' discharge in Paris. Now, realizing that the developments of the past year had changed the way in which Britain viewed him, Law hoped uneasily that 'His Majesty will have no scruple to order a second expedition of it [the pardon]'. But he was worried enough about his reception to flex his political muscle and stress menacingly how damaging a refusal to let him return might be. 'It would be very much contrary to the interest of my country to refuse me the retreat I desire there . . . I have received offers from very powerful Princes, which would tempt one that had either the passion of ambition or revenge. England may retrieve her credit, if no other state pretend to rival her in it; but if I should fail to work with a prince that has means, authority, and resolution, I can change the face of the affairs of Europe.'

Since leaving France, Law had certainly received offers of employment from Denmark and Russia, which so far he had turned down. But his threat was far from idle: if England refused him entry and Orléans continued to deny him funds to settle his debts, he would have no choice but to 'look for a protector to avoid a prison sentence, which might endure all my life'. The threat of debtor's prison was ever present, and presumably the experience of Newgate in his youth heightened his terror of returning. Significantly, a stipulation of his request to return was that his creditors in Britain should allow him a few months' grace to arrange his affairs before pressing for payment. The total loss to Londonderry from a drastic wager made in Paris, which anticipated that East India stock would fall, was nearly £600,000 and his inability to repay it had forced Middleton, his banker, to close his business at around the same time that Law left Paris.

Londonderry and Ilay contacted Lord Carteret, who

conferred with the King, but when by late summer there was still no clear decision and his creditors were clamouring ever more menacingly, Law decided, with typical impulsiveness, to risk it. Later he wrote, 'I had no invitation from the King nor from his ministers but the situation of my affairs made me take the course of going there with these uncertainties.'

Leaving Venice at the end of August, and carefully avoiding Holland and parts of Germany where he knew angry creditors might apprehend him, Law took a circuitous route through Bohemia to Hanover, then northwards to Copenhagen. He had intended to spend some time in the Danish court – the diplomat Guldenstein was an old friend who, since Law's departure from France, had repeatedly offered him a role in government. Law had refused on the grounds that his plan was to live quietly: 'having worked in the most beautiful theatre in Europe under the most enlightened Prince, having taken my project to the point where it could make a nation happy, and having little to support me against the cabals of court and the factions of the state I will take no more engagements.'

The English Baltic squadron was anchored at Elsinore and preparing to sail home before winter, so there was no time to see Guldenstein at the Danish court. Admiral John Norris, commander of the fleet, allowed Law to board his vessel *Sandwich* for the return passage. The ship set sail on 6 October, arriving a fortnight later at the naval base of the Nore in the Thames estuary. It was the first time Law had set foot on English soil for twenty-six years.

His friends Ilay and Londonderry were waiting for him and escorted him to London where, as he had feared, there were mixed feelings about the prodigal's return. On arrival he wrote to Katherine: 'I don't expect to be well received at court; for which reason I think not to go, having nothing to ask.' Apart from the South Sea catastrophe, for which he was widely blamed, it was also feared 'his stay in London could only help people with evil intentions to whip up jealousies' – that France would frown on England for offering Law sanctuary. The controversy was sufficiently fierce to be raised twice in the House of Lords, Earl Coningsby complaining that Law 'had done so much mischief in a neighbouring kingdom; and [who] being so immensely rich as he was reported to be, might do a great deal more hurt here, by tampering with many who were grown desperate by being involved in the calamity occasioned by the fatal imitation of his pernicious projects.' Above all, stated Coningsby, Law should be shunned for renouncing 'not only his natural affection to his country, and his allegiance to his lawful sovereign by being naturalized in France, and openly countenancing the Pretender's friends; but which was worst of all, and weighed most with him, that he had also renounced his God by turning into a Roman Catholic.' Carteret stood up for Law. He was here having received the benefit of the King's clemency, he was no longer a fugitive from British justice, having been granted his pardon in 1717, and it was the right of every subject to return to his native land.

By November the ferment had begun to settle as Law's influential supporters gained ground, and persuaded the establishment that, far from endangering the relationship with France, Law might actually help it. The diplomat Sutton noted, 'The retreat of Mr Law to England does not seem to displease the court . . . Law will do nothing to trouble the good intelligence and harmony between the two courts.' By the end of the month this argument had prevailed, and Law was permitted to return to the bar of the King's Bench to plead pardon, attended by the Duke of Argyll, the Earl of Ilay and several other influential friends. The *London Journal* of 2 December contained the following report of the momentous event: 'On Tuesday November 28 (the last day of term) the famous Mr Law appeared at the King's Bench Bar, and pleaded his pardon for the Murder of Beau Wilson on his knees.'

Thus officially pardoned, Law took lodgings in Conduit Street. He still longed to see Katherine and hoped that his move might help: 'I can't think the Regent will detain you when he knows I'm first here. I think His Royal Highness and those who serve him honestly should be pleased that I am here, where I may be useful to him; knowing his intentions to live in friendship with the King.'

Although he had been granted a modest pension by the Regent, and London bankers restored limited credit to his accounts, he still battled for settlement of debts incurred on the company's behalf, for which many held him personally responsible. He was distraught that his brother's friend, the London banker George Middleton, had been forced into bankruptcy as a result of his losses on Law's account, and had already tried to speed up the settlement of these debts from Venice: 'I would have you get the Marquis de Lassay and my brother to meet with you, to concert what can be done to satisfy M. Middleton, I have wrote to M. le Duc, who will speak to the Regent about what is due by the King, his R.H. had agreed to have a million per month given out of the 15 millions the company was to pay . . .' he had written to Katherine. But the Regent had seemingly forgotten his promises and, despite numerous letters to Bourbon, Dubois (the French first minister), Lassay and others, nothing was done.

Little by little Law was welcomed back into fashionable London society. People were fascinated by his reputation, longed for the opportunity to meet him – and were invariably charmed by him when they did. Writing to the Earl of Oxford, William Stratford noted,

I was fetched from the Audit House yesterday to three gentlemen who had brought me a letter from Dr Cheyney. I was once thinking not to have gone home, but when I did, the gentlemen proved to be the famous Mr Law and his son, and

Lord Sommerville, a young Scotch lord. Though I was no
stranger to Law's character, yet I did not grudge a bottle of wine,
for the sake of a little conversation with one who has made so
much noise in the world.

In the new year of 1722 he was a regular visitor at court. He
spoke frequently with the King, presumably in German since
George spoke little English, and mingled with the Prince of
Wales and other royal offspring. To Katherine he described the
royal children as 'handsome, genteel, and well fashioned. If my
daughter was here I believe [she] would be liked by them.' In
between the social rounds he spent his time quietly, enjoying
a regular ride with his son on the horses they had acquired; he
told Katherine that he felt much revived by the exercise.

But the passing months brought little real improvement.
His financial affairs were still unresolved; the company debts
remained unsettled. One creditor, a money-lender called
Mendez to whom Middleton had been forced to turn to raise
money against Law's debts, had now taken out a writ against
him and could have him arrested at any time. Despite repeated
applications for a passport, Katherine was still refused permission to leave France. 'I own to you these reflections animate
me sometimes to that degree, that I'm not master of my
passion,' he wrote helplessly, valiantly trying to rekindle her
hope that they would soon be reunited with the suggestion that
yet another refusal to grant her passport might mean he would
soon be recalled to France, 'I'm in hopes to hear the Regent
will allow you to come out of France; if not, I suppose his
intention may be to have me go over, for I hear the people of
that country are much changed in their way of thinking upon
my subject.' At other times, when his sense of desperation was
overwhelming, he vented his wretchedness in letters to Orléans
or Bourbon. 'I am aware of the treatment I have had from
France. The imprisonment of my brother and of those who

showed some attachment to me, the retention of Mme Law and my daughter, but above all the indifference that Your Royal Highness has shown on my subject has hurt me more than the state to which I am reduced,' he wrote to the Regent, who as usual failed to respond.

Added to concerns about his financial affairs and Katherine, his relationship with his brother William had become severely strained. As soon as Law had left France, William had written long, grumbling letters to him in Venice, to which Law had sternly replied, 'I would have you reflect that what you have had has been by my means, and if I have engaged you in measures that you don't now approve, I have followed these measures for myself and children, reproaches are not proper at present, you should propose expedients.' The divide widened after William's arrest, when he had recklessly sent his wife Rebecca to Venice to beg for help. Rebecca was pregnant and Law referred to the journey as '*la sottise*', foolishness. Nonetheless he provided her with statements detailing his involvement and shared what little money he had – borrowed from Lassay – with her. Since Law's return to Britain the rancour between the brothers had deepened further over outstanding debts and disagreements about property bought by Middleton. At first Law had felt that the hardship of his incarceration excused his brother: 'My brother must have gone mad; perhaps prison has turned his head,' he suggested to a friend. Middleton had tried to intervene, telling William of 'some conversation I have had lately with your brother. I find him a little disobliged with you, which I believe proceeds in some measure from your writing him in a way or manner not altogether agreeable to him.' Middleton urged William to make up his differences with Law. 'Now as he was by far the most valuable friend you possibly could have, and still expressed himself with much concern for you, 'till of very late, I humbly think you would do well to consider sedately, how far it may be proper for you to disoblige him, as well as how much the world will blame you.' But Middleton's letter seems to have had little if any effect, and Law was infuriated to discover that some of the malicious and unfounded rumours concerning his supposed secret funds outside France had originated from William. 'What must my enemies think when they see the conduct of my brother?' he wondered. Even when the situation in France improved slightly and his brother's release was imminent, a frostiness remained, and, compared with letters to other friends, Law's tone in letters to William was markedly detached. 'I have wrote several times to the Regent, and to the Cardinal [Dubois] about your enlargement; and I expect to have heard of your being at liberty. I suppose you will soon, his R.H. having promised to do me and you justice.'

Watching developments closely was Sir Robert Walpole, the First Lord of the Treasury and Chancellor of the Exchequer, who, having risen to power in the aftermath of the South Sea débâcle, was now Britain's prime minister in all but name. Despite Law's financial vulnerability, Walpole felt that he might soon be invited back to France. 'If the Duke of Orleans is disposed to recall him [Law] as Mr Law's friends here are very sanguine in hoping,' he wrote to the diplomat Sir Luke Schaub,

> it is not our business to obstruct it . . . If Mr Law does not return there can be no doubt but that the power might fall into worse hands; and if any who are neither Englishmen by birth or affection should prevail, we should have a less chance than by admitting one who has sundry ties to wish well to his native country.

The conviction that he would soon be back in power also helped buy time from Law's creditors. Some money-lenders had enough confidence in his prospects to offer him primes option loans: for a £10 loan he would repay £100, but only if he returned to France. He admitted he would be tempted by the offer 'if they wanted to give me enough to settle my commitments'.

The pace of progress was excruciatingly slow. Eventually, in October 1723, almost two years after his arrival in London, Law's departure for Paris, accompanied by Walpole's brother, seemed imminent. 'I have so ordered my brother's journey to Paris with him that he thinks Horace goes with his advice,' wrote Walpole. But it was not to be. Preparations were under way and Law was awaiting final instructions from Paris when, on 2 December, inauspicious news reached London. Orléans, worn out by debauchery and the pressures of government, had suffered a massive heart-attack at the age of forty-nine, and collapsed and died in the arms of one of his mistresses, the Duchesse Marie Thérèse de Falaris.

Law's hopes of return to France died with him. Bourbon took over the reins of power, but his ambitious and scheming mistress, Madame de Prie, who had lent Law her coach when he escaped from France, had grown hostile to him. The recall for which he had hoped never came, and payment of his pension was suspended. The charity of friends and wins at the tables were again his only means of support. Profound humiliation shines through his letter to the Countess of Suffolk: 'Can you not prevail on the Duke to help me something more than the half year? Or is there nobody that could have the good nature enough to lend me one thousand pounds? I beg that, if nothing of this can be done, that it may only be betwixt us two, as I take you as my great friend.'

A poignant letter to Bourbon from the following summer of 1724 resounds with turmoil at his circumstances: 'there is scarcely an example, perhaps not one instance, of a foreigner like him [Law], who acquired in so high a degree the confidence of the Prince, who made so large a fortune in so upright a manner, and who, on leaving France, reserved nothing for himself and his family, not even what he had brought into the kingdom with him'. As time passed, rancour at this injustice yielded to a sense of remorse at the opportunities he had let slip:

> *I have sacrificed everything, even my property and my credit, being now bankrupt not only in France but also in all other countries. For them I have sacrificed the interests of my children, whom I tenderly love, and who are deserving of all my affection; these children, once courted by the most considerable families in France, are now destitute of fortune and of assets. I had it in my power to have settled my daughter in marriage in the first houses of Italy, Germany, and England; but I refused all offers of that nature, thinking it inconsistent with my duty.*

Desperate for money, worried that he might be thrown into debtor's prison at any moment, and hopeful that if he were employed by the English authorities they might take up his case with France, Law now turned to Walpole for a diplomatic post. Although as a Catholic he was barred from holding an official diplomatic position, Walpole agreed. Law was delighted: 'I will do all I can so that his majesty and his ministers are satisfied with my services,' he wrote a few days before leaving.

Having received his first payment from the government, presumably with much relief, John Law crossed the channel on 9 August 1725, accompanied by his nephew. He had been instructed to head for the spa of Aix-la-Chapelle, and take the waters while awaiting further orders. His role was to be far from orthodox: he was to journey through Europe, pretending to be a traveller but in reality acting as an undercover agent, reporting anything of interest he noticed. France's 'meteor' was poised at the age of fifty-four to embark on a new career as a spy.

Chapter Eighteen

Venetian Sunset

I stood in Venice, on the Bridge of Sighs;
A palace and a prison on each hand:
I saw from out the waves her structures rise
As from the stroke of the enchanter's wand:
A thousand years their cloudy wings expand
Around me, and a dying Glory smiles
O'er the far times, when many a subject land
Look'd to the winged Lion's marble piles,
Where Venice sate in state, throned on her hundred isles!
Byron, *Childe Harold's Pilgrimage, Canto the fourth*

LAW ALWAYS RELISHED PLAYING THE MAN OF MYSTERY. Relieved to have a distraction from his problems in France he threw himself into the subterfuge with typical enthusiasm. He arrived, as planned, in the German resort of Aix-la-Chapelle in early September to await orders. Aix-la-Chapelle, or Aachen as it was also known, was one of Europe's most famous spas, where the fashionable congregated to take the sulphur waters, socialize and, happily for Law, to gamble. He made no attempt to conceal his identity, and visitors to the chic watering-hole were enchanted to meet and quiz the international celebrity – little suspecting that while they were trying to extract snippets about his system he was pumping them for political insights. The Elector of Cologne and Prince Theodore, his brother, were passing through incognito when they heard Law was in town and immediately sent word to his lodging inviting him to wait on them. Law was still in bed when his valet informed him 'that the Elector desired to see me' but, conscious of his duties as a secret agent, dressed hastily and rushed to pay his respects, then reported the encounter back to Whitehall.

A month later he was still waiting for instructions, and the suspicion that his assistance was not quite as crucial to the British authorities as he had presumed was beginning to grow. To jolt them into action he despatched a sharp reminder that his fame in Europe was undimmed and offered entrée to the highest circles. 'The work I did in France and the confidence that the Duc d'Orléans had in me excites curiosity. I see that in Vienna ministers and even the Emperor wanted to speak to me on the business that passed between my hands.' Although to English eyes the imperial court at Vienna was of particular interest – Austria had recently broken her alliance with England and France and forged new ties with Spain – Law was much too high-profile and contentious a figure to be trusted to dabble in such delicate matters. Eventually he was given the far less crucial job of visiting Munich to try to persuade the Elector of Bavaria to break with Vienna and favour the English alliance.

Leaving Aix-la-Chapelle in early December, he broke the journey in Augsburg, where he had arranged for letters from France to be sent. Again, mindful of his new position, he took every opportunity to mingle in political circles. The ambassador of Savoy to France, Monsieur de Courtance, was in town and eager to talk. Law made diligent use of the opportunity at hand: 'I made him see that the Alliance of Spain and Portugal won't be a great help to the Emperor; that his British Majesty was today the only maritime power, who could put more vessels to sea than all the other powers combined, that Spain and Portugal risk much with regards America if they enter into war with England.' Like everyone else in Europe, Courtance was hungry to find the secret of Law's moneymaking. Law hated to be viewed as a failed conjuror, but could rarely resist an opportunity to hold forth on his pet subject. Discussions such as these meant he could justify his actions – probably to himself as much as to those listening – and gave him a sounding board for new ideas.

> *I made him see that he was mistaken in believing that luxury in England was to be feared. Luxury is not to be feared unless it makes the state a debtor to other countries, by a consumption of foreign goods which exceeded the debit of export goods. But if industry improves in a larger proportion than luxury, and if the balance sheet overall between the countries is larger than it has ever been then the state is in a most flourishing situation.*

On New Year's Day Law's party left Augsburg for the short journey to Munich and the court of Elector Maximilian Emmanuel of Bavaria. Munich was generally thought to be one of the most pleasant of German courts. 'The splendour and beauty of its buildings both public and private . . . surpasses anything in Germany,' wrote one eighteenth-century tourist. And, as an added attraction, the carnival was in full swing. Law, still fired with commitment to his assignment, and eager at last to have the chance to get on with it, ignored the entertainments and headed straight for the electoral palace. Maximilian had been indisposed for several days with 'a type of rheumatism in his neck which greatly torments him and prevents him from sleeping, and forces him to remain in bed.' Nevertheless, news of the arrival of the illustrious Law cheered him and the following day Law was summoned to his bedchamber.

Greeting him warmly, Maximilian questioned why, when Law had passed through Munich on his departure from France four years earlier, he had failed to visit. Law alluded vaguely to his dilemma with creditors: 'I had then reasons for passing without being known.' But the fact that he was now lingering in international resorts, living the life of a well-to-do tourist, can only have added further fuel to the rumours that he had a hidden cache of funds somewhere. Maximilian, in common with most of Europe, was under the impression that Law was still fabulously wealthy, and as keen as everyone else to get him on to the subject of money. Bemoaning the high interest he was being forced to pay on loans, he wondered whether Law might help him out. Law replied frankly: 'I took the occasion to tell him that if I was in a position to do so I would lend to His Excellency with pleasure, and at a reasonable rate of interest, but that I had nothing outside France, and that since my affairs were still undecided I had my own difficulties.'

After promising initial discussions, Law left the ailing Elector without tackling the question of the English alliance, but the intention on both sides was that the talks should continue soon. The following day the Elector's health seemed improved and 'he had slept better last night than on preceding ones,' but he was not well enough to receive visitors. Law passed the time meticulously reporting the details of his first meeting back to London. He was still frantic for news from France, and the letter begins and ends with entreaties to the Duke of Newcastle and Walpole to intercede on his behalf with the Duc de Bourbon.

A week later the Elector's health deteriorated. The pains spread from his neck to his stomach and were so severe that it was feared his life was endangered. More medical advice was urgently sought, and leading physicians were summoned. A French doctor pronounced the illness not life-threatening and promised to restore him to full health, but despite his confident prognosis, a fortnight later Maximilian was dead.

Uncertain what he should do next, Law remained in Munich. Ostensibly he was still fulfilling his role as undercover agent, dispatching information about the armies of Bavaria and the neighbouring state of Hesse Cassel, and waiting for further instruction. His presence in Bavaria drew several influential visitors, among them Count von Sinzendorff, an Austrian minister to whom Law gave a copy of a memoir explaining his ideas which, he said, would prove the scheme 'well founded and that it would have lasted if extraordinary events had not intervened'. Despite his sufferings his idealistic approach to money remained unchanged, and when von Sinzendorff asked him about state lotteries, Law, still haunted by visions of the rue Quincampoix tumult, replied disapprovingly that they encouraged debauchery, whereas 'wealth should be acquired by industry not by luck or gambling'. Bearing in mind that, apart from his salary from the British government, he relied heavily on gambling for his own income, it seems Law was far from gratified or easy with the life he had been forced to lead.

As months passed, his presence in Munich seemed increasingly futile. The new Elector Charles Albert had no intention of joining forces with Britain against Austria. No further assignments were proposed. There was no indication that anyone in England paid heed to his reports. When, eventually, Law grew tired of waiting and tendered his resignation to the British government, it was accepted without any apparent dismay. Venice, the city in which he had always felt at home, beckoned once more.

Henry James once wrote that only by living in Venice from day to day does one feel the fullness of its charm. It is, he said, as 'changeable and nervous as a woman, and you know it only when you know all the aspects of its beauty'. In 1726, as Law returned for the third and final time to the city of canals, campaniles and card games, similar sentiments must have struck him. Venice's artistic riches, its Bacchanalian masqued balls, regattas, pageants and processions, which had first entranced him and Katherine a quarter of a century ago, were comfortably familiar but captivating still. As time passed, and his affairs in France remained unresolved, the city's tranquil beauty must also have brought solace from the clouds of disillusionment.

Creditors remained an overwhelming worry. Some were patient in their demands, others made menacing threats against his life and that of his son if they were not refunded. Defenceless in the face of financial demands he could not hope to meet, and desperate to find a surreptitious way to leave something to his family, he began to invest surplus winnings in art and dabble in picture-dealing. Katherine may have helped the burgeoning collection by sending some of his paintings from Paris before their household effects were seized. Within two years he had assembled a collection of nearly 500 works, including paintings by Titian, Raphael, Tintoretto, Veronese, Holbein, Michelangelo, Poussin and Leonardo.

In exploring the art market Law was again revealing his highly original business acumen. At the time paintings were viewed as symbols of status and signals of good taste rather than as a sound investment. Burges, the English resident (government agent), was typical of the age in failing to perceive the intrinsic value in art, and wrote disparagingly of Law's dealings, 'No man alive believes that his pictures when they come to be sold will bring half the money they cost him.' Law, he felt, had been badly cheated. 'I think it is generally agreed he bought his pictures very ill and was horribly imposed on in every bargain he made'. Time proved Law correct. Today such a collection would be far beyond the reach of all but a handful of multi-millionaires.

On his return to Venice, perhaps as a memento for Burges or his family, Law commissioned a portrait of himself by the Dutch artist John Verelst. Last seen on the open market in the 1960s and now in an unknown private collection, the portrait is a world away from the image painted when he was at the height of his power. He is plainly dressed in an unbuttoned velvet jacket and white cravat, classically posed, with one arm bent and the other holding a glove. The stance is taken, appropriately, from the great Venetian artist Titian. The face that broods disconcertingly away from the viewer has filled out. The wig, no longer the ripplingly extravagant peruke of earlier days, is in the new shorter style known as a *perruque à noeuds*, powdered a pale grey suggestive of advancing years. He was now fifty-six. For all that, it is still a face of distinction and allure: the wide forehead, heavy eyebrows and extravagantly beaked nose are marked as in every portrait of him; the mouth is sensually full and half smiles, as if at some remembered diversion. But the air of placid, well-to-do contentment it conveys is deceiving.

Law's pleasure was tinged progressively with despair, but until the end, when the façade finally fell, few realized his underlying melancholy. When the celebrated writer and political philosopher Montesquieu came to call a year after the portrait was painted, on 29 August 1728, Law retraced the early days of the bank and company and 'pretended that the fall of his system came about because of suspicion with regard to his *arrêt* (which divided the notes) so that it was revoked, and the public could no longer have confidence in him after he had been flouted in such a way'. Montesquieu was struck by Law's argumentativeness: 'The whole force of [his] arguments is to attempt to turn your reply against you, by finding some objection in it,' he recalled. Montesquieu had never been sympathetic to Law: in 1721 he had anonymously published *The Persian Letters*, a savage satire on the excesses of the regency in which he had scathingly attacked Law. In Venice, after spending two hours with Law, even though he declared him to be 'more in love with his ideas than his money', his suspicions remained. Law, wrote Montesquieu, was 'still the same man, with small means but playing high and boldly, his mind occupied with projects, his head filled with calculations'.

But, even if Montesquieu failed to realize it, Law was profoundly changed. After seven long years the scrutinizing of his affairs in France dragged relentlessly on, no closer to conclusion. Having sustained his belief that eventually justice would prevail, the news that a further commission had been appointed to re-examine his accounts forced him to the depressing conclusion that matters would never be resolved in his lifetime. With the realization, despair descended and his health became frail. As winter passed and another carnival drew to a close, Law fell gravely ill with pneumonia. He had suffered from a weak chest, rheumatism and recurrent fevers for some years, and the dampness of the winter months in Venice must have made it worse. At the end of February he developed 'a shivering cold fit which lasted him five or six hours, and that was succeeded by a violent hot one, which has never intermitted but continued upon him ever since'. Despite the usual medical ministrations of emetics and bleeding his condition worsened. Everyone who saw him knew that his life was drawing to a close.

Death held no fears for him. On the contrary, he was 'very desirous to die; believing his death would be of greater service to his family at this juncture than any other'. Only then, he confided to Burges, did he believe that the hounding of him and his family would end: 'They will be more inclined to do him justice in France when they shall know how poor he dies, and that he has nothing in any part of the world but in that country and in the King's hands.' Pragmatic to the last, he instructed his twenty-two-year-old son to go to France immediately after his death and throw himself on the King's mercy.

Both Burges and the French ambassador, Gergy, realizing that the end was near, hovered round him, anxious that the minute his life was over they should be the first to examine his papers. He had mentioned in earlier letters to France that he was working on writing a history of his system, and they presumed that this document would be found among his papers. The French feared that if details of the system's intricacies fell into the wrong hands, Bourbon and other powerful members of the French establishment might be embarrassed. It was also thought that the papers would include details of the secret fortune with which everyone still believed he had escaped. Gergy enlisted Jesuits to administer the last sacrament and keep vigil over the invalid. Despite a slight rally at the beginning of March, which gave 'some sort of hope of Mr Law's recovery', his strength continued to wane, and two weeks later Burges reported him 'so ill that nobody expects his recovery'.

Nonetheless, he remained mentally alert and well enough to make a will in which he left his entire estate to Katherine. Although the fact that they had never married could not have been entirely secret, the elopement had been generally forgotten. The world at large believed Katherine to be his wife. Because she was not, and presumably to spare her embarrassment, Law made the bequest to her in the form of a deed of gift to Lady Katherine Knowles. There was no mention in the document of their children, nor of the fact that she was his common-law wife.

Two days later, on 21 March 1729, a month before his fifty-eighth birthday, the end came peacefully. 'Mr Law is dead, after struggling seven or eight and twenty days with his distemper, which was judged mortal by his physicians from the very beginning; he died with great calmness and constancy and is spoke of here with much esteem,' recorded Burges, whose affection for the colourful exile had grown over the past years. The epitaph in the March edition of the *State of Europe* was less decisive in its tribute, describing him as 'a gentleman who has made himself so famous in the world by the enchanted project of the Mississippi and other fatal schemes that were copied after it, that his name . . . will be remembered to the end of the world'.

For young John Law, who had been at his father's bedside when he died, the sorrow of bereavement was profound. He wrote poignantly to his mother, describing Law as both father and friend and outlining his bequest. 'He departed this life on Monday last 21st of this month, giving us all his blessing; and has made a general gift to your ladyship of all he had and all pretensions whatsoever, with full power of disposing, acting, contracting, etc., in short doing what you think proper of all.'

To spare young John the pain of remaining in the house in which his beloved father had died, Gergy sympathetically invited him to stay. In truth he was more concerned about 'the secret papers which 'tis reported Mr Law has lodged in the hands of a friend' and the contents of the will than the boy's suffering, and hoped that with John close he would soon get a chance to examine them. John voluntarily handed over to him several of his father's letter books, one of which survives in the Bibliothèque de Méjanes in Aix-en-Provence, but, anxious that the French might try to appropriate the art collection, tried to keep the contents of the deed-of-gift document secret. As soon as he was installed in Gergy's residence and safely out of the way, Gergy found and copied the will and sent it to the French Minister of Foreign Affairs: 'I wished to be informed surreptitiously concerning the testament which everyone said the deceased had made, there fell into my hands a copy (which I take the liberty of sending you) of a deed of gift executed on the 19th of this month, of all M. Law possessed in favour of her who passes as his wife, although, as you will see he does not describe her as such in this deed.'

A day after his death, John Law's body was taken to the ancient Venetian church of San Gemignano in the Piazza San Marco. He was buried the next day following a requiem mass sung by the papal nuncio. Nearly eight decades later, while Venice was under Napoleon's rule, the church was ordered to be demolished. By a strange quirk of fate, one of the French governors of the city was John Law's great-nephew, Alexander Law. Before the church was razed he ordered that his illustrious forebear's remains be moved to the nearby church of San Moise. His tomb remains there still – a stone's throw from Florian's and the Ridotto, where once he passed his days – a fitting resting-place for a man who spent so much of his life in sampling the city's pleasurable pursuits, and who, in the end, became a tourist attraction himself.

Even in death Law's wishes were thwarted. His brother William's resentment still burned, and the news of John Law's death and unconventional will offered a final outlet for his rancour. William disputed the deed of gift and claimed Law's estate for himself. His grounds were that Katherine had never been married to his brother, that her children were illegitimate, and therefore he, as next-of-kin, was Law's legal heir. The French judiciary found against Katherine but, since William was not naturalized, declared that his children, John Law's nephews, who had been born in France and were thus French citizens, should inherit.

One can hardly imagine Katherine's reaction to the news of Law's death and his brother's subsequent actions. Apart from the sorrow of Law's death after such a prolonged separation, she had to endure the embarrassment of scrutiny of their private circumstances, exactly what Law had tried to avoid. She had visited and supported William while in prison, and helped her sister-in-law as far as she could. To be repaid in such a manner must have seemed a desperately cruel blow. There was further calamity to come. When the precious art collection was being sent by boat from Venice to Holland a few months after Law's death, a storm brewed, the boat sprang a leak and was forced back to port, by which time the paintings were so seriously damaged that they needed restoration that would take several years to complete.

In the midst of the ascendant sorrows, Katherine derived one significant advantage from Law's death and unconventional last testament. As he had predicted, his death helped his family: the authorities were at last convinced that no funds were hidden abroad and dropped all outstanding claims against him. Katherine and her daughter were issued with passports and, with pitifully few assets, were at last able to leave France. Young John had secured a commission in an Austrian dragoon regiment and to be near him she settled first in Brussels then Utrecht. Tragically, only five years after his father's death, the son contracted smallpox in Maastricht and died. Having somehow managed to secure part of the art collection, Katherine sold fifteen pictures and moved into a convent, where she lived until her death in 1747.

Fate dealt more kindly with Law's beloved daughter Kate, who married her cousin Lord Wallingford and lived the life of a doyenne of London society, in a grand house in Grosvenor Street. Horace Walpole admired her good looks and remarked how similar she was to her father, whose portrait by Rosalba Carriera graced his famous picture gallery at Strawberry Hill.

Epilogue

Our age is the most parochial since Homer. I speak not of any geographical parish: the inhabitants of Mudcombe-in-the-Meer are more aware than at any former time of what is being done and thought at Praha, at Gorki, or at Peiping. It is in the chronological sense that we are parochial: as the new names conceal the historic cities of Prague, Nijni-Novgorod, and Pekin, so new catchwords hide from us the thoughts and feelings of our ancestors, even when they differed little from our own. We imagine ourselves at the apex of intelligence, and cannot believe that the quaint clothes and cumbrous phrases of former times can have invested people and thoughts that are still worthy of our attention.

Bertrand Russell, *On Being Modern-Minded*

WITH JOHN LAW'S DEATH EUROPE DREW BREATH. HE HAD come to France prosperous, captivating, brimming with dynamic energy and ambition, confident that he could engender an economic revival. While he had seemed set to succeed he had been the people's hero, by his own admission one of the wealthiest, and certainly among the most powerful men in Europe.

In his eyes he had failed not because of any flaw inherent in his ideas or ability but because of his own impatience: 'I do not pretend that I have not made mistakes, I admit that I have made them, and if I could start again I would act otherwise. I would go more slowly but more carefully; and I would expose neither the state nor myself to the dangers which must necessarily accompany disorder of the general system.' Yet this was only part of the reason for his downfall. The road to hell, so the old proverb warns, is paved with good intentions. In Law's case the more fundamental defect he could never bear to face was his own idealism. In dreaming of Utopia he ignored human frailty and never imagined that he was unleashing several monstrous genies – people's desire to make as much money for as little effort as possible, their instinct to follow the herd, to hoard when threatened, to panic if confidence was shaken. These elemental, uncontrollable human traits, together with the enmity of the establishment and the tragedy of the plague, were ultimately what toppled him.

In the aftermath of his departure and the collapse of the paper-money system, a draconian return to the coinage took place. Along with his paper money the reactionary backlash swept away most of the tax reforms he had engineered. But the effect of his system remained indelible. He had created rampant but, for the Crown, highly beneficial inflation, which devalued Crown debt by two-thirds, and in so doing relieved the need for high taxation. France was left with a viable economy that allowed the monarchy to survive for a few more generations. The cost was to those who had held government debt in the form of bonds, annuities or Mississippi shares, who found themselves ruined. His manipulation of finance had two further significant consequences: on the one hand profound distrust that made a state bank impossible to establish before the revolution; on the other, increasing demand for transparency. There were no published royal accounts until Necker's *Comte Rendu* of 1781, which became a bestseller as a result. In creating a financial boom and making shares so widely accessible, Law had sown a seed of financial equality that the *ancien régime* could never entirely obliterate. Significantly, banknotes next returned to France eighty years later, when paper money known as *assignats* based on the value of land – a scheme that echoed one of Law's earliest proposals – was issued by the French National Assembly at the beginning of the Revolution.

In hindsight Law captivates as much for his flaws and naïveté as for his flashy brilliance. It was not always so. For years his failure overshadowed his vision. Great eighteenth-century economists such as Adam Smith and Sir James Steuart acknowledged his significance but frowned on his actions. Smith called his system 'the most extravagant project both of banking and stock-jobbing that perhaps the world ever saw', and Steuart felt 'the best way to guard against it [being repeated], is to be apprised of the delusion of it, and to see through the springs and motives by which the Mississippi bank was conducted'. The eighteenth-century philosopher and essayist David Hume must have learned something from Law's mistakes when he wrote: 'The greater or less plenty of money is of no consequence; since the prices of commodities are always proportioned to the plenty of money, and a crown in Harry VII's time served the same purpose as a pound does at present.' Suspicion reverberated throughout the next two centuries. The nineteenth-century writer Charles Mackay included a vivid account of Law's life in a volume entitled *Memoirs of Extraordinary Popular Delusions*, in which he figures alongside chapters on Tulipmania and duels. Karl Marx saw him slightly more sympathetically as 'the pleasant character mixture of swindler and prophet'.

In this century infamy has turned mainly to neglect, even if, in the specialist world of economic historians, respect for him has increased as time has passed. Norman Angell, author of the famous *The Story of Money*, published in 1930, described him 'juggle(ing) like a master magician with shares, premiums, instalments and issues'. J.K. Galbraith, Emeritus Professor of Economics at Harvard, writing in the 1970s, said that Law 'showed, perhaps better than any man since, what a bank could do with and to money', while his most recent and detailed analyst, Professor Antoin Murphy, called him an 'effervescent spirit who made quantum leaps in economic theory'. Beyond such specialist realms, Law, once one of the world's most famous and powerful figures, is largely forgotten.

In an age of innovation, when one man's vision and energy could surmount any constraint and change the world, John Law did. He was what would colloquially be called a mover and shaker. Many of his ideas were avant-garde. The idea of conglomerate corporations with multiple interests and sources of income is as ordinary today as it was extraordinary then. The marketing and propaganda techniques he employed were similarly innovative then but familiar now. The realization that art represented not only status but money was also exceptional for its time. Most of all, in conceiving a paper currency that operated independently of gold, he anticipated a development that is now taken for granted.

Often after time the message in past events is more easily read. Unravelling Law's story three centuries on, one cannot help but feel a sense of *plus ça change plus c'est la même chose* – nothing really has changed. Today paper and plastic are unthinkingly accepted as valuable, and at the press of a button millions of dollars move around the world. But time's passage has seemingly brought little in the way of additional invulnerability to the giant institutions public investment has created. Even with regulators, central bank reserves and aeons of experience, stock exchanges, banks and economies still collapse and threaten the stability of those elsewhere. The economic cycle, that our forebears probably thought of as the wheel of fortune, has in recent history resulted in the meteoric rise and collapse of the Asian economies, Russia's financial breakdown, and uncertainty surrounding the fate of China and Brazil. In the world of banking and finance the spectre of financial calamity looms as intimidatingly as ever it did to investors in Regency Paris or in Georgian London. Maverick financiers can still rock governments, financial landslides on telephone-number scale still happen – recent years have seen mega-losses in unregulated hedge funds, and vast losses generated by Nick Leeson at Baring's.

Similarly, speculation contagion still periodically infects vast swathes of society. As in the days of the Mississippi, equities are no longer an élitist investment. Nowadays anyone with money invested in a pension, a tax-exempt savings scheme, a mutual fund or a building-society account is likely to have a vested interest in the share market, and to feel, directly or indirectly, the effect of huge spikes and falls in share prices. Recently, speculation fervour has fantastically bubbled NASDAQ Internet company shares.

Most amazingly of all, the driving force that causes the swell and burst of bubbles seems little altered. Within our high-tech information-technology universe, the hunch remains as much a part of the pundit's repertoire as ever, the herd instinct if anything more able to effect terrifying vacillations in markets. Monetary Utopia, John Law would be amazed to see, remains as elusive as ever.

Acknowledgements

I WOULD LIKE TO THANK THE FOLLOWING FRIENDS AND experts, many of whom have patiently shared their knowledge and read and commented on early drafts of the book: Nicholas Carn of Alliance Capital; Antoin Murphy of Trinity College, Dublin; David Bowen; Virginia Hewitt, Lorna Goldsmith and Dr Barrie Cook in the Coins and Medals Department at the British Museum; Dr Francis Harris, Department of Manuscripts at the British Library; Professor Walter Eltis, Exeter College, Oxford; Sophie Angonin, CICL; Guy Holborn, Librarian Lincoln's Inn; Gavin Kealey QC; Christine Battle; Al Senter; staff at the Bank of England Museum, especially John Keyworth; Amanda Straw, curator of Knowsley Estate; Jacob Simon at the National Portrait Gallery; stock market historian David Schwartz; Peter Furtado at *History Today*; Dr Munro Price, Department of European Studies, University of Bradford; Dr Peter Campbell, Department of European Studies, University of Sussex; staff at the Bibliothèque Méjanes, Bibliothèque Nationale, Public Record Office, West Hill Library, the London Library, the British Library, the Heinz archive at the National Portrait Gallery;

my enthusiastic and efficient publishers at Transworld, especially Sally Gaminara; literary agent sans pareil Chris Little; and my husband Paul Gleeson, whose career in the financial markets helped spark my fascination with John Law in the first place.

Sources

LAW HAS LONG ATTRACTED THE ATTENTION OF BIOGRAPHERS AND economic historians. Many of his most important writings have been published by Paul Harsin in *Les Oeuvres complètes de John Law*. The earliest biography of John Law was published in 1721 by W. Gray; the first detailed biography written after his death was that by J. P. Wood, written in 1824. Law's financial activities were recounted by several eighteenth-century economists, including Marmont du Hautchamp, Sir James Steuart, Du Tot and others. The regency period in France, John Law's career and the social effect of his policies are vividly documented in the numerous journals, letters and diaries of the times, including the letters of the Regent's mother Charlotte Elizabeth, the Princess Palatine; and the journals and memoirs of the Duc de Saint-Simon, Barbier, Buvat, d'Argenson, and Marais. The effect of his policies is also richly reflected in diplomatic correspondence preserved in the Public Record Office. The most poignant record of Law's escape from France and final years in exile are the letters contained in his letter book at the Bibliothèque Méjanes, Aix-en-Provence.

As this is intended as a book for the general reader I have deliberately simplified the sometimes mind-bogglingly complex financial details, and kept numbers to a minimum. The figures quoted in the text are mostly taken from those published in Professor Antoin Murphy's recent scholarly analysis of Law's economic theories and policies. The following notes detail the chief sources for the narrative. Fuller details of these and other relevant publications are listed in the bibliography that follows.

Chapter 1 A Man Apart

Law's gambling activities in Paris: du Hautchamp, *Histoire du système*.
Rules of faro: *Gambling*, Wykes.
D'Argenson's personality: Saint-Simon, *Memoirs*.
Expulsion from Paris because of paper-money scheme and Torcy's interest in: Hamilton, *John Law of Lauriston*.

Chapter 2 Gilded Youth

Family background: Fairley, *Lauriston Castle*; Wood, *Life of John Law of Lauriston*.
Edinburgh: McKean, *Edinburgh*; Defoe, *Journey Through the Whole Island of Great Britain*.
Goldsmith banking: Chandler, *Four Centuries of Banking*; Williams, *Money: A History*; Galbraith, *Money: Whence It Came, Where It Went*.
Lithotomy operations: Lister, *A Journey to Paris in the Year 1698*; Pepys, *Diary*.
Description of Law: du Hautchamp.
Law's professed dislike of work: ms Méjanes
Lockhart's reminiscence of Law: Lockhart: *Memoirs*.
Journey to London: Hibbert, *The English*.

Chapter 3 London

London life: Ward, *London Spy*.
History of Bloomsbury: Chancellor, *The History of the Squares of London*.
Mrs Lawrence: *Proceedings of the King and Queen's Commissions*.
Thomas Neale: Ward; Hyde, *John Law: the History of an Honest Adventurer*; *Dictionary of National Biography*.
Probability: Bernstein, *Against the Gods*; Ashton, *History of Gambling in England*; Wykes.
Royal Mint: Chandler, *Four Centuries of Banking*.
'Public lotteries are less bad than private ones . . .': AS Turin Law to the Duke of Savoy, 7 December 1715, quoted by Hamilton and Murphy.

Chapter 4 The Duel

The events leading to the duel: *Proceedings of the King and Queen's Commissions*.
Wilson: Evelyn, *Diary*.

'took a great house . . .': Gray, *The Memoirs, Life and Character of the Great Mr Law and his Brother at Paris*.

Description of prison life: Ward, *London Spy*; Anthony Babington, *The English Bastille*.

'The mixtures of scents . . .': Ward.

Lovell's personality: West, *The Life and Surprising Adventures of Daniel Defoe*.

Legal procedures: Baker, *The Legal Profession and the Common Law*; Beattie, *Crime and the Courts in England 1660–1800*.

'An accidental thing, Mr Wilson drawing first . . .' *Proceedings of the King and Queen's Commissions*.

Chapter 5 Escape

'Mr Laws knows best how he made his escape . . .' PRO SP 35/20.

Duelling: Kiernan, *The Duel in European History*.

William's order to keep Wilson's family informed: State Papers 22 April 1694.

Warriston letters, detailing Law's trial and escape: PRO SP 35/18 fo 118; PRO SP 35/20–21.

Appeal trial reports recorded by: Leach; Skinner; Carthew; Comerbach.

Traditional version of Law's escape: Gray, *The Memoirs, Life and Character of the Great Mr Law and his Brother at Paris*.

Escape attempt: Luttrell, *A Brief Historical Relation of State Affairs*.

Escape theories: *The Unknown Lady's Pacquet of Letters*; Hyde; alternative version discussed in Murphy, *John Law*.

Chapter 6 The Exile

Law's travels: du Hautchamp; Gray; Wood.

Bank of Amsterdam: Williams; Galbraith; Angell, *The Story of Money*.

Swedish banking: Williams.

American banking: Angell.

'The present poverty . . .': ibid.

Paris in the late seventeenth century: Lister; J. Black, *The British Abroad*; C. Hibbert, *The Grand Tour*.

'a perpetual diversion . . .': Lister.

'It is a great misfortune for a stranger': Andrew Mitchell quoted by Hibbert, *Grand Tour*.

'never carried less than two bags filled with gold coins . . .': du Hautchamp.

Katherine Knowles: Gray; Wood; Hyde; Murphy, *John Law*; Saint-Simon.

'a man is in general better pleased . . .': S. Johnson, quoted by Hibbert, *Grand Tour*.

Law's problems with authorities, and elopement with Katherine: Gray.

'Women, men and persons of all conditions . . .': Evelyn, *Diary*.

'They dismiss the gamesters . . .': quoted by Hibbert, *Grand Tour*.

Queen Anne petition: HMC Portland vol. VIII, pp. 320–21.

Money and Trade Considered: reprinted in Harsin (ed.), *Les Oeuvres complètes de John Law*.

Greg report and account of duel: HMC Portland vol. IV, pp. 195, 208–209.

Miniature of Law: Earl of Derby's collection, Knowsley; interestingly the miniature is recorded as having been acquired (lot 46) at the famous Horace Walpole Strawberry Hill sale in 1842, when a Rosalba Carriera pastel of Law was also sold (and subsequently lost). Literature: George Scharf, *Catalogue of the Collection of Pictures at Knowsley Hall*, 1875.

Chapter 7 The Root of All Evil

Conditions in France: Cronin, *Louis XIV*; Perkins, *France Under the Regency*; Charlotte Elizabeth, *Letters*.

Louis XIV's financial problems and difficulty raising loans: Murphy, *John Law*.

Visits to Paris and letters: Harsin.

Character of Orléans: Pevitt, *The Man Who Would Be King*; Charlotte Elizabeth; Saint-Simon.

Drummond letter: April 1713, HMC Portland vol. V, p. 287.

Lotteries in Holland: Hamilton.

Desmarets' letters: Harsin.

'A Scot named Law . . .': quoted by Hamilton.

Stair's visit and petitions, February 1715: Murray, *Stair Annals*, p. 265; Hardwicke, *State Papers*.

Halifax letter 14 February 1715: *Stair Annals*, p. 264.

Stanhope's fury: ms Méjanes, 79v–80.

Chapter 8 The Bank

'*Your Royal Highness* . . .': Harsin.

Public opinion about the bank: Barthélemy, *Gazette de la Régence*.

'an intruder put by the hand . . .': Saint-Simon.

Economic problems and debts: Murphy, *John Law*.

'We found the estate of our Crown . . .': Pevitt, p. 180.

'The convenience will be such . . .': Saint-Simon, vol. IV, p. 68.

Duc d'Antin support: quoted by Murphy, p. 143.

'The use of banks . . .': Harsin, p. 260.

'I could still be useful': ibid., p. 245.

'I have need of nothing having enough . . .': ibid.

'If Spain had ceded the Indies . . .': ibid., p. 265.

Visa: Perkins; Murphy, *John Law*; Hyde; Mackay, *Memoirs of Extraordinary Popular Delusions*.

Revaluation of currency: Murphy, pp. 152–3; Mayhew, *Coinage in France from the Dark Ages to Napoleon*.

Galleys: Perkins; Evelyn.

Structure and progress of the bank: Saint-Simon; Murphy, *John Law*; Hyde.

'The bank promises to pay . . .': Wood.

Attempts to exhaust reserves: Hyde; Murphy, *John Law*.

Chapter 9 King of Half America

'But the bank is not the only . . .': Harsin, p. 37.

Pitt diamond: Saint-Simon.

Mississippi colony history: Heinrich, *Louisiane*; Perkins.

Launch of Mississippi Company: Hyde; Murphy, *John Law*; Wood; Mackay.

'Natural love of indirect ways . . .': Saint-Simon, p. 137.

'The Parlement are still doing all they can . . .': HMC Stuart, vol VII, 24 August 1718.

'sent immediate orders to the foot and horse guards . . .': HMC Stuart, vol. VI.

Chapter 10 Finding the Philosopher's Stone

Takeover of bank: Steuart, *Principles of Oeconomy*; Murphy, *John Law*; Shennan, *Philippe, Duke of Orleans*.

Law's acquisitions: Buvat, *Journal de la Régence*.

William Law: Healey, *Coutts & Co*; Wood.

Tobacco: Minton, *John Law, Father of Paper Money*.

'jealous of the credit . . .': Harsin.

'On Monday night I did not sleep . . .': Harsin.

Tax system: Shennan; Murphy, *John Law*; Black, *Dictionary of Eighteenth Century History*.

Opposition to Law: Murphy.

'The public had run upon this new subscription . . .': Hardwicke, *State Papers*.

Contemporary descriptions and anecdotes of rue Quincampoix: Defoe; Buvat; Barbier; Saint-Simon; Charlotte Elizabeth, etc.; Wood, Cochut and Mackay also relate many.

'It is certain that the commerce . . .': PRO SP78 166/88a.

Chapter 11 The First Millionaire

Anecdotes about Law: chiefly in Wood; Saint-Simon; Charlotte Elizabeth; Mackay.

'Every day I had a hundred impertinent demands . . .': ms Méjanes, 195v.

Rumours of Law's infidelities: Soulavie; Barbier; Buvat.

'never discussed politics with a whore . . .': quoted by Pevitt.

'Law is in love with Mlle de Nail . . .': HMC Stuart vol. VI

'If you want your choice of duchesses . . .': Wood.

Law's freedom of Edinburgh: *Political State*, September 1719.

Investments recorded in Buvat, Barbier, etc.; diamonds: Healey.

Art: *Journal de Rosalba Carriera*.

Design of ceiling: Buchan, *Frozen Desire*.

Economic reforms: Buvat; Shennan; Perkins.

'the people being generally so oppressed with taxes . . .': Veryard, *An Account of Diverse Choice Remarks*.

'When it pleases Your Majesty to create an office . . .': quoted by Cronin.

Abolition of offices: Shennan

'the richest subject in Europe . . .': Law frequently describes himself thus in ms Méjanes, e.g. 149v.

Share price rises: Murphy, *John Law*.

'had built a seven-storey building . . .': quoted by Perkins.

Throws money to the crowd: Soulavie.

Stair's growing animosity: Hardwicke, *State Papers*; Murray, *Stair Annals*.

'The Regent has already reaped many solid advantages . . .': letter from Bladen to Stanhope 16 October 1719, PRO 78/166/38.

'He spared no occasion . . .': PRO SP 78/166.

Friendship with Jacobites Dillon, Mar, etc.: letters in HMC Stuart vol. IV and V.

Sotheby's portrait of Law appeared in Woolton House sale 6–7 December 1993, lot 584, attributed to Herman Vandermyn.

Chapter 12 Mississippi Madness

Mississippi colony: Heinrich; Steuart, *Principles of Political Oeconomy*, Book IV.

Cantillon and Law: Murphy, *Cantillon*; Minton, *John Law*.

Account of the arrival of Law expedition: Bib Nat Fran MS 14613.

'With regard to my Louisiana colony . . .': ms Méjanes, 192.

Pulteney's account of India Company's progress: PRO SP 78/166 92.

Transportations recorded in Buvat, Saint-Simon, and many other published memoirs.

Allocations of concessions, transportations and Law declared controller general: PRO SP 78/166 95.

Chapter 13 Descent

'I have spoken to a Frenchman who is lately come from the Mississippi . . .': PRO 78/166.

Share prices and introductions of primes: PRO SP 78/166 110; significance of primes discussed in Murphy, *John Law*.

'I am told that most things are considerably dearer . . .': PRO SP 166/78 176.

'Constraint is contrary to the principles . . .': quoted in Shennan.

Acquisition of royal shares: ibid.

'The rage of the people is so violent and so universal . . .': Hardwicke, *State Papers*.

Law's breakdown: ibid.

Chapter 14 The Storms of Fate

'The silver is to be employed in such foreign trades . . .': PRO SP 78/166.

Crime and civil unrest in Paris: recounted in Defoe and numerous French memoirs including Buvat, Marais, Saint-Simon.

Monetary policy: Murphy, *John Law*; du Hautchamp; Pulteney's letters, PRO SP 78/166.

'When M. le D demanded the revocation . . .': ms Méjanes, 130.

Chapter 15 Reprieve

'*Lundi j'acheti des actions* . . .': anon, quoted in Hyde.

Law's arrest and audience with the Regent: Fauré, *La Banqueroute de Law*; Murphy, *John Law*; Hyde.

'the only man capable of getting them out of the maze they were in': Duc d'Antin memoirs, quoted by Fauré.

'We saw this day a rare thing . . .': ibid.

Changes following Law's reinstatement: Marais.

'It is thought he will influence the commissaries a point to take Mr Law's accounts . . .': PRO SP 78/166.

South Sea Bubble: Carswell, *The South Sea Bubble*.

'The hurry of our stock-jobbing . . .': quoted by Angell.

Burning of notes and desire for cash: Buvat, Marais, etc.

Drop in exchange rate: Murphy, *John Law*.

Riots at bank: PRO SP 78/166 266; Buvat; Defoe, etc.

Plague: Defoe; Buvat; Marais; PRO SP 78/166 420.

Quarantine restrictions: Carswell.

'One cannot say what effect the demand for silver had . . .': Harsin.

Chapter 16 The Whirligig of Time

Satirical prints: British Museum, *Catalogue of Prints & Drawings, Political and Personal Satires.*

'The idea came to me . . .': ms Méjanes.

New building projects: Buvat.

The anonymous pamphlet and Law's appraisal of his achievement: Murphy.

Pulteney's letter: PRO SP/78/166, quoted by Murphy.

Cantillon: Murphy, *Cantillon*; Pulteney's letter PRO SP 78/166 420.

'You promise much . . .': quoted in Lemontey, Marais and Murphy.

Threat to Law's safety: PRO SP78/166 420.

'The distress people are under by the excessive prices of all things . . .': PRO SP 78/166 301.

Anecdotes relating to Law's family in Barbier, Marais, and Buvat.

New orders demanding compulsory payments detailed in diplomatic correspondence, PRO SP 78/166.

'The Regent only follows this course to amuse himself . . .': letter, 27 November 1720, PRO SP 78/166 436.

Rumours surrounding Law's departure: PRO SP 78/169 311.

'He did not see among the French anyone who had enough intelligence . . .': quoted by Fauré.

Appointment of de la Houssaye and investigations of bank: PRO SP78/166450.

Law's last days in Paris: PRO SP 78/169/315.

Chapter 17 The Prodigal's Return

'It is difficult to decide between the desire . . .': ms Méjanes, 13.

'I cannot sufficiently express my grief on your departure . . .': quoted by Murphy, *John Law.*

'My enemies act with passion . . .': ms Méjanes

'Perhaps my distance will soften them . . .': ibid.

Crawford's report: PRO SP 78/169 321–5.

'I have learned today that I have been accused of having aided the Pretender . . .': ms Méjanes.

Law's departure from France: PRO SP 78/169 327.

Law's finances when leaving: Harsin.

Details of journey to Brussels: ms Méjanes.

'I had hoped to be able to pass through here without being known . . .': ms
  Méjanes, 17–19.

'This conduct attracts attention': PRO SP78/169.

Rumours relating to Law's misappropriation of funds: Barbier.

'What could have given rise to this rumour were the dispatches of silver . . .':
  Harsin, p. 253.

Law's problems with creditors: Hyde; Charlotte Elizabeth.

'I am sensible that you suffer extremely by the resolution I have taken . . .':
  ms Méjanes.

Arrival in Venice noted by Burges: PRO SP99/62 561.

'It is better to return to the old system of finance . . .': ms Méjanes.

'We often think of you, your brother and I . . .': ibid.

'I find myself well, being alone without valet . . .': ibid.

'What has happened is very extraordinary, but doesn't surprise me . . .': ibid.

Playing 'from morning to night . . .': Murphy, *John Law*, p. 38.

Games invented by Law: Hamilton; Murphy, *John Law*; Hyde.

'I can only believe that you will agree to what I have the honour of
  proposing . . .': Barbier.

Details of investigations and brother's arrest: Soulavie; Buvat; Barbier; Marais.

Censure of Law: PRO SP 78/166 452.

'I want your company and to live as we used to before I engaged in public
  business . . .': ms Méjanes.

'Mme Law writes that they find me a debtor of 7 million to the bank . . .':
  ms Méjanes.

'Mr Law . . . has sent a new project': PRO SP78/166.

'His Majesty will have no scruple to order a second expedition of it . . .': ms
  Méjanes, 92v.

'It would be very much contrary to the interest of my country . . .': ibid.

'having worked in the most beautiful theatre in Europe . . .': ibid.

'I had no invitation . . .': ms Méjanes.

Return to England and opposition in House of Lords: *The Political State*, vol.
  XXII, October 1721, p. 393 *et seq*.

'I don't expect to be well received . . .': ms Méjanes.

'The retreat of Mr Law to England . . .': PRO SP78/166.

'I can't think the Regent will detain you . . .': ibid.

'I would have you get the Marquis de Lassay and my brother to meet with
  you . . .': ibid.

'I was fetched from the Audit House yesterday . . .': HMC Portland, vol. VII.

'handsome, genteel, and well fashioned': ms Méjanes.

'I own to you these reflections animate me . . .': ms Méjanes.

'I am aware . . .': ms Méjanes.

Rebecca Law's visit to Venice: PRO SP 78/170.

'My brother must have gone mad . . .': ms Méjanes.

'some conversation I have had lately with your brother . . .': quoted by Healey.

'I have wrote several times to the Regent, and to the Cardinal about your enlargement . . .': ms Méjanes, 204.

'If the Duke of Orleans is disposed to recall him . . .': Sir Robert Walpole to Sir Luke Schaub, 10 April 1723, quoted in Wood, pp. 173–5.

Offers of loans: ms Méjanes, 198v.

'I have so ordered my brother's journey to Paris with him . . .': Walpole to Lord Townshend, 12 October 1723, quoted in Wood, p. 175.

'Can you not prevail on the Duke to help me . . .': *Letters to and from Henrietta, Countess of Suffolk 1712–1767*, vol. 1.

'there is scarcely an example, perhaps not one instance . . .': Harsin.

'I have sacrificed everything . . .': Harsin.

'I will do all I can so that his majesty and his ministers are satisfied . . .': PRO SP 81/91.

Chapter 18 Venetian Sunset

Dispatches to Whitehall: PRO SP 81/91.

'The splendour and beauty . . .': quoted by Hibbert, *Grand Tour*.

Law and the art market: Murphy; Hamilton.

'No man alive believes that his pictures when they come to be sold . . .': Burges to Lord Londonderry 21 October 1729; PRO SPc108/415, quoted in Murphy.

Painting of Law by Verelst: sold Christie's 16 December 1966, lot 291. Signed and dated 1727, ex-collection Sir H. Steward.

Montesquieu's visit: *Voyages de Montesquieu*, vol. 1, p. 59.

'a shivering cold fit which lasted him five or six hours . . .': Burges, Venice, 4 March 1729, PRO SP 99/63 91.

'Mr Law is dead, after struggling seven or eight and twenty days . . .': Burges, Venice, 25 March 1729, PRO SP 99/63 95.

'He departed this life on Monday last . . .': letter from John Law Jr to Katherine Knowles, quoted by Murphy.

'I wished to be informed surreptitiously concerning the testament which everyone said the deceased had made . . .': letter from de Gergy to Chauvelin, French Minister of Foreign Affairs, 26 March 1729, quoted in Hyde.

Bibliography

Angell, Norman, *The Story of Money*, 1929

Argenson, Marquis d' (ed. E.J.B. Rathery), *Journals et mémoires*, 1859

Ashton, J., *History of Gambling in England*, 1898

Babington, Anthony, *The English Bastille*, 1971

Baker, J.H., *The Legal Profession and the Common Law*, 1986

Barbier, E.F.J., *Journal d'un bourgeois de Paris sous le règne de Louis XV*, 1857

Barthélemy, E. de, *Gazette de la Régence janvier 1715–juin 1719*, 1887

Beattie, J.M., *Crime and the Courts in England 1660–1800*, 1986

Berkeley, George, *Works of* (ed. A.C. Fraser), 1871

Bernstein, Peter L., *Against the Gods: The Remarkable Story of Risk*, 1996

Black, Jeremy, *The British Abroad: The Grand Tour in the Eighteenth Century*, 1992; *Dictionary of Eighteenth Century History* (ed. with Roy Porter), 1994

British Museum, *Catalogue of Prints & Drawings, Political and Personal Satires*, vol. II 1689–1733, 1873

Buchan, James, *Frozen Desire*, 1997

Buvat, J., *Journal de la Régence*, 1865

Calendar of State Papers Domestic, 1694–9, 1906

Campbell, Peter R., *Power and Politics in Old Regime France 1720–1745*, 1996; unpublished Ph.D. thesis, 1985.

Carriera, Rosalba, *Journal de*, 1865

Carswell, John, *The South Sea Bubble*, 1960

Carthew, Thomas, *Report of Cases Adjudged in the Court of King's Bench*, 1728

Chancellor, Beresford, *The History of the Squares of London*, 1907

Chandler, George, *Four Centuries of Banking*, 1964

Charlotte Elizabeth, *The Letters of Madame*, translated and edited by Gertrude Scott Stevenson, vol. II, 1925

Cochut, P.A., *Law: son système et son époque*, 1853

Comerbach, Roger, *The Report of Several Cases Argued and Adjudged in the Court of King's Bench at Westminster*, 1724

Cronin, Vincent, *Louis XIV*, 1964

Daridan, Jean, *John Law, père de l'inflation*, 1938

Davies, Glyn, *A History of Money*, 1994

Davies, Norman, *Europe: A History*, 1997

Defoe, Daniel, *His Life and Recently Discovered Writings* (ed. William Lee), 1869; *Journey Through the Whole Island of Great Britain* (ed. P. Rogers), 1971

Duclos, *Mémoires Secrets sur les Règnes de Louis XIV et de Louis XV*, 1829

Du Tot, *Réflexions politiques sur les finances et le commerce* (ed. P. Harsin), 1935

Evelyn, John, *The Diary of* (ed. E.S. de Beer), 1955

Fairley, John A., *Lauriston Castle*, 1925

Fauré, Edgar, *La Banqueroute de Law*, 1977

Galbraith, John Kenneth, *Money: Whence It Came, Where It Went*, 1975

Giraud, M., *Histoire de la Louisiane française*, 1953

Grant, James, *Cassell's Old and New Edinburgh*, 1881

Gray, W., *The Memoirs, Life and Character of the Great Mr Law and his Brother at Paris*, 1721

Green, E., *Banking: An Illustrated History*, 1989

Hamilton, Earl, 'John Law', *International Encyclopedia of the Social Sciences*, vol. ix, 1968; 'John Law of Lauriston: Banker, Gamester, Merchant, Chief?', *American Economic Review*, vol. lvii, 1967; 'The Political Economy of France at the time of John Law', *History of Political Economy*, vol.1, 1969.

Hardwicke, S. (ed.), *Miscellaneous State Papers from 1501–1726*, 1778

Harsin, Paul (ed.), *Les Oeuvres complètes de John Law*, 1934

Hart, Albert Bushnell (ed.), *American History told by Contemporaries, vol.II, 1689–1783*, 1898

Hautchamp, Marmont du, *Histoire du système de finances*, 1739

Healey, Edna, *Coutts & Co: The Portrait of a Private Bank*, 1992

Heinrich, Pierre, *La Louisiane sous la Compagnie des Indes 1717–1731*, 1907

Hibbert, Christopher, *London*, 1997; *The English, A Social history 1066–1945*, 1987; *The Grand Tour*, 1987

Historic Manuscripts Commission, Portland vol. IV, V, VII, VIII, 1897–1907; Stuart, vol. IV, V, VI, VII, 1916–1923

Hume, David, *Essays, Literary, Moral and Political*, 1875

Hyde, H. Montgomery, *John Law: the History of an Honest Adventurer*, 1969

Kent, W., *An Encyclopaedia of London*, 1951

Kiernan, V.G., *The Duel in European History*, 1988

Lande, L., *The Rise and Fall of John Law 1716–20*, 1982

Leach, Thomas, *Modern Reports or Select Cases Adjudged in the Courts of King's Bench, vol. IV*, 1793

Lemontey, P.E., *Histoire de la Régence et de la minorité de Louis XV*, 1832

Levasseur, Emile, *Recherches Historiques sur le Système de Law*, 1854

Lister, Dr Martin, *A Journey to Paris in the Year 1698*, reprinted in *A General Collection of the Best and Most Interesting Voyages and Travels* (ed. J. Pinkerton), vol. IV, 1809

Lockhart, George, *Memoirs concerning the Affairs of Scotland*, 1707

Lough, John, *France Observed in the Seventeenth Century*, 1984

Luttrell, Narcissus, *A Brief Historical Relation of State Affairs*, 1857

Mackay, Charles, *Memoirs of Extraordinary Popular Delusions and the Madness of Crowds*, 1841

Marais, Mathieu, *Journal et mémoires de* (ed. M. de Lescure), 1863

Mayhew, Nicholas, *Coinage in France from the Dark Ages to Napoleon*, 1988

McKinnon, R., *The Jacobite Rebellion*, 1973

McKean, Charles, *Edinburgh: Portrait of a City*, 1991

McCusker, John J., *Money and Exchange in Europe and America 1600–1775*, 1978

Mémoire sur la Louisiane ou le Mississippi, published in *Recueil, A.*, 1745

Meyer, Jean, *La vie quotidienne en France au temps de la Régence*, 1979

Minton, Robert, *John Law, Father of Paper Money*, 1975

Montesquieu, Charles S., *Oeuvres Complètes de Montesquieu* (ed. André Mason) 1950; *Voyages*, 1896

Murphy, Antoin, *Cantillon: Entrepreneur and Economist*, 1986; *John Law: Economic Theorist and Policy Maker*, 1997

Murray, Graham John, *Annals and Correspondence of the Viscount and the First and Second Earls of Stair*, 1875

Norwich, John Julius, *Venice: a Travellers' Companion*, 1990

Oudard, Georges (trans., ed.), *John Law: a Fantastic Financier 1671–1729*, 1928

Pepys, Samuel, *The Diary of* (ed. R. C. Latham and W. Matthews), 1970

Perkins, J.B., *France Under the Regency*, 1892

Pevitt, Christine, *The Man Who Would Be King*, 1998

Piper, David, *Catalogue of Seventeenth-century Portraits in the National Portrait Gallery 1625–1714*, 1965

Plumb, J.H., *England in the Eighteenth Century*, 1963

Political State, vol. VIII, September 1719; vol. XXII, October 1721

Poellnitz, Carl Ludwig von, Baron, *Memoirs, vol.1*, 1737

Price, Jacob M., *France and the Chesapeake*, 1973

Proceedings of the King and Queen's Commissions 18–20 April, 1694

Saint-Simon, Duc de, *Memoirs* (trans. K.P. Wormley), 1909

Shennan, J.H., *Philippe, Duke of Orléans*, 1979

Skinner, Robert, *Reports of Cases Adjudged in the Court of King's Bench*, 1728

State of Europe, 1720, 1721, 1729

Steuart, Sir James, *An Inquiry into the Principles of Political Oeconomy*, 1770

Soulavie, *Pièces Inédites sur les Règnes de Louis XIV, Louis XV et Louis XVI*, 1891

Suffolk, Countess of, *Letters to and from Henrietta, Countess of Suffolk, and her second husband, the Hon. George Berkeley, 1712–1767*, 1824

The Unknown Lady's Pacquet of Letters included in Mme d'Aulnoy, *Memoirs of the Court of England*, 1707.

Veryard, Ellis, *An Account of Diverse Choice Remarks*, 1701

Vilar, Pierre, *A History of Gold and Money*, 1976

Voltaire, *Correspondence*, 1977; *Essays on Literature, Philosophy, Art, History*, vol. XIX, 1931

Ward, Ned, *London Spy*, 1703

West, Richard, *The Life and Surprising Adventures of Daniel Defoe*, 1998

Williams, Johnathan (ed.), *Money: a History*, 1997

Wodrow, Robert, *The Life of Rev. James Wodrow*, 1828

Wood, John Philip, *The History of the Parish of Cramond*, 1794; *Memoirs of the Life of John Law of Lauriston*, 1824

Wykes, Alan, *Gambling*, 1964

Index

Certain DIOGENE moderne,
Cherchant dans tout le genre humain
Quelqu'un que la raison gouverne,
Vint à PARIS un beau matin :
Il portoit en main sa lanterne.
Quel spectacle s'offre à ses yeux !
QUINQUENPOIX un fourbe odieux
Qui merite qu'un coup de berne
Lui montre le faubourg des Cieux.
Je trouve, dit-il, dans ces lieux
Des foux de plus d'une maniere.
Il fut surpris d'une chaudiere :
Elle bouilloit sur un foïer :
Un Diable y bruloit du papier,
Billets d'ETAT, et de MONNOIE,
Primes du WEST, Primes du SUD,
PAPIERS plus faux que le TALMUD,
Il en faisoit un feu de joie.
Dans la CHAUDIERE, à pleine main,
Un fou jettoit, sur l'esperance
D'Une ambitieuse opulence,
Son or et l'argent du prochain.
Quand la matiere étoit fondue ;
Qu'en sortoit il ? PAPIERS nouveaux,
Billets de banque des plus beaux,
Marchandise bien cher vendue.
L'Extravagante VANITÉ
Montroit pour devise un icare,
Vrai symbole du sort bizarre
D'Un QUINQUENPOIX decredité.